NEW DIRECTIONS

assessment and preparation of Hispanic college students

Bilingual Press/Editorial Bilingüe

Publisher
Gary Francisco Keller

Executive Editor
Karen S. Van Hooft

Address
Bilingual Press
Hispanic Research Center
Arizona State University
PO Box 875303
Tempe, Arizona 85287-5303
(480) 965-3867

NEW DIRECTIONS

assessment and
preparation
of Hispanic
college students

EDITED BY

Alfredo G. de los Santos Jr.

Laura I. Rendón

Gary Francisco Keller

Alberto Acereda

Estela Mara Bensimón

Richard J. Tannenbaum

Bilingual Press/Editorial Bilingüe
TEMPE, ARIZONA

Library of Congress Cataloging in Publication Control Number: 2017043764

ISBN (cloth) 978-1-939743-23-7
ISBN (paper) 978-1-939743-24-4

PRINTED IN THE UNITED STATES OF AMERICA

Cover art: *Scholarship Activism Justice* (2004), silkscreen, by Malaquías Montoya
Cover and interior design: John Wincek

Jorge Chapa

Jorge Chapa, professor of Latino/Latina Studies at the University of Illinois at Urbana-Champaign, died unexpectedly on Monday, October 19, 2015. Jorge, his wife Belinda De La Rosa, and Blanca Rincón were working on their article for *New Directions: Assessment and Preparation of Hispanic College Students* when he died.

A prolific writer, Jorge was author, editor, coauthor, or coeditor of twelve books; he also published fifteen articles in refereed journals and eighteen book chapters as well as book reviews, documentaries, computer models, and more. His 2004 book *Apple Pie and Enchiladas*, coauthored with Ann V. Millard, has become the standard treatment for the very important demographic, political, and social changes in the Midwest.

His first book, *The Burden of Support: Young Latinos in an Aging Society*, was a groundbreaking treatise on the consequences of Latino population growth and won the 1989 *Choice* Outstanding Academic Book Award.

He was a great scholar, our best demographer, a gentle giant of a man, an activist, a thinker, a great teacher and mentor, *un hombre de compromiso* who sought equal opportunity for all, an expert witness, a loving husband and father, a wonderful friend . . . y mucho más. He will be missed.

We were delighted that Blanca and Belinda continued to work on the article, which is an important contribution to *New Directions*.

Table of Contents

PART I   ASSESSMENT

PART II   ACADEMIC PREPARATION

Download the index for this book at https://bilingualpress.clas.asu.edu/book
/new-directions-assessment-and-preparation-hispanic-college-students

Foreword

Walt MacDonald, PRESIDENT AND CEO, EDUCATIONAL TESTING SERVICE

How will the United States' Hispanic-Serving Institutions (HSIs) support, expand, and sustain educational and workplace opportunities for college aspirants of Hispanic heritage? It is an urgent question, and not just for HSIs and their students. For the answer will have a direct and substantial impact on the prospects and well-being of the 57 million Americans of Hispanic heritage and, by extension, on the long-term outlook for the United States as a whole.

In the articles that form *New Directions: Assessment and Preparation of Hispanic College Students,* more than two dozen distinguished Hispanic academics, researchers, and thinkers examine the question from two perspectives—academic preparation and assessment in Hispanic higher education.

Among the specific issues the authors address is a fundamental one for HSIs: What exactly does it mean to be a Hispanic-Serving Institution? The answer would seem obvious and depend on nothing more than whether the institution meets the criteria set forth in the Higher Education Act regarding accreditation, nonprofit status, ethnicity, and income. But as made clear by the authors of the article "Signaling Success for Hispanic Students in a Changing Higher Education Landscape," the answer involves more than demographic data. It is bound up with institutional identity, mission, and priorities.

Other core issues that are examined in these pages include the lived experience of and unique challenges faced by Hispanic faculty; the often overlooked cultural and familial factors that influence high-achieving Hispanic students' college-selection decisions; the need for a truly integrated K–16 system that better prepares Hispanic students for college-level work and success, including raising the rate at which Hispanic students transfer from community colleges to four-year programs; and the role of assessment in strengthening both student achievement and institutional performance.

If there is an overarching theme in these articles, it is the imperative of raising the rates at which Hispanic students attain an effective, high-quality higher education that prepares them for an intensely competitive, knowledge-driven workplace and world. And if there is an underlying theme, it is the imperative for *institutions* to adapt to the unique backgrounds, experiences, and learning styles of their students and not the other way around. It is a change of perspective that is long overdue.

In these pages, you will find not just a review of the challenges facing Hispanic higher education, but an abundance of specific, carefully considered, thoroughly researched proposals for meeting these challenges, including ways for academics to bring their expertise to bear on public policy. It is that coequal emphasis on research and results that makes this volume so timely and so valuable.

New Directions: Assessment and Preparation of Hispanic College Students is one of two books published by Bilingual Press as part of a partnership between Educational Testing Service (ETS) and Arizona State University's Hispanic Research Center, which works closely with the ASU-based American Association of Hispanics in Higher Education (AAHHE). The other volume is *Moving Forward: Policies, Planning, and Promoting Access of Hispanic College Students.*

The two books represent just the latest products of our collaboration. For more than three decades, ETS and the Hispanic Research Center at ASU have worked together to promote the success of Latino students. Our organizations joined forces in 2005 to convene an invitational conference devoted to Latino achievement in the STEM fields. Five of the research papers published for that conference appeared in the *Journal of Hispanic Higher Education* in July of 2006, and an *ETS Policy Notes* research bulletin that summer also highlighted these issues. I anticipate that these two new books will help inform and shape our discussions at the 2017 AAHHE conference. Also, I am confident that these books will and should inform discussions among decision makers—from higher education leaders and boards to state and federal legislatures.

The United States is undergoing an evolution that, like any evolutionary process, has been long in the making. The demographic data are there for all to see. The time has come to put these data and the changes they reflect to work for our shared future as Americans. For ETS, the success of Hispanic students and Hispanic-Serving Institutions is integral to our mission to advance quality and equity in education for all learners, regardless of their backgrounds or circumstances, through research, assessment, and advocacy. We are proud to be part of this collaboration and the positive change to which it will contribute.

Introduction

Alfredo G. de los Santos Jr. and Gary Francisco Keller

ONE PROJECT IN TWO VOLUMES

The two volumes that we introduce here, *New Directions: Assessment and Preparation of Hispanic College Students* and *Moving Forward: Policies, Planning, and Promoting Access of Hispanic College Students*, are the product of a larger undertaking that includes not only these publications but also an academic conference and an alliance of professors and other specialists in fields related to assessment, academic preparation, and access. The overall project is known as the New Directions project (ND). ND is an academic alliance that covers many dimensions of research, policy, and advocacy about Hispanic student assessment and achievement. Our twenty-six papers were written separately and coterminously with each other. This New Directions project and its resultant two volumes are not intended as publications with separate chapters that each build upon the other, working incrementally toward a cumulative effect and final conclusion. Quite to the contrary, the project has a number of separate and related conclusions reflecting the multiculturalism and language registers of numerous contributors from all over our nation. ND reflects all of the Hispanic cultures that make up the vibrant Hispanic population of the entire United States. They are not intended to blend every strain of our multicultural nation into a single, homogenous, and nicely packaged product. We take seriously the overarching reality of the Hispanic communities of the United States: *juntos pero no revueltos*.

Thus, unified by our common ground that encompasses the entire nation, each contributor has produced a paper that is internally coherent, self-standing, and individually cogent. Each contributor was master of her or

1

his house; the authors produced their work independently of each other, addressing particular broad themes of the ND alliance. No wonder, then, that both the ND project and the two volumes we have produced reflect heterogeneity and inclusiveness within the academic world. The edited collection reflects a variety of papers by a wide spectrum of academics ranging from professors with endowed chairs through full professors, associate professors, and tenure-track assistant professors to advanced graduate students. In addition, research scientists and policy experts at the Educational Testing Service (ETS) and two national organizations based in Washington, DC—Education Trust and *Excelencia* in Education—contributed papers. By design, the papers before you reflect the Hispanic within multiculturalism and the distinctive emphases and registers of the Hispanic communities and interest groups that populate every region of our nation.

The kernel, the acorn from which these multiple oaks grew, as it were, came from the inspiration of Beth M. Bouloukos, PhD, senior acquisitions editor at the State University of New York (SUNY) Press.

In 1991 SUNY Press published a book on which the current volumes have been loosely modeled: *Assessment and Access: Hispanics in Higher Education*, edited by Gary D. Keller, James R. Deneen, and Rafael G. Magallán. This volume was a landmark that was well received and highly influential. The publication had substantive participation from ETS and the College Board in that coeditors James R. Deneen and Rafael G. Magallán were senior administrators of the ETS and the College Board, respectively.

Assessment and Access led to decades of valuable collaboration among Arizona State University (ASU), the College Board, and ETS, which in November 2005 celebrated their twenty-six years of partnership with a seminal conference, "Latino Achievement in the Sciences, Technology, Engineering, and Mathematics." The conference, in turn, led to the publication of a special issue of *ETS Policy Notes: News from the ETS Policy Information Center* devoted entirely to the theme of the conference. The conference papers were published in the July 2006 issue of the *Journal of Hispanic Higher Education*. The guest editors for the issue—Alfredo G. de los Santos Jr., Gary D. Keller, Michael T. Nettles, and Rose Payán—represented the three organizations that organized the conference.

Now, approximately twenty-five years have transpired and much has been achieved that urgently cries for elucidation. In 2014, Beth Bouloukos suggested to Gary Keller that it would be desirable and exciting for a new book to be published that would update developments in the field. Keller was enthusiastic and in turn contacted his colleague, Alfredo G. de los Santos Jr., a research professor in the ASU Hispanic Research Center

(HRC) and emeritus vice-chancellor of the Maricopa County Community College District.

De los Santos, with equal enthusiasm and in addition an extraordinary network of contacts, brought these two volumes to fruition. He was key in identifying the contributors whose scholarship and advocacy grace these pages. He developed a list of some thirty possible authors and assumed the role of lead editor, culling information about the proposed contributors' interests and publications to facilitate development of the proposed contents. His early involvement as founding vice president in the creation of the American Association of Hispanics in Higher Education (AAHHE) and his long working relationship with Loui Olivas, AAHHE founding president and professor emeritus at ASU, provided another invaluable source of possible contributors: the programs for AAHHE's annual conferences.

During the discussion of what we sometimes playfully called "Assessment and Access 2.0," we mutually agreed that, in addition to inviting senior scholars to contribute to the book, we would provide professional development opportunities for junior faculty and emerging scholars. We are proud of the fact that many professors and associate professors involved either assistant professors or graduate students in the preparation of their contributions to the books. In a few instances, a graduate student took the lead, under the guidance and supervision of the professor, and is listed as the lead author. We are also pleased that the authors represent a wide range of institutions and organizations from around the entire nation.

Once the proposed volume was complete, the final articles were submitted to SUNY Press as a single manuscript. Beth Bouloukos viewed the contributions as the extraordinary result of an ambitious analysis of the key elements pertaining to the academic preparation, assessment, and promotion of access and achievement of Hispanic students. Equally extraordinary was the response from the academic community to the editors' invitation to contribute to this project. Beth judged that, as a matter of practicality, the project in its entirety should be published as two separate, closely related volumes, and the editors agreed. The revised proposal for two separate books was enthusiastically accepted by the SUNY Press editorial board. The five original organizing sections for the entire research publication appear in the two volumes as follows: assessment and academic preparation in the *New Directions* volume, and policies, planning, and progress in *Moving Forward*.

And then an unexpected development! Originally anticipating publication by SUNY Press, the six coeditors signed a contract for the two volumes. Unfortunately, issues of timing and control over design suddenly loomed large. The American Association of Hispanics in Higher Education (AAHHE), ably led by Prof. Loui Olivas, decided to make a major investment in the books and to feature them at its annual conference in 2018. The president of ETS, Walter D. MacDonald, committed to write the foreword to *New Directions* and to give the keynote at one of the plenary sessions at the conference, and the chancellor of the California State University System, Timothy P. White, agreed to do the same with respect to *Moving Forward*. Selected authors representing both volumes will present their papers during the conference's concurrent sessions.

As the date of the AAHHE conference is highly time sensitive, the organization's major involvement in the project led to the necessity of having both volumes published relatively quickly by academic standards. A distinctively Hispanic design was called for with respect to the book covers and interior pages. Both a casebound and a softcover book were needed. At our request, SUNY Press graciously agreed to cancel our contract, and the result is that the Bilingual Press, which only publishes Hispanic-related texts—over 250 titles—has undertaken the project. The issue of timing is further facilitated because editors de los Santos and Keller, AAHHE and its leader Loui Olivas, and executive editor Karen Van Hooft and the editorial offices of the Bilingual Press are all housed together in the Hispanic Research Center (HRC) of Arizona State University.

THE EDITORS

Alfredo G. de los Santos Jr., the lead editor of these volumes, is a research professor at the Hispanic Research Center of Arizona State University. He is emeritus vice-chancellor of the Maricopa Community College District and the founding president of El Paso Community College. In addition, he was a founding vice president of AAHHE, which established the Dr. Alfredo G. de los Santos Jr. Distinguished Leadership in Higher Education Award in his honor. He has been a member of the board of trustees of the College Board, the Educational Testing Service, the United States Open University, the Carnegie Foundation for the Advancement of Teaching, the Council for Higher Education Accreditation, the Tomás Rivera Policy Institute at the University of Southern California, the American Association of Community Colleges, the American Association for Higher Education, American College Testing, and the American Council on Education. He is the recipient of the 1998 Harold W. McGraw Jr. Prize in Education, the Lifelong Dedication to Hispanic Education Award from the Hispanic Association of Colleges and Universities, the Profesor Honorario Award from the Universidad Autónoma de Guadalajara, and the 1993 Education Achievement Award from the National Science Foundation.

Laura I. Rendón, University of Texas at San Antonio professor emerita of educational leadership and policy studies, was named in 2013 one of the Most Powerful and Influential Women in Texas by the National Diversity Council. Rendón is also a nationally recognized education theorist, speaker, and advocate for low-income, first-generation students. She developed the theory of validation that faculty and student affairs practitioners have employed as a student success framework. Rendón is also a teaching and learning thought leader. She is the author of the book *Sentipensante (Sensing/Thinking) Pedagogy: Educating for Wholeness, Social Justice and Liberation* (2009). As a leader in the field of college access and achievement, Rendón's research has been featured in the *Chronicle of Higher Education* and the PBS documentary *The College Track*. She is cofounder and past board chair of the National Council for Community and Education Partnerships and past president of the Association for the Study of Higher Education (ASHE), a leading scholarly organization focusing on higher education research.

Gary Francisco Keller is Regents' Professor and director of the Hispanic Research Center at Arizona State University. He is the author of over thirty books and more than one hundred articles on Latino literature, film, art, linguistics, and language policy. In addition, he has received grants from the National Endowment for the Arts, National Science Foundation, US Department of Education, US Department of Energy, and numerous private foundations. Keller was the lead editor of *Assessment and Access: Hispanics in Higher Education* (SUNY Press, 1991), which was an inspiration for the New Directions project. In 1993 he was awarded a $50,000 prize for "Pioneering Achievement in Education" from the Charles A. Dana Foundation for his design and successful administration of Project 1000. He was featured in a 1989 issue of *Hispanic Business* magazine as among the "one hundred of the nation's most influential Hispanics." Keller received the 2006 National Association for Chicana and Chicano Studies (NACCS) Distinguished Scholar Award. In 2017 he was awarded the Dr. Loui Olivas Distinguished Leadership in Higher Education Award by The Victoria Foundation, and in 2018 he received the first AAHHE President's Award of the American Association of Hispanics in Higher Education.

Alberto Acereda is Senior Director, Global Education, at the Educational Testing Service (ETS) in Princeton, New Jersey. He provides overall leadership for business development initiatives and academic outreach in global and higher education. Prior to joining ETS in 2012, he spent two decades at various universities across the United States. Just before joining ETS he was at Arizona State University, where he was professor of Spanish and Latin American literatures and cultures, chair of the Program of Spanish and Portuguese, director of Graduate Studies at the School of International Letters and Cultures, member of the ASU provost's executive committee, and president of the senate of the College of Liberal Arts and Sciences. He is a member of the North American Academy of the Spanish Language (Academia Norteamericana de la Lengua Española), a branch of the Real Academia Española. He is currently a faculty affiliate at Arizona State University's Hispanic Research Center.

Estela Mara Bensimón is professor of higher education and director of the Center for Urban Education (CUE) at the University of Southern California Rossier School of Education. Her current research is on issues of racial equity in higher education from the perspective of organizational learning and sociocultural practice theories. Dr. Bensimón has held the highest leadership positions in the Association for the Study of Higher Education (President, 2005–2006) and the American Education Research Association–Division on Postsecondary Education (Vice President, 1992–1994). In 2011 she was inducted as an AERA Fellow in recognition of excellence in research. In 2013 she was presented with the Association for the Study of Higher Education Research Achievement Award, and in 2015 she received the American Association of Hispanics in Higher Education Outstanding Latino/a Faculty in Higher Education (Research Institutions) Award. In 2017 she was elected to the National Academy of Education; that same year she was presented with the Social Justice in Education Award by the American Education Research Association.

Richard J. Tannenbaum is a principal research director in the Research and Development Division of the Educational Testing Service (ETS). He has strategic oversight for multiple Centers of Research that include more than 100 directors, scientists, and research associates. These centers address foundational and applied research in the areas of academic-to-career readiness, English language learning and assessment (both domestic and international), and K-12 student assessment and teacher credentialing. Prior to this position, Richard was the senior research director for the Center for Validity Research at ETS. He holds a PhD in Industrial/Organizational Psychology from Old Dominion University. He has published numerous articles, book chapters, and technical papers. His areas of expertise include assessment development, licensure and certification, standard setting and alignment, and validation.

ABOUT THE ARTICLES IN *NEW DIRECTIONS*

Assessment

Alberto Acereda, Joseph A. Ríos, Ross Markle, María Elena Oliveri, and Ou Lydia Liu, "Signaling Success for Hispanic Students in a Changing Higher Education Landscape." Assessment and academic preparation are at the heart of the New Directions project. Educational Testing Service is the leading national and international provider of academic assessment, and this volume begins with a major article by ETS written by five leading researchers and administrators at that institution. This paper, which includes an ample and valuable bibliography, focuses on a variety of issues and strategies that have great potential for improving educational attainment and competitiveness in the job market for Hispanic students. Among the strategies, of special significance is a new approach to communicating nontraditional skills called "digital badges."

Rebecca A. Beals and Roberto A. Ibarra, "Multicontextuality: A Framework for Access and Assessment of Underrepresented STEM Students" addresses how, in a political climate marked by the diminished impact of affirmative action and race-based admissions to programs, alternative multicontextual models that focus on interaction, utilization of space, and other factors can challenge typical assimilationist models for student development. Such models have the potential to reframe departmental and institutional culture to promote systemic success for underrepresented STEM students.

Blanca Rincón, Belinda De La Rosa, and Jorge Chapa, "A State of Neglect: Latino Educational Attainment." The late Jorge Chapa, whose sudden death caused us shock and grief, was the leading demographer of Latino educational attainment. The coauthors of this article, including his wife Blanca De La Rosa, have taken up his mantle. Making ample use of U.S. Census Bureau and U.S. Department of Education data, they document how the Latino population has changed over the last twenty-five years, analyze educational attainment over time, and provide an overview of the salient sociodemographic characteristics of Latinos that are highly correlated with educational outcomes.

Lindsey E. Malcom-Piqueux and Estela Mara Bensimón, "Five Design Principles for Equity and Excellence in Hispanic-Serving Institutions" focuses on the critical issues related to Hispanic-Serving Institutions (HSIs). There is currently a lack of consensus on what it means to be an HSI. The authors take on this issue in depth, and they offer design principles for equity and excellence at HSIs that may be used to assess the extent to which those institutions with HSI designations are genuinely serving Latino/a students.

Melissa A. Martínez, "From Student to Professor: How Hispanics Are Faring as Faculty in Higher Education" provides a timely review on the current state of Hispanics in the professorate. Using up-to-date data, Martínez concludes that not only is there a continued need to recruit and retain more Hispanics in higher education, but we need to offer the necessary supports and make vital changes to the culture of academia in order to retain Latina/o faculty.

Academic Preparation

Gilda L. Ochoa, " 'That's Just Like Here, at Our College': Tracking Latina/o Inequality from High School Programs to Honors Colleges." Politicians and social commentators emphasize academic achievement gaps. However, they neglect other more important issues, namely social, racial/ethnic, economic, and opportunity gaps. Ochoa maintains that the academic and political debates focus on the product of schooling rather than the multiple processes that foster those very gaps. She examines how various K–12 practices prepare students for disparate paths and how these are often replicated and similarly unquestioned at colleges and universities through a hierarchy of colleges and proliferation of honors programs.

Ebelia Hernández and Antonio G. Estudillo, "The College Choice Process for High-Achieving Latinas" is a field-research study that explores the decision-making processes of a number of high-achieving Latinas in the US Northeast who ultimately chose to attend a public, selective, research-intensive institution. Utilizing critical race theory (CRT), the researchers draw conclusions about the individuals, policies, and institutional factors that informed the Latinas' decision-making processes, what information was used, and the advantages and constraints that influenced the college choice process.

Frances Contreras and Gilbert Contreras, "Latino Community College Students in California: Challenges and Opportunities for Leadership" explores the central challenges that exist for Latino students who attend community colleges in California, home to the largest community college system in the nation. The cohort analysis shows high developmental education rates and low completion rates for Latinos. In addition, the data suggests that persistence and the completion of thirty college units may be relatively high for Latinos, but this marker of success does not lead to community college completion and transfer of the students to four-year colleges.

Nancy Acevedo-Gil, "Latina/o Students Navigating the Labyrinth: Persistence in Community College Developmental Education" presents a case study on the condition of California's Latinas/os in developmental education. The study concludes that there is a major disconnection between the academic preparation received in K–12 and college-readiness. Moreover, education stakeholders need to address the institutional obstacles in developmental education in order to eliminate this major exit point in the higher education pipeline.

José Del Real Viramontes and Luis Urrieta Jr., "Un cuento de nunca acabar: Exploring the Transfer Conditions for Latinx Tejanx Community College Students in Texas" draws attention to current transfer policies and practices at six top public universities in Texas and evaluates their efforts to increase access, retention, and graduation rates for Texas Latinx community college students. The study provides a series of recommendations for addressing and improving those transfer policies and practices.

Laura I. Rendón, Vijay Kanagala, and Ripsimé K. Bledsoe, "Shattering the Deficit Grand Narrative: Toward a Culturally Validating Latino Student Success Framework" reviews the last three decades of research and practice on Latino college access and completion and finds that the dominant deficit-based model is simply not working, inappropriate, and even harmful for Latino students. The authors challenge deficit-based thinking and call for a Latino-centric perspective that provides an asset-based model incorporating contemporary, culturally validating features of student success.

Louie F. Rodríguez, "Nuestra Excelencia: Building an Institutional Culture of Excellence through a Latina/o Excellence Pedagogy at the Post-Secondary Level" recognizes that merely enrolling Latina/o students does not necessarily equate to serving this population. The author proposes an excellence-based pedagogical framework that addresses the challenges facing Latina/o college students and promotes a college/university culture that facilitates their success.

Acknowledgments

We acknowledge the advice and help from colleagues at Arizona State University's Hispanic Research Center (HRC), including Michael J. Sullivan, Karen S. Van Hooft, Melanie Magisos, and Ana María Regalado.

Michael, Executive Director for Science, Technology, Engineering, and Mathematics, has the uncanny ability to define problems clearly and succinctly, and based on that, to suggest the optimal solution. He also has a healthy and positive approach to problems: "Things will work out."

Karen, who has been with the HRC's Bilingual Press for four decades, first as Managing Editor and then Executive Editor, handled the extensive editorial queries and other communications with authors to produce the final manuscript as well as directing the books' physical production. Melanie, Executive Producer, Publishing and Product Development, also participated in the editorial and production processes.

We thank our coeditors, who include two old friends, Laura I. Rendón and Estela Mara Bensimón, and our colleagues at Educational Testing Service, Alberto Acereda and Richard J. Tannenbaum. They provided advice and counsel that helped the project move forward.

And finally, but not least, we thank Ana María Regalado, Director of Strategic Initiatives at the Hispanic Research Center, who provided organizational support for the project. This involved preparing the initial invitation letter to potential authors, receiving the manuscripts, keeping track of detailed information for more than 50 authors, receiving and filing the authors' biographical sketches, and more. As issues came up, Ana's response was positive and she always found a way to deal with the issue at hand. Without her help, this two-book project would not have happened.

PART

I

assessment

Signaling Success for Hispanic Students in a Changing Higher Education Landscape

*Alberto Acereda, Joseph A. Ríos, Ross Markle,
María Elena Oliveri, and Ou Lydia Liu*

This article explores how changes to the higher education landscape have the potential to improve educational attainment and competitiveness in the job market for Hispanic students. We discuss the lower attainment rates in higher education for Hispanic students, review literature that may explain some of the unique barriers that these students face, and highlight the role of Hispanic-Serving Institutions (HSIs) in increasing educational opportunity and attainment. Our discussion then shifts to changes in the higher education landscape, which include nontraditional pathways to credentials, an increased interest in nontraditional skills in higher education, and last, a new approach to communicating attainment of nontraditional skills, referred to as 'digital badges'. Although these changes can benefit all students, particular focus will be placed on the Hispanic context.

US HIGHER EDUCATION IN A GLOBAL KNOWLEDGE ECONOMY

In this digital age, society is in the midst of a great transformation, something economists have defined as the "knowledge economy." The term describes a shift from economies that focus on the production of goods to those in which the production and use of knowledge are paramount. Academic institutions are important foundations of such a system, not only for their production of knowledge but for their role in training knowledge producers in the skills necessary for success in this environment. However, due to decreasing investment in public higher education by state and federal governments in the United States, academic institutions have faced falling revenues, which have led to tuition increases for students. This increased cost has not only led to issues of accessibility for many students, but has also generated a public demand for a greater return on investment in a degree (Henry, Pagano, Puckett, and Wilson 2014). In fact, misplaced institutional priorities have led to too many students not graduating on time, and, for those who do graduate, many are found to lack adequate preparation (see for example Goodman, Sands, and Coley 2015) and are burdened by record debt (American Council of Trustees and Alumni 2014).

Without acknowledging and acting on the current issues in higher education, the United States risks falling behind in a global race for innovation and talent. Organizations like the Lumina Foundation (2013) believe that, unless actions are taken now to significantly increase postsecondary attainment, we will fail to produce a highly educated populace that will strengthen America's democracy and economy. That is why the Lumina Foundation has focused its resources on seeking 60 percent postsecondary degree or certificate attainment among American adults by the year 2025. Projections by the Georgetown Center on Education and the Workforce show that more than 65 percent of US jobs will require some form of postsecondary credential by the end of this decade (Carnevale, Smith, and Strohl 2014). And yet, according to the Lumina Foundation's (2015) annual Stronger Nation report on postsecondary attainment rates, only 40 percent of working-age adults (ages 25 to 64) now hold at least a two-year degree.

Furthermore, this report demonstrates a persistent and widening gap in degree attainment (at least a two-year degree) among ethnic groups. As an example, both Asian American and White adults aged 25 to 64 possess much higher degree attainment (60.1 percent and 44.5 percent, respectively) than do educationally underrepresented minority groups of the same ages, such as African Americans (28.1 percent), Native Americans (23.9 percent), and Hispanics (20.3 percent). Clearly, to reach the goal of having the highest concentration of adults with postsecondary degrees in the world, the United States must do a better job in closing this attainment gap among ethnic groups. One way to do this is to accelerate the rate of higher education attainment for Hispanics, who are one of the fastest growing ethnic groups in the country (Brown 2014).

BARRIERS TO POSTSECONDARY ATTAINMENT FOR HISPANIC STUDENTS

In 2012, Hispanics were the second largest ethnic group in the United States, making up 17 percent of the total population, and they are expected to have continued growth (Lumina Foundation 2013). By 2050, it is estimated that they will constitute more than 33 percent of the US population under five years old, and 30 percent (119 million) of the general population by 2060 (Colby and Ortman 2015). In terms of education, 70 percent of Hispanic high school seniors enrolled in college in 2012, and the number of bachelor's degrees conferred on Hispanics has increased by more than 50 percent over the past five years (*Excelencia* in Education 2015). Nonetheless, Hispanics have consistently had the highest percentage of high school droupouts and the lowest percentage of college graduates (Capello 2015). As a result, it is no surprise that Hispanics have high rates of unemployment, fewer individuals in the highest-paying occupations, and overrepresentation in lower-paying service jobs. These facts are particularly troubling, as Hispanics are projected to have a 2.5 percent increase in labor participation by 2022, compared to just 0.2 percent for non-Hispanic White students (*Excelencia* in Education 2015).

While there have been encouraging developments over the past decade, such as an exponential increase in the number of Hispanics enrolling in higher education (Fry 2011) and increased attainment of college degrees (*Excelencia* in Education 2015), this group largely remains underserved across virtually all areas of higher education, with many barriers to postsecondary attainment. These barriers include a lack of knowledge about college, concerns over affordability, and family and work obligations, to name a few (Kelley, Schneider, and Carey 2010; Liu 2011). Research has shown each one of these barriers to have direct implications for Hispanic student persistence in obtaining a college degree.

One of the biggest barriers that academically qualified Hispanic students face in enrolling in college is a lack of resources to make informed decisions about the college process. In a qualitative analysis of Hispanic high school seniors, Immerwahr (2003) found that students had little knowledge of higher education and no direct or clear adult guidance from parents, teachers, or counselors in making educational choices. They were misinformed about how to apply to college, and believed that higher education was useful only for an individual who had already decided on a particular career. As a result, Hispanic students tend to be unaware of institutions that are both academically and financially within reach, and, if they do enroll in college, often choose less selective schools than they might be qualified to attend (Smith, Pender, and Howell 2012). This direction may in turn lead to low educational attainment, as Hispanic student graduation rates have been found to be strongly related to institutional selectivity; that is, as admission selectivity increases, so do Hispanic graduation rates (Kelley, Schneider, and Carey 2010). Although this outcome may be partly due to precollege factors, such as lack of quality and rigor in the high school curriculum (Warburton, Bugarin, and Núñez 2001), it may be due mostly to a lack of institutional focus on retention and graduation rates (Kelley, Schneider, and Carey 2010).

An additional barrier to higher education attainment for Hispanics is the concern over cost. This concern tends to be coupled with that of fulfilling family responsibilities and work. As noted by Immerwahr (2003), many Hispanic students work between 20 and 40 hours per week while in high school. The concern over diverting energy from making an income often leaves many students unsure about whether higher education is the right choice for them. Of those Hispanic high school students who do decide to enroll, nearly 50 percent attend two-year colleges (*Excelencia* in Education 2015). From an economic standpoint, attending an in-state community college can save students on average of $5,281 on tuition and fees over an in-state four-year university, and an average of $8,549 on room and board if they commute from home (College Board 2011). However, contrary to general belief, community colleges have not traditionally served as a gateway to transferring to a four-year college and obtaining a bachelor's degree (Arbona and Nora 2007). In fact, a longitudinal study of transfer rates showed that only 6 percent of Hispanic students had obtained a bachelor's degree six years after enrolling in community college, although 23 percent wanted to obtain a four-year degree (Hoachlander, Sikora, Horn, and Carroll 2003).

The low instance of successful transfers has generally been attributed to several causes: lowering of students' educational expectations while at two-year colleges (Clark 1960), a shift by community colleges from pre-transfer education to vocational programs (Dougherty 1994), poor academic preparedness for upper-division courses (Dougherty 1994), an inability to secure financial aid (Dougherty 1994), and loss of academic credit when transferring (Monaghan and Attewell 2014). Furthermore, the need to fulfill family responsibilities and work while going to college affects enrollment status by encouraging part-time over full-time enrollment, limiting students' academic integration and involvement on campus, and taking focus away from academic performance (depending on the type of employment)—all factors that influence Hispanic students' persistence in college, and ultimately, their educational attainment (see for example Lee, Mackie-Lewis, and Marks 1993; Nora and Wedham 1991; and Wassmer, Moore, and Shulock 2004). Taken together, these results suggest that Hispanic students face many barriers that directly and negatively affect their educational attainment. To address these issues, Hispanic-Serving Institutions have been tasked with increasing educational opportunity and attainment among Hispanic students.

THE ROLE OF THE HISPANIC-SERVING INSTITUTION (HSI)

HSIs are higher education institutions that (a) are accredited and nonprofit, (b) have student bodies that consist of at least 25 percent Hispanic undergraduates enrolled full-time, and (c) possess a 50-percent Hispanic student population that is low income. Currently, 435 educational institutions, comprising 13 percent of total institutions in the United States and Puerto Rico, have been designated as HSIs by the US Department of Education. These institutions are almost evenly divided between two- and four-year colleges (219 and 216, respectively) and are based in 18 states and Puerto Rico. Since the 1994–1995 academic year, the number of HSIs has grown by 130 percent, and it appears that the number will continue to grow as there are, at the time of this writing, 310 emerging HSIs (defined as institutions with Hispanic full-time-equivalent enrollments between 15 and 24 percent). In total, 62 percent of Hispanic undergraduates (about 1,750,000 students) are enrolled in HSIs, and they comprise on average 46 percent of the total student population at these institutions. For further information about HSIs, see *Excelencia* in Education (2016).

Since HSIs enroll such a large percentage of Hispanic undergraduates, Title V funding from the US Department of Education is available on a competitive basis to assist in retaining and graduating Hispanic students at these institutions. That is, institutions are eligible to submit a grant proposal to obtain five-year funding to (a) improve student support services (e.g., academic tutoring or counseling, financial aid, and/or community college transfer services), (b) construct or renovate instructional facilities, (c) purchase educational materials (e.g., scientific or laboratory equipment for teaching), (d) develop innovative and customized instruction courses (e.g., distance learning academic instruction), and (e) invest in faculty development, to name a few. For the 2015 fiscal year, the US Department of Education awarded 96 new five-year grants averaging $544,941 per grant for a total of $51,066,641 (US Department of Education 2016). However, the question remains, how successful have HSIs been in increasing educational opportunity and attainment among Hispanic students?

HISPANIC GRADUATION RATES AT HSIs

Data on graduation rates for HSIs have shown that the gap between Hispanics and Whites is smaller than at non-HSIs. However, this is not due to increased Hispanic graduation rates, but rather to Whites graduating at a below-average rate (Kelley, Schneider, and Carey 2010). In reality, HSIs have nearly identical retention rates to non-HSIs, 67 and 66 percent respectively (Postsecondary National Policy Institute 2015), and when controlling for admissions criteria, HSIs graduate Hispanic students at about the same rate as other institutions (Kelley, Schneider, and Carey 2010). Such statistics suggest that in general HSIs are not necessarily meeting their task of increasing educational opportunity and attainment rates among Hispanic students, and that, to some degree, they perpetuate many of the inequities in student persistence, degree completion, and lack of participation in high-demand fields that they purport to address (Contreras, Malcom and Bensimon 2008; Malcom-Piqueux and Bensimon 2015; Malcom-Piqueux, Suro, Bensimon and Fischer 2013).

One reason for the lack of improvements in Hispanic educational outcomes at HSIs is that, with few exceptions, the HSI designation does not correlate to an institution's identity, mission, and priorities (Malcom-Piqueux and Bensimon 2015). Instead, HSI designation is entirely based on the demographic makeup of the student population, rather than on any institutional priority to facilitate academic success for Hispanic students. Consequently, some have argued for changes: one is a national dialogue on what it means to be truly Hispanic-serving (Malcom-Piqueux and Bensimon 2015); another is that HSI designation and Title V funding should be tied to institutional performance on outcomes for Hispanic students, such as retention, graduation, and labor-market success (Kelley, Schneider, and Carey 2010). Regardless, improving the state of HSIs is extremely important to advancing the agenda of decreasing the unemployment and poverty rates for Hispanics in this country (Nora and Crisp 2009).

CHANGES IN THE HIGHER EDUCATION LANDSCAPE THAT MAY BENEFIT HISPANIC STUDENTS

The sections that follow describe how three areas of change in the higher education landscape may be beneficial to improving both educational attainment and competitiveness in the job market for Hispanic students: (a) nontraditional pathways to credentialing, (b) a focus on expanding nontraditional skills, and (c) microcredentialing.

Nontraditional Pathways to Credentialing

Technological changes have facilitated the rise of nontraditional educational models, which are needed to create greater accessibility, flexibility, and affordability in higher education for Hispanic students. Traditionally, many institutions have organized their schedules, policies, services, and curricular pathways around traditional first-time, full-time students (Hess, 2011); yet, a large number of Hispanic students may not fit this profile as many may be nontraditional students due to family and work obligations and/or the need to obtain additional postsecondary training upon embarking on a career. These Hispanic students are part of a general nontraditional student population that has seen rapid growth, leading to projections that such students will make up 73% of the college population by 2018 (Hussar & Bailey, 2009). Consequently, distance education (also referred to as distance learning or e-learning), which allows for teaching outside the traditional classroom setting, may provide greater flexibility and accessibility for Hispanic students.

The number of HSIs providing at least one distance education course has been found to be equivalent to the national average; however, the number of Hispanic students enrolling in these courses has been found to be lower than non-Hispanic students at HSIs (US General Accounting Office, 2003). Lower participation rates may largely be related to negative perceptions of distance education credibility (Saltzman, 2014) and a lack of academic support, as Hispanic students have been found to perform better in a traditional class environment when compared to online instruction (Figlio, Rush, & Yin, 2013). To address this discrepancy, HSIs have actively sought Title V funding to improve access to distance education for Hispanic students by increasing teacher training in using this modality, improving technological capabilities, and most importantly, developing and providing online academic support services for students enrolled in distance education courses or programs (US Department of Education 2016). Clearly, more research is needed to understand the effectiveness of these efforts, but distance education, if used thoughtfully, can assist in providing more accessible and equitable education for Hispanic students.

Another educational model that has drawn increasing interest is competency-based education (CBE). CBE has gained favor because of its potential to propel students to degree completion faster, more economically, and on a more flexible schedule. This is possible for two reasons. First, CBE models are not subject- or content-based. Rather, they focus on the skills and abilities that students should possess. Second, CBE models are not temporally based. That is, CBE models define learning by achievement and not the time spent in a course. Thus, entering students can complete a program if they have received no instruction or other interventions from the educational program but can demonstrate all the required program outcomes. With such flexibility and opportunities for acceleration (for example, obtaining credit without instruction), CBE programs have the potential to drive down the cost of a degree, which is particularly beneficial to Hispanic students who view cost as a barrier to higher education attainment. In fact, increasing educational access for economically disadvantaged students and reducing inequities in student outcomes has been one of the main drivers for implementing CBE programs throughout the country (Steele et al. 2014). This new focus on competency-based learning has grown dramatically, and in early 2016 there were 600 colleges or universities in the United States experimenting with the model, including HSIs such as Brandman University, which currently offers a CBE bachelor's degree of business administration. Taken together, nontraditional educational models such as distance and competency-based education have the potential to reduce some of the barriers (e.g., cost, flexibility, and accessibility) that Hispanic students face in the traditional university educational model.

Expanding Skills in Higher Education

Although nontraditional educational models may assist in improving educational attainment for Hispanic students, simply possessing a college degree may not make these individuals competitive in the job market. In fact, research has shown that wage gaps for Hispanics in the labor force are largely predicted by lower levels of nontraditional or noncognitive skills (Petre 2014). Therefore, to improve the labor-market success of Hispanic students, there is a clear need to focus not only on the technical skills associated with a college degree but also on the additional skills needed to thrive in the workforce. The paragraphs that follow provide a description of the historical reasons for a shift in the need for these skills, the current deficiencies in the preparation of students to enter the workforce, the efforts within higher education to improve these skills, and the assessment efforts intended to hold institutions such as HSIs accountable for developing these skills.

Over the last several decades, there has been a clearly stated need for college graduates to demonstrate more diverse and complex skills, including critical thinking, communication, interpersonal skills, and creativity. In some ways, calls for greater focus on these skills emerge at the intersection of global economic trends and increased accountability of higher education. In other ways, there are direct calls from employers for clear demonstration of these factors in their new employees (i.e., recent college graduates). Still others might argue that these are the characteristics at the heart of a liberal education that colleges and universities have been providing all along. Regardless of the impetus, it is clear that college graduates need a different set of skills to meet the needs of a 21st century workforce. These skills include more complex versions of traditional skills (e.g., communication, problem solving, critical thinking, quantitative literacy, information literacy) as well as so-called noncognitive factors that have rarely been explicit parts of curricula, instruction, or learning outcomes.

The skills required of college graduates to succeed in the labor market have changed over the past 30 years in response to changes in the economy (Autor, Levy, and Murnane 2003). These economic changes include a loss of manufacturing jobs, the introduction of more sophisticated work technologies, and an increased demand for workers in the service sector (Murphy and Welch 1995). The impact of technological innovation on the skills rewarded in the labor market is a prevailing view for many of the structural changes to the economy (Autor, Katz, and Kearny 2008; Kirsch, Braun, and Yamamoto 2007). These technological changes have been collectively referred to as skill-biased technological change by Mooalen, Goos, and Manny (2003) and are replacing many facets of work once performed by human workers. As routine tasks have become more highly automated, and as the shift from a manufacturing to a service economy has taken place, the unique skills performed by highly skilled human workers have come to hold a premium in the labor market (Levy and Murnane 2005).

Within this environment, highly skilled workers with complex thinking and interpersonal skills are needed, as the new economy requires problem-solving, integration of knowledge, and strong communication skills (National Research Council 2008). As Autor, Levy, and Murnane (2003) note, computers did not take over all aspects of work, as once feared, but their widespread use crystallized the aspects of work that require a highly skilled workforce. Technological innovation also drove the globalization of work; as the means of production and technical knowledge and information became more easily transmitted, there was increasing competition for fewer jobs and ever greater demand for technological skill (Walters 2005).

While this new economy favored college-educated workers over high school graduates (Katz 2003), new skills were required from college-educated workers as well (Partnership for 21st Century Skills 2003). In this new knowledge- or information-based economy, content knowledge was no longer sufficient; employers were asking for college educated workers with advanced critical thinking and noncognitive skills who could produce in a knowledge-based service economy (Casner, Lotto, and Bennington 2006).

With these changes has emerged a "skills gap." Whereas changes to the labor market began in the eighties, it took some time before the demands of the labor market reached higher education, as the mismatch between the product of higher education and the requirements of the workforce became apparent (Casner et al. 2006). Accordingly, the landscape of higher education changed to address the preparation of a more diverse workforce for a labor market requiring more highly skilled workers with both cognitive and noncognitive skills.

Much of the evidence of these needed skills comes from the voices of employers. For example, various surveys have shown that relatively few employers (28 percent) feel that four-year colleges and universities are preparing students adequately for the modern workforce (Hart Research Associates 2010). In general, employers feel that there is a shortage of qualified applicants with sufficient skills (Manyika et al. 2011), and that critical complex skills (e.g., oral and written communication, teamwork/collaboration, professionalism/work ethic, and critical thinking/problem solving) are centrally important for college graduates (Casner-Lotto and Benner 2006). Although there are many hypotheses about potential causes, it is clear that employers are not thoroughly pleased with the human capital that higher education is producing.

The business community has been by no means alone in calling for new skills; members of the higher education community have also identified key skills that require additional attention. Rather than noting gaps in skills, literature in this arena tends to focus on the need to redefine and reestablish key learning outcomes for colleges and universities. The many examples include the Liberal Education and America's Promise (LEAP) initiative of the Association of American Colleges and Universities (2011), the degree qualifications profile put forth by the Lumina Foundation (Adelman, Ewell, Gaston, and Geary Schneider 2014), the Council for the Advancement of Standards in Higher Education (Strayhorn 2006), and the Assessment and Teaching of 21st Century Skills (ATC21S 2012). Each of these models not only presents expanded sets of complex skills, but also provides robust frameworks and defines student learning outcomes in several domains.

Ultimately, whether the motivation for addressing such skills comes from the workforce or from within higher education, one of the key challenges is not just to identify these skills, but to provide tools that can provide data, insight, and measures of achievement to develop and improve them (Markle et al. 2013). Here, recent work by the Educational Testing Service has notably sought to advance the field and help both institutions and students.

Signaling Success in Learning

To help higher education institutions such as HSIs assess these newly expected skills both for improvement and accountability, ETS started an initiative to (a) identify the most important student learning outcomes valued by institutions and (b) develop next generation assessments for these outcomes by leveraging advanced theories, practices, and psychometric techniques. In addressing the first objective, researchers relied on a broad-based review of existing frameworks for student learning in higher education, as well as input from institutional provosts and vice presidents regarding the learning outcomes they expected of their college graduates. Some of the key frameworks considered were the Framework for Higher Education Qualifications, European Higher Education Area Competencies, Liberal Education and America's Promise, Framework for Learning and Development Outcomes, the Degree Qualifications Profile, the Assessment and Teaching of 21st Century Skills instrument, and the General Competency Model Framework of the ETA Competency Model Clearinghouse (for a review of each framework, see Markle, Brenneman, Jackson, Burrus, and Robbins 2013). In addition to the efforts already cited, ETS surveyed more than 220 administrators of two- and four-year, profit and nonprofit, and public and private institutions.

From the review and survey, ETS identified six key learning outcomes: critical thinking, written communication, quantitative literacy, digital and information literacy, civic competency and engagement, and intercultural competency and diversity. These domains are diverse in that they cover skills that have been traditionally evaluated as student learning outcomes (e.g., written communication and quantitative literacy) as well as those that have seen increased interest in both higher education and the workforce (e.g., digital and information literacy, civic competency and engagement, and intercultural competency and diversity; Association of American Colleges & Universities 2011; Hart Research Associates 2013).

However, many of the nontraditional or noncognitive skills identified present distinctive measurement concerns. For example, it may be challenging to provide a clear operational definition for noncognitive skills, to develop items that are genuine indicators of these skills, and to reduce socially desirable responding for dispositional or attitudinal skill components. It is factors such as these that have limited the development of large-scale assessments for such skills and constitute a major obstacle to deriving valid measures of these learning outcomes. To address this challenge, ETS took a research-driven approach to assessment design. The process consisted of four broad procedures for each skill domain: 1) review influential frameworks, 2) evaluate existing assessments in regard to assessment design and validity evidence, 3) develop an operational definition by involving external consultants who are experts in the domain of interest, and 4) consider assessment design considerations, such as test length and types of data preferred, which were informed by recommendations from external experts, provosts, and deans.

For a thorough description of the literature review and assessment efforts within various domains, the reader is referred to reports on test development endeavors in intercultural competency and diversity (Griffith, Wolfeld, Armon, Rios, & Liu 2016), written communication (Sparks, Song, Brantley, & Liu 2014), critical thinking (Liu, Frankel, & Roohr 2014), quantitative literacy (Roohr, Graf, & Liu 2014), and civic competency and engagement (Toney-Purta, Cabrera, Roohr, Liu, & Rios 2015). Taken together, these efforts highlight ETS's commitment to redefining key learning outcomes for colleges and universities as well as developing assessment tools to assist in improving accountability.

Microcredentialing

With the development of assessments that measure complex traditional and noncognitive skills, the next issue that arises is how to present stakeholders with certification of Hispanic students' achievement in these areas. Traditional certification in higher education, such as degrees and transcripts, has largely been associated with the amount of time spent learning or the number of course credits obtained. Olneck (2012) has suggested that this form of certification is related to the "genericism," or orientation toward generic skills, that has grown over time within universities. However, as there has been a push by employers for universities to develop skills in students that are useful within the workforce, such traditional credentialing is inappropriate, as the granularity provided by transcripts and degrees lacks the specificity necessary for employers to make informed hiring decisions (Riconscente, Kamarainen, and Honey 2013). An alternative proposed by researchers such as Shanker (1988) and Baker (2007) is to provide credentialing for skills that are obtained at a more granular-level than those obtained by convential degrees and transcripts, which is referred to as microcredentialing (Yu, Dyjur, Miltenburg, and Saito 2015). One way that a student can express her microcredentials is through digital badges.

Digital badges. A digital badge can be generally defined as an online validated credential of an accomplishment or skill earned through a variety of online or offline learning environments. The origin of the digital badge is associated with the traditional physical merit badges worn by members of the military and scouting organizations for young people (Gibson, Ostashewski, Flintoff, Grant, and Knight 2013). However, a digital badge offers greater advantages in that metadata can be embedded in the badge image file to provide information to any stakeholder, a potential employer for example. Metadata could provide descriptions of the issuer, the skill obtained, the method of assessment, the proficiency criteria against which the student was measured, the quality of performance, the date of expiration (if applicable), and information as to whether ongoing study or experience is needed to maintain the badge. In terms of documenting the validity of digital badges via metadata, the Mozilla Foundation has been influential in designing and maintaining the technical infrastructure that any organization can use to create, issue, and verify the authenticity of digital badges.[1] In addition, this infrastructure allows students to combine multiple digital badges obtained from diverse issuers and display them via the Internet to potential employers in what has been called a "digital backpack." This approach allows the individual student to fully control whether all badges or only a subset of badges should be shared when considering a particular audience (e.g., peers or a potential employer). The next section will highlight the proposed advantages of digital badges for students, higher education institutions, and employers, respectively.

Advantages of digital badges. From the student's perspective, microcredentialing allows for one to capture, validate, and provide evidence of skills that are increasingly gaining interest in higher education and industry (Davidson 2011). These skills can then act as supplementary information to traditional credentials to improve competitiveness in the job market (Rughiniç 2013). Additionally, with the infrastructure of digital backpacks students can easily visualize previously accomplished goals, reflect on their progress, and plan for future learning experiences throughout their life (Hickey, Otto, Itow, Schenke, Tran, and Chow 2014). From an institutional perspective, microcredentialing is advantageous in that it allows institutions to (a) explicitly state the connections between learning opportunities offered, (b) communicate valued knowledge and skills to stakeholders, and (c) increase visibility to prospective students when granting badges for skills in high demand by employers (Knight 2012; Riconscente, Kamarainen, and Honey 2013).

Finally, employers can benefit from microcredentialing by using digital badges as an indicator of prospective employee capacities. This would allow employers to narrow an applicant pool to those individuals that possess digital badges for the skills necessary or desired for the job of interest (Devedžić and Jovanović 2015). However, this would require (a) that employers identify

---

1. For other platforms that address the design and development of digital badges, including issuing and validating them, see openbadges.org/participating-issuers.

the limited and specific qualities that they are seeking and (b) that digital badges correspond to those qualities exist (Olneck 2012). If these requirements can be met, traditional academic credentials such as transcripts and degrees could serve as preliminary requirements for job entry, while digital badges could provide evidence of skills that cannot be observed through grades or degrees. Such information may be vital, as only 38 percent of employers have stated that there is a strong relationship between academic performance and job preparedness (Raish and Rimland 2016).

Current uses of digital badges. Given these advantages, it is of no surprise that Hispanic-serving universities, such as the University of Texas Rio Grande Valley, are already offering digital badges (Corbeil, Corbeil, and Rodríguez 2015). Furthermore, HSIs such as Chaffey College in Rancho Cucamonga, California, and La Guardia Community College in New York City have received Title V funding to increase their badging capability to serve their largely Hispanic student populations. In addition, large-scale initiatives have been developed to generally increase digital badging in higher education. For example, the Education Design Lab has partnered with higher education institutions and employers to (a) identify skills that are most desired by employers and (b) design digital badges that are competency-based (i.e., not participation based), allow for assessment, and are transparent in terms of the requirements necessary for obtainment of the badge.[2] An additional initiative partnered by the Clinton Global Initiative, the MacArthur Foundation, Mozilla, and HASTAC (Humanities, Arts, Science, and Technology Alliance and Collaboratory) has been undertaken to provide outreach and technical assistance to universities and employers to incorporate digital badges for admissions, obtaining academic credit, hiring, and promotions.[3]

Although microcredentialing is clearly gaining momentum, there is no literature to date regarding the adoption rate of digital badges by human resource or hiring professionals. However, the majority of employers surveyed have stated that their level of interest in digital badges is largely dependent on learning more about microcredentialing (Raish and Rimland 2016). Their concern may be due to the fact that there has been only limited research on the definitions, assumptions, assessment, and credibility of microcredentialing (Riconscente, Kamarainen, and Honey 2013).

---

2. See eddesignlab.org/badgingchallenge.

3. For the MacArthur Foundation initiatives, see macfound.org/press/press-releases/better-futures-2-million-americans-through-open-badges.

Digital badge limitations and directions for future research. Many of the issues associated with digital badges are related to the push for an open credentialing system in which essentially any organization can grant badges. This system has led to a lack of standardization across the most basic principles underlying digital badges. As an example, in conducting interviews with 40 representatives of badge initiatives, reviewing literature published in academic journals and blog posts, as well as obtaining feedback during a meeting of 100 national leaders associated with the badge movement, Riconscente, Kamarainen, and Honey (2013) found a substantial variation in badge definitions and assumptions. Specifically, badges were assumed to be a new form of assessment as opposed to a new form of credentialing, and, as a new form of assessment, digital badges were suggested to be an innately more valid and reliable approach when compared to traditional credentialing and assessment practices. The authors also found that a major concern raised about microcredentialing was related to the assessment practices in badge implementations. As noted by Devedži and Jovanović (2015), the acceptance of badges as a valid indicator of the associated knowledge or skill is highly related to whether alternative forms of assessment (for example, performance-based tests, e-portfolios, and peer assessment) are accepted by employers. In a review of 30 badge development initiatives, Hickey et al. (2014) found that there were no standardized assessment design practices shared. As an example, initiatives differed in terms of using leveled badge systems, aligning assessment activities to standards, using scoring rubrics, employing formative feedback, enhancing validity arguments with expert judges, designing assessments with built-in mastery learning (giving practice until mastery is met), and involving students in assessment design.

Such findings highlight one of the biggest issues associated with digital badges: perceived credibility. That is, due to the focus on open credentialing, a mechanism for establishing the credibility of badges does not at present exist. Without such a mechanism, employers may wonder whether a badge is a valid indicator of the knowledge or skills that a potential employee possesses. Consequently, the value of a badge may largely be dependent on its perceived credibility (Riconscente, Kamarainen, and Honey 2013). To address this concern, Hamilton (2014) has suggested that the credibility of a digital badge may lie in its endorsement by established companies and educational institutions. However, some fear that this process of endorsement would lead to large organizations holding control over smaller entities, which could lead to credibility being tied to partnerships and marketing as opposed to assessment practices and research (Riconscente et al. 2013). To avoid this potential pitfall, Knight (2013) suggested that digital badges should undergo traditional accreditation in which standards, evaluation, and evidence would serve as the pillars of credibility. However, to implement such an accreditation system, a number of organizational and technical challenges would have to be overcome (Devedžić and Jovanović 2015). Consequently, it is apparent that greater adoption of digital badges requires further research and outreach to higher education institutions and employers. If we can overcome these challenges, digital badges have the potential to document and validate knowledge and skills that have previously been underappreciated in higher education and can supplement traditional credentials to make Hispanic students more competitive in the job market.

Conclusion

Hispanics are the largest and one of the fastest-growing ethnic groups in the United States. However, they are also one of the most undereducated populations in the country, and as a result possess high rates of unemployment, fewer individuals in the highest-paying occupations, and overrepresentation in lower-paying service jobs. This is largely attributed to barriers that Hispanics face in higher education such as questions over affordability, flexibility, and accessibility, which lead to inequitable outcomes (e.g., persistence, degree completion, and participation in high-demand fields) even at Hispanic-Serving Institutions.

To address these issues, this article has highlighted potential changes to the higher education landscape that have the potential to improve degree attainment and labor market success for Hispanics. Specific focus was placed on how nontraditional pathways, such as distance and competency-based education programs, might provide a more affordable, accessible, and flexible education to Hispanics. Furthermore, we also discussed how a focus on nontraditional skills and microcredentialing by higher education institutions have the potential to improve labor market success for Hispanics by supplementing traditional college credentials, such as degrees, with microcredentials of highly desirable skills from industry. However, as these changes to the higher education landscape are relatively new, it is unclear how impactful they have been, and as result, they require further research. Regardless, we need continued improvements in educational policies and practices that target Hispanic educational attainment and labor market success. The economic vitality and strength of democracy in the United States is and will be further determined by how well we serve our Hispanic population (Kelley, Schneider, and Carey 2010).

REFERENCES

Adelman, C., P. Ewell, P. Gaston, and C. Geary Schneider. 2014. *The Degree Qualifications Profile.* Washington, DC: The Lumina Foundation.

American Council of Trustees and Alumni. 2014. *Education or Reputation? A Look at America's Top-Ranked Liberal Arts Colleges,* https://www.goacta.org/images/download/education_or_reputation.pdf.

Arbona, C., and A. Nora. 2007."The Influence of Academic and Environmental Factors on Hispanic College Degree Attainment." *Review of Higher Education* 30: 247–269.

Association of American Colleges and Universities (AAC&U). 2011. *The LEAP Vision for Learning: Outcomes, Practices, Impact, and Employers' Views.* Washington, DC.

Autor, D. H., L. F. Katz, and M. S. Kearney. 2008. "Trends in US Wage Inequality: Revising the Revisionists." *Review of Economics and Statistics* 90: 300–323.

Autor, D. H., F. Levy, and R. J. Murnane. 2003. "The Skill Content of Recent Technological Change: An Empirical Exploration." *The Quarterly Journal of Economics* 118: 1279-1333.

Baker, E. L. 2007. "Presidential Address: The End(s) of Testing." *Educational Researcher* 36: 309–317.

Brown, A. 2014. *US Hispanic and Asian Populations Growing, But for Different Reasons.* Retrieved from http://www.pewresearch.org/fact-tank/2014/06/26/u-s-hispanic-and-asian-populations-growing-but-for-different-reasons/.

Carnevale, Anthony P., Nicole Smith, and Jeff Strohl. 2014. *Recovery: Job Growth and Education Requirements through 2020.* Washington, DC: Georgetown Public Policy Institute, Center on Education and the Workforce.

Casner-Lotto, J., and L. Barrington. 2006. *Are They Really Ready to Work?* Washington, DC: Partnership for 21st Century Skills.

Cappello, L. 2015. *Educational Attainment in the United States and Six Major Metropolitan Areas, 1990–2010: A Quantitative Study by Race, Ethnicity, and Sex.* New York: Graduate Center, CUNY, Center for Latin American, Caribbean & Latino Studies, http://clacls.gc.cuny.edu/files/2015/11/Educational-Attainment-US-and-Metro-Areas-1990-2010.pdf

Clark, B. A. 1960. "The 'Cooling-Out' Function in Higher Education." *American Journal of Sociology* 65: 569–576.

Colby, S. L., and J. M. Ortman. 2015. *Projections of the Size and Composition of the US Population: 2014 to 2060.* Current Population Reports, P25-1143. Washington, DC: US Census Bureau.

College Board. 2011. *Trends in College Pricing: 2011.* New York, NY: College Board.

Contreras, F. E., L. E. Malcom, and E. M. Bensimon. 2008. Hispanic-Serving Institutions: Closeted Identity and the Production of Equitable Outcomes for Latino/A Students. In *Interdisciplinary Approaches to Understanding Minority Serving Institutions,* edited by M. Gasman, B. Baez, and C. Turner, 71–90. Albany: SUNY Press.

Corbeil, M. E., J. R. Corbeil, I. E. Rodríguez. 2015. "Digital Badges in Higher Education: A Three-Phase Study on the Implementation of Digital Badges in an Online Undergraduate Program." *Issues in Information Systems* 16: 1–9.

Davidson, C. N. 2016. *Why Badges Work Better Than Grades* (2011). Humanities, Arts, Science, and Technology Alliance and Collaboratory (HASTAC), http://hastac.org/blogs/cathy-davidson/why-badges-work-better-grades.

Devedžić, V., and J. Jovanović. 2015. "Developing Open Badges: A Comprehensive Approach." *Educational Technology Research and Development* 63: 1–18.

Dougherty, K. J. 1994. *The Contradictory College: The Conflicting Origins, Impacts, and Futures of the Community College.* Albany: State University of New York Press.

Excelencia in Education. 2015. *The Condition of Latinos in Education: 2015 Factbook.* Washington, DC: Excelencia in Education.

_____. 2016. *Hispanic-Serving Institutions (HSIs): 2014-2015 at a Glance.* Washington, DC: Excelencia in Education .

Figlio, D., M. Rush, and L. Yin. 2014. "Is It Live or Is It Internet? Experimental Estimates of the Effects of Online Instruction on Student Learning." *Journal of Labor Economics* 31: 763–784.

Fry, R. 2011. *Hispanic College Enrollment Spikes, Narrowing Gaps With Other Groups.* Washington, DC: Pew Research Center.

Gibson, D., N. Ostashewski, K. Flintoff, S. Grant, and E. Knight. 2015. "Digital Badges in Education." *Education and Information Technologies* 20: 403–410.

Goodman, M. J., A. M. Sands, and R. J. Coley. 2015. *America's Skills Challenge: Millenials and the Future.* Princeton: ETS Center for Research on Human Capital and Education.

Griffith, R. L., L. Wolfeld, B. Armon, J. A. Ríos, and O. L. Liu. 2016. "Assessing Intercultural Competence in Higher Education: Existing Research and Future Research." Unpublished manuscript.

Hamilton, G. 2014. *Evidencing Employability Skills with Open Badges.* JISC RSC Scotland e-Assessment, http://goo.gl/eiBlim.

Hart Research Associates. 2010. *Raising the Bar: Employers' Views on College Learning in The Wake of The Economic Downturn.* Washington, DC: Association of American Colleges and Universities.

_____. 2013. *It Takes More Than A Major: Employer Priorities for College Learning and Student Success,* an online survey among employers conducted on behalf of the Association of American Colleges and Universities, http://www.aacu.org/leap/documents/2013_EmployerSurvey.pdf.

Henry, T., J. Pagano, J. Puckett, and J. Wilson. 2014. *Five Trends to Watch in Higher Education.* Boston Consulting Group, https://www.bcgperspectives.com.

Hess, F. 2011. "Old School: College's Most Important Trend Is The Rise of The Adult Student." *The Atlantic* (September 28), http://www.theatlantic.com/business/archive/2011/09/old-school-colleges-most-important-trend-is-the-rise-of-the-adult-student/245823/.

Hickey, D. T., N. Otto, R. Itow, K. Schenke, C. Tran, and C. Chow. 2014. *Badges Design Principles Documentation* (Indiana University, Center for Research on Learning and Technology, DPD, Interim Project Report, http://iudpd.indiana.edu/JanuaryReport.

Hoachlander, G., A. C. Sikora, L. Horn, and C. D. Carroll. 2003. *Community College Students: Students at Risk and The Pipeline to Higher Education* (NCES 98–094). Washington, DC: US Department of Education, National Center for Education Statistics.

Hussar, W. J., and T. M. Bailey. 2009. *Projections of Education Statistics to 2018.* NCES 2009-062. Washington, DC: National Center for Education Statistics.

Immerwahr, J. 2003. *With Diploma in Hand: Hispanic High School Seniors Talk about Their Futures.* San Jose: National Center for Public Policy and Higher Education.

Kelley, A. P., M. Schneider, and K. Carey. 2010. *Rising to the Challenge: Hispanic College Graduation Rates as a National Priority.* Washington, DC: American Enterprise Institute.

Kirsch, I., H. Braun, K. Yamamoto, and A. Sum. 2007. *America's Perfect Storm: Three Forces Changing Our Nation's Future.* Princeton: Educational Testing Service.

Knight, E. 2012. *Open Badges for Lifelong Learning.* Mozilla Foundation white paper, https://wiki.mozilla.org/images/5/59/OpenBadges-Working-Paper_012312.pdf.

_____. 2013. *An Open, Distributed System for Badge Validation.* Mozilla Foundation white paper, http://bit.ly/badgevalidation.

Lee, V. E., C. Mackie-Lewis, and H. Marks. 1993. "Persistence to the Baccalaureate Degree for Students Who Transfer from Community College." *American Journal of Education* 102: 80–114.

Levy, F., and R. J. Murnane. 2005. *The New Division of Labor: How Computers Are Creating the Next Job Market.* Princeton: Princeton University Press.

Liu, M. C. 2011. *Investing in Higher Education for Latinos: Trends in Latino College Access and Success.* Washington, DC: National Conference of State Legislatures.

Lumina Foundation. 2013. *Strategic Plan: 2013–2016,* https://www.luminafoundation.org/files/file/2013-lumina-strategic-plan.pdf.

Malcom-Piqueux, L. E., and E. M. Bensimon. 2015. *Design Principles for Equity and Excellence at Hispanic-Serving Institutions.* San Antonio: University of Texas at San Antonio, Center for Research and Policy in Education.

Malcom-Piqueux, L. E., R. Suro, E. M. Bensimon, and A. Fischer. 2012. *Addressing Latino/a Outcomes at California's Hispanic-Serving Institutions.* Los Angeles: University of Southern California, Center for Urban Education and Tomás Rivera Policy Institute.

Manyika, J., S. Lund, B. Auguste, L. Mendonca, T. Welsh, and S. Ramaswamy. 2011. *An Economy That Works: Job Creation and America's Future.* Washington D.C.: McKinsey Global Institute.

Markle, R., M. Brenneman, T. Jackson, J. Burrus, and S. Robbins. 2013. *Synthesizing Frameworks of Higher Education Student Learning Outcomes* (ETS RR 13-22). Princeton: Educational Testing Service.

Monaghan, D. B., and B. Attewell. 2014. "The Community College Route to the Bachelor's Degree." *Educational Evaluation and Policy Analysis* 37: 1–22.

Nora, A., and G. Crisp. 2009. *Hispanics and Higher Education: An Overview of Research, Theory, and Practice in Higher Education. Handbook of Theory and Research*, edited by J. C. Smart, 317–353. Netherlands: Springer.

Nora, A., and E. Wedham. 1991. *Off-Campus Experiences: The Pull Factors Affecting Freshman-Year Attrition on A Commuter Campus*. Paper presented at the 1991 annual meeting of the American Educational Research Association, Chicago.

Olneck, M. 2012. *Insurgent Credentials: A Challenge to Established Institutions of Higher Education*, HASTAC, http://www.hastac.org/files/insurgentcredentials michaelolneck2012.pdf.

Petre, M. C. 2014. "Essays on the Impact of Cognitive and Noncognitive Skills on Labor Market Outcomes." PhD diss. University of Texas at Austin.

Postsecondary National Policy Institute. 2015. *Hispanic-Serving Institutions: A Background Primer*, https://www.newamerica.org/postsecondary-national-policy-institute /hispanic-serving-institutions-hsis/.

Raish, V., and E. Rimland. 2016. "Employer Perceptions of Critical Information Literacy Skills and Digital Badges." *College & Research Libraries* 20: 87–113.

Riconscente, M. M., A. Kamarainen, and M. Honey. 2013. *STEM Badges: Current Terrain and the Road Ahead*. New York: New York Hall of Science, http:// badgesnysci.files.wordpress.com/2013/08/nsf_stembadges_final_report.pdf

Roohr, K. C., E. A. Graf, and O. L. Liu. 2014. *Assessing Quantitative Literacy in Higher Education: An Overview of Existing Research and Assessments with Recommendations for Next-Generation Assessment* (ETS RR 14-22). Princeton: Educational Testing Service.

Rughiniç, R. 2013. "Talkative Objects in Need of Interpretation: Rethinking Digital Badges in Education." In *CHI '13 Extended Abstracts on Human Factors in Computing Systems, CHI EA '13*, edited by W. E. Mackay, S. Brewster, and S. Bødker, 2099–2108. New York: Association for Computing Machinery.

Saltzman, G. M. 2014. "The Economics of MOOCs." In *NEA 2014 Almanac of Higher Education*, edited by H. S. Wechsler, 19–29. Washington, DC: National Education Association.

Shanker, A. 2012. "Restructuring Our Schools." *Peabody Journal of Education* 65: 88–100.

Smith, J., M. Pender, and J. Howell. 2012. *The Full Extent of Student-College Academic Undermatch*. Newtown, PA: College Board.

Sparks, J. R., Y. Song, W. Brantley, and O. L. Liu. *Assessing Written Communication in Higher Education: Review and Recommendations for Next-Generation Assessment* (ETS RR 14-37). Princeton: Educational Testing Service.

Steele, J. L., M. W. Lewis, L. Santibañez, S. Faxon-Mills, M. Rudnick, B. M. Stecher, and L. S. Hamilton. 2014. *Competency-Based Education in Three Pilot Programs: Examining Implementation and Outcomes*. Santa Monica: RAND Corporation.

Strayhorn, T. L. 2006. *Frameworks for Assessing Learning and Development Outcomes*. Washington, DC: Council for the Advancement of Standards in Higher Education.

Toney-Purta, J., J. C. Cabrera, K. C. Roohr, O. L. Liu, and J. A. Ríos. 2015. *Assessing Civic Competency and Engagement in Higher Education: Research Background, Frameworks, and Directions for Next-Generation Assessment* (ETS RR 15-34). Princeton: Educational Testing Service.

US Department of Education. 2016. *Developing Hispanic-Serving Institutions Program—Title V*, http://www2.ed.gov/programs/idueshsi/awards.html.

US General Accounting Office. 2003. *Distance Education: More Data Could Improve Education's Ability to Track Technology at Minority Serving Institutions*. Washington DC: US General Accounting Office .

Warburton, E. C., R. Bugarin, and A-M. Núñez. 2001. *Bridging the Gap: Academic Preparation and Postsecondary Success of First-Generation Students*. Washington, DC: National Center for Education Statistics.

Wassmer, R., C. Moore, and N. Shulock. 2004. "Effect of Racial/Ethic Composition on Transfer Rates in Community Colleges: Implications for Policy and Practice." *Research in Higher Education* 45: 651–672.

Yu, L., P. Dyjur, J. Miltenburg, and K. Saito. 2015. "Micro-Credentialing: Digital Badges in Faculty Professional Development." In *Proceedings of the IDEAS: Designing Responsive Pedagogy*, edited by Armando Babb, Miwa Takeuchi, and Jennifer Lock, 82–89. Calgary: University of Calgary.

Multicontextuality

A FRAMEWORK FOR ACCESS AND ASSESSMENT OF UNDERREPRESENTED STEM STUDENTS

Rebecca A. Beals and Roberto A. Ibarra

Research in education suggests that racial and ethnic minority students complete advanced degrees in the fields of science, technology, engineering, and math (STEM) at lower rates than their white counterparts do. With the aim of addressing this imbalance, we examine how *multicontextual* academic environments offer both nontraditional means for assessing the promise of underrepresented minority students and benefits to these students once they start work in a lab. The diminished impact of affirmative action and race-based admissions to programs in current and future political climates necessitates a new framework for minority student access and assessment. Multicontextual models for increasing minority student success in STEM offer a cutting edge and accessible diversity model that challenge typical assimilationist models for student development and benefit all individuals, regardless of race, class and gender.

The data for this article is derived using mixed methods, including in-depth interviews with 58 students, faculty, and program administrators and 211 student survey responses from various STEM installations across four states and five institutions in the US Southwest. We discuss how multicontextual academic environments attract students to STEM fields and help them thrive as they advance toward their graduate education by focusing specifically on interaction, space, association, learning, and systems.

Research shows that women and underrepresented racial minority students in STEM fields are completing undergraduate degrees, graduate degrees, and entering academia and the workforce at much lower rates than their white male counterparts despite equal education aspirations upon entering college and the higher proportion of female enrollees (National Science Foundation 2010). A variety of nationally funded programs from the National Institutes of Health (NIH), the National Science Foundation (NSF), and the Department of Education (DoE) to increase the representation of underrepresented racial minority students in STEM fields have shown success. However, even the most successful of these programs cannot demonstrate deep understanding of what it is that they are doing that works. This is because typical program evaluations include only the process and summative components that will enable them to secure subsequent funding from their national funding agencies. Thus, they offer relatively superficial ideas about how programs work, and why some are successful while others are not (Clewell, Cohen, Tsui, and Deterding 2006; Moorehead and Barrios, n.d.).

The weakness of the evaluations may be due to the overemphasis of affirmative action principles of access and retention models in typical program evaluations in higher education. Tinto's model of student departure (Tinto 1993) or Weidman's model of socialization (Weidman 1989; Weidman, Twale, and Stein 2001) is used as a theoretical framework through which to examine programs. Tinto's model is based on the assimilationist idea that students will stay in postsecondary schools and succeed if they are integrated into the social and intellectual fabric of the institution. Weidman's model of socialization is useful in that it takes into account students' experiences in higher education, recognizes the importance of academic disciplines and departments, and calls attention to issues of engagement and investment by students. However, it still emphasizes promoting integration by changing the student to fit the social and intellectual fabric of the institution, rather than promoting change in an institution's approach.

The traditional socialization and retention models help us understand minority student success in only a limited way. In both models, students who learn how to "fit in" in the academic environment will succeed. While these models put the burden of this task on both students and the institution, they focus ultimately on identifying how students need to change in order to be successful in higher education. Both models were developed in the early 1990s when access and retention ("pipeline models") were the major components of diversity models in higher education. Access and retention models are similarly assimilationist models of student retention that seek to identify specific barriers faced by underrepresented racial minority students and subsequently to help students assimilate into a dominant academic cultural context by promoting persistence and achievement.

Recently, the National Science Foundation has called for a more comprehensive understanding, not only of how to only increase success of minority students in STEM, but also of how to foster systemic change within institutions of higher education that will result in large-scale, long-term effects. This article supports that effort by addressing the pitfalls of relying solely on access and retention models. We offer an empirically tested alternative framework, called *multicontextuality* (Ibarra 2001, 2003) for understanding minority student success in STEM that also fosters the systemic, long-term institutional change desired by national funding agencies.

CHALLENGING TRADITIONAL SOCIALIZATION MODELS: ACCESS AND RETENTION

Classic student retention and socialization models, including Tinto's (1993) model of student departure and Weidman's theory of socialization (Weidman 1989; Weidman, Twale, and Stein 2001), often employ concepts like "social capital" (Coleman 1988, 1990), "cultural capital" (Bourdieu 1973), and "cultural reproduction" (Bourdieu 1973). Here, socialization and cultural reproduction are discussed in terms of '*habitus*,' which consists primarily of imprinted cultural values, beliefs, behaviors, and knowledge of how the social world is arranged. It is largely developed by primary relationships within family and social institutions close to the individual, operating beneath the level of the conscience.

Institutions also have a habitus, reflected in organizational culture and climate (Berger and Milem 2000; Foor, Walden and Trytten 2007; Ibarra 2001; Johnson 2007; Tierney and Bensimon 1996) and reified when certain practices and policies are valued and encouraged over others. Those students whose habitus matches that of the school system, it is argued, will be more successful within that system because they enter the institution with their individual habitus already aligned with the organizational habitus of the institution. Affirmative action policies focusing on access (reaching out to nontraditional students) and retention (changing the student to fit into the institutional fabric) in a general way reflect the process of cultural reproduction, thereby legitimating the cultural capital of a privileged class from which the institution was established. Beyond the problems of an unchallenged and unchanging institution, the current tenets of affirmative action policy—access and retention—are problematic in and of themselves. The institution remains unchanged while the focus of change remains on the growing number of nontraditional students entering the system. By focusing the impetus of change at the individual level, the institution remains unchallenged and unchanged. Opportunities for long-term success are diminished and a need for affirmative action initiatives remains.

First, retention via the use of cultural reproduction can be interpreted as culturally deterministic and applied as a cultural deficit model. The cultural reproduction process can also influence individuals from underrepresented backgrounds negatively, by subtly suggesting that the cultural capital that comes from their cultural setting is not what is valued within highly legitimated social institutions, like higher education. In effect, it can have a negative impact on a student's lived experience within the system of education. This can promote feelings that the student does not belong, leading to early departure (Austin 2002; Brickhouse 2001; Chen 2012; Clewell and Campbell 2002; Espinosa 2011; Foor, Walden and Trytten 2007; Johnson 2007; Malone and Barabino 2009; Ong, Wright, Espinosa, and Orfield 2011.) Bringing social and cultural reproduction to bear in such a deterministic way is problematic and may contribute to the overemphasis on access and retention in higher education. Carter (2005) notes that as individuals confront a system dominated by white middle-class values and beliefs, they may have a more difficult time finding where they fit and how they might succeed.

MULTICONTEXTUALITY: TRANSFORMATION THROUGH ATTRACTION AND PERSISTENCE

Multicontextuality, an alternative framework for understanding student success in higher education, was developed by Roberto Ibarra in his work with Latinos in graduate education across the United States. It utilizes theories on learning, cognition, cross-cultural communication, and higher education to present an alternative to traditional models of access and retention. A multicontextual framework focuses on imbalances in educational systems and ways to transform institutions systemically, reaching beyond the individual affirmative-action tenets of access and retention. Student departure becomes a consequence of cultural conflict within an imbalanced system of higher education. By shifting the focus away from individual student failure and toward consideration of structural imbalance, we can begin to understand how organizational dynamics can be applied to improve access, experience and outcomes for underrepresented minorities in STEM environments. Thus, the framework bypasses traditional models of access and retention to emphasize attracting students to multicontextual environments where they will persist and thrive.

In considering a multicontextual framework, the context surrounding interaction is of primary importance. Context is the "information that surrounds a [cultural process] and is inextricably bound up with the meaning of that event . . ." (Hall and Hall, 1990, in Ibarra 2001, 52. Subsequent page numbers refer to the latter work.) Individuals get sorted into populations based on how they perceive and communicate with one another. The relationship is between the information surrounding a particular cultural process. Those from high context cultures make meaning and learn using "multiple streams of information which surround an event, situation, or interaction" (53). Those from low-context cultures "filter out conditions surrounding an event and focus on words and objective facts" (53). Within a multicontextual framework, context can be described as high, low, or a combination of the two (multicontextual). High-context cultures (HC) identified in the United States as comprised predominantly of ethnic minorities and females, tend to focus on the streams of information that surround an event, situation, or interaction to determine meaning. In contrast, low-context cultures (LC), predominantly northern European ethnic groups and majority males, tend to filter out conditions surrounding an event or interaction to focus as much as possible on words and facts (53). See Table 1 for examples of "low" and "high" context characteristics.

TABLE 1. Selected characteristics of high- and low-context cultures

Low-Context (LC)		High-Context (HC)
Interaction	Long term interpersonal feedback	Short term interpersonal feedback
	They avoid interfering with or intervening in others' lives. They take colleagues' mood shifts for granted, attributing them to personal problems that should be ignored.	Constant checking on emotional status of others is important for group morale. Though this characteristic is attributed to women, HC people in general are especially attuned to slight mood changes among friends and colleagues.
Space	More spatial boundaries	Space is more communal
	LC people need more social distance for interaction, with little if any touching or contact during conversation. Personal space is compartmentalized, individualized, and private.	HC people are more comfortable interacting within close social distances, and constant non-intimate touching during conversation is normal. Personal space is shared, and involvement with others is encouraged.
Association	Low commitment to others	Commitment to others is high
	Relationships start and end quickly. Many people can be inside one's circle, but boundaries are blurred. They are often highly committed to their job or career. Written contracts are important.	Relationships depend on trust, build up slowly, and are stable. They are careful to distinguish who is in their circle. People are deeply involved with each other. They have a strong tendency to build lifetime relationships. Written contracts are less important than bonds of personal trust.

continued on following page

TABLE 1. Continued.

Low-Context (LC)	High-Context (HC)
Learning	**Learn best by following directions** They assemble or combine facts according to rules they memorize. Ideas are spelled out. Explanations are explicit, even in an apprenticeship model. Theoretical and philosophical problems are treated as real.	**They learn best by demonstration** They learn by hands-on methods: observing and mimicking others, practicing it mentally and physically, demonstrating it to others, and by apprenticeship. Real-life problems are as important as theoretical and philosophical ones.
Learning	**Learning oriented toward the individual** They prefer to approach tasks and learning individually. They tend to work and learn apart from others. Teamwork means that individuals are assigned specific tasks to accomplish.	**Learning is group oriented** They prefer to work in groups to learn and solve problems. Some groups prefer constant talking (interacting) in close proximity when working or learning.
Time	**Time is monochronic** They emphasize schedules, compartmentalization, and promptness. They do one thing at a time and may equate time with money and status. Change happens fast.	**Time is polychronic** They emphasize people and completion of transactions. They do many things at once (multi-tasking) and do not equate time with money or status. Change happens slowly, for things are rooted in the past.
Culture	**Formal culture is team-oriented** Teams consist of individuals with specific skills who are brought together to work on projects or tasks. Their work may be linked, but tasks are sequential, compartmentalized, and designed to be handed off to others.	**Informal culture is group-oriented** Individuals with general and/or specific skills come together to work as a group to complete projects. Work is interactive, and individuals are not territorial about specific tasks.
Systems	**Disciplines and areas of interest** They may favor traditional scientific fields that tend to conduct analysis with methods that often eliminate context, or separate information from context. Research analysis usually deals with large numbers of quantitative and easily measured variables; results are more deterministic and context is less important. New research projects are directed toward strongly projected, predetermined outcomes.	**HC Disciplines** They may favor disciplines that are more directly involved with contextual thinking and research about livings systems and people. Research analysis is more qualitative and probabilistic and requires attention to variables in which cultural context is important. New research projects are clear about the direction and methods of analysis, but projected outcomes are open-ended and flexible.
Systems	**Scientific thinking is emphasized** They value examining ideas rather than broad comprehension of real-world applications. Linear thinking is ultra-specific and inhibits a broad mutual understanding of multilayered events.	**Practical thinking is valued** They value application of knowledge in real world events (social skills). Interconnected thinking fosters creativity and broad comprehension of multilayered events.

Source: Modified from R. Ibarra, *Beyond Affirmative Action: Reframing the Context of Higher Education* (Madison: University of Wisconsin Press, 2001), chap. 3, 69–76.

Higher education and STEM disciplines alike operate with a preferred contextual style. Born from the German research model and characterized by linear processes wherein abstract thinking, competition, impersonal relationships and individual learning are prioritized, higher education, specifically in STEM fields, is noted for operating primarily within a low-context framework—one that validates low-context individuals. Student departure or failure to become socialized into such environments is explained as a result of a cultural conflict; high-context individuals confront a stubborn, unchanging low-context environment, and then decide to leave, feeling like they do not belong (Espinosa 2011). Students such as these are more likely to be engaged in fields that value and promote high-context or multicontextual characteristics—this allows them to connect to each other and also connect what they are doing to the communities they come from or to other humans. Data confirms that within STEM disciplines more women and minorities opt for degrees in biology and medicine, in which humans and living organisms are the unit of analysis, than in technology and physics, which are more abstract and less closely connected to human life. Students with a preference for high-context environments can learn to be successful by developing a sense of "bicognition" (Ramirez 1999), or multicontextual practices and behaviors.

While low-context and high-context cultures are not superior or inferior to each other, the cultural imbalance in STEM fields that favor low-context learning modes and styles works to exclude large numbers of individuals who prefer more high-context environments (17). To serve a more diverse student body, academic departments and institutions must reframe their contexts and cultures by fostering multicontextual cultural environments. Doing so will create a more balanced institutional environment wherein individuals with a diversity of learning styles can be successful.

In this article, we chose as the case for analysis a federally funded program called Promoting Minority Participation in the Sciences (PMPS), which has demonstrated a high degree of success in increasing the representation of racial and ethnic minorities in STEM fields over the past 25 years. We focus on the elements of the program framework that aid students in achieving long-term success and on the impact that the related activities have on the program participants. The program was established in the early 1990s at the height of the popularity of access and retention models of affirmative action. We were curious to find out whether these traditional components remained within the program or if over time a new framework for success had emerged.

PMPS Methods

PMPS is headquartered at a large research-intensive university in the Southwest. The program has demonstrated continuous success in graduating underrepresented racial minority students in STEM fields since its founding in 1991. Evaluations indicate that the program consistently produces the outputs that it desires. PMPS operates across five states in the Southwest with branch programs at 30 institutions, varying from Research 1 schools to community colleges. The program works by funding small, individual research proposals written by faculty with the intention of funding undergraduate students to work on research projects.

Sampling

Using a non-probability purposive sampling technique, we selected five institutions from the 30 that participate in the PMPS program. We used non-probability purposive sampling techniques to select individuals for in-depth interviews, relying on enrollment information provided by PMPS program staff. We completed 58 interviews during the course of our fieldwork activities. Student interviews accounted for 33 of the interviews; 25 interviews were with faculty participants. An online survey was distributed to all of the students affiliated with the PMPS program in April 2015, and a total of 211 students completed the survey by September 2015.

Data

We used a mixed-method design to collect both qualitative and quantitative data. Qualitative data came from 58 in-depth interviews with students and faculty mentors participating in a program funded by the National Science Foundation and designed to increase the representation of underrepresented minority students in STEM fields. Qualitative data were used to uncover major themes from participants about their experiences and are presented to add depth and detail to quantitative results. Quantitative data came from 211 online survey responses of student participants in this program. The survey was constructed using the themes that emerged from the interviews. Quantitative data were used to assess the generalizability and frequency of these themes from a larger population of participants.

Findings and Discussion

Findings from this study suggest that the program operates within a multicontextual framework. The major concepts of *multicontext theory* (MC) that emerged from the interviews and were supported by the quantitative survey results will be discussed individually in the remainder of this article. They include Interaction, Space, Association, Learning, and Systems. Qualitative and quantitative data are presented together as each theme is presented separately and represented in tables that support each theme. Each table represents one concept of multicontext theory that emerged from the qualitative data. For each concept, we have included a short description from multi-context theory, followed by the behaviors and practices that participants discussed during interviews. Tables 2-6 contain the survey question relating to the multicontext concept measured and descriptive data from the survey. The percentages of respondents who disagree or agree with statements measuring the concept are also included in the tables. Numbers in parentheses in the text refer to the raw number of individuals who were interviewed that discussed the particular theme.

Interaction and Space: Community and Mentorship

One major tenet of multicontext theory is the importance of interaction that occurs between players in a cultural space. In a low-context environment, interaction can be characterized as lacking in personal emotion: it emphasizes the avoidance of interference in colleagues' personal lives. In a high-context environment, recognition of personal emotions—checking in on the emotional status of individuals, for example—is seen as an important element for group morale. While the university and STEM disciplines in particular are characterized as low-context insofar as interaction, we found that participants in the PMPS program often discussed their interactions in a more high-context manner and that this facilitated the development of community among faculty and students.

Interaction

Table 2, Interaction, presents evidence suggesting a multicontextual approach to interactions in PMPS. Over 70 percent of student participants agreed that participating in PMPS gave them an opportunity to be a part of a campus community within which they developed deep, personal connections to a faculty mentor. Of the respondents, 65 percent agreed that the connections they developed with peers and faculty were "family-like." The university can sometimes be seen as an impersonal place where individualism is celebrated, but nearly 80 percent of respondents mentioned that being a part of a community on campus was important to them, suggesting that these individuals value a high-context approach to interaction in higher education.

TABLE 2. Interaction

Interaction	Description Short term interpersonal feedback	Practice Checking in on emotions, multicultural mentors		
Percentage:		**Disagree**	**Neutral**	**Agree**
As a result of PMPS, I developed a close connection with a faculty member in my field of interest.		9.94	18.71	71.35
PMPS provided me an opportunity to be a part of a community.		4.71	21.76	73.53
During my time in PMPS, I developed deep, family-like connections with faculty and students.		13.09	21.43	65.47
A faculty approached me and invited me to do research with him/her that was funded by PMPS.		33.93	10.12	55.95
Before PMPS, I felt like I did not belong at my institution.		60.11	20.83	19.05
Being part of a campus community is important to me.		8.33	13.64	78.03

During interviews, students noted that their relationships with their PMPS faculty were different from their relationships with faculty outside the program. Some students mentioned feeling intimidated by non-PMPS faculty, as if they were just one face in a large crowd of students. One senior student noted, "I feel like [PMPS] helped me look at faculty members the same now. But I felt really intimidated beforehand. . . . It's made me feel more comfortable in an academic setting than I ever have before." One woman's interaction with her PMPS faculty mentor challenged her to deconstruct what she described as "the wall" she had put between herself and faculty members in the past. By deconstructing this wall, she was finally able to visualize herself as a future faculty member, "Honestly, it felt like there was a wall between being a student and knowing a faculty member . . . you don't really see them as a peer. So I think the PMPS program has really helped that relationship [and made me feel] that I am going to be that, and almost like I am." Before their PMPS experience, many students felt intimidated by faculty and sensed an invisible barrier between who they were and where faculties are professionally. However, their work with PMPS faculty mentors gave them the opportunity to know faculty on a more personal level and realize that they were not fundamentally different from the students. Deconstructing this invisible wall allowed students to better see themselves as faculty members in the future.

In addition, interview participants also mentioned the exposure to a community of like-minded scientists, and the support that comes from that community, as a benefit to their participation (40—in other words, 40 of the individuals we interviewed mentioned the exposure to and support from like-minded scientists as a benefit to their participation. This pattern continues throughout the discussion). This community included the research lab environment, which consisted of at least one faculty mentor, graduate students (12) who play a role in mentoring the undergraduate students, other undergraduates with various levels of experience who participate in co-mentoring activities (10), and other underrepresented minorities at all levels (undergraduate and graduate students, and faculty).

Space

The concept of "space" in multicontext theory is inextricably related to interaction. Interaction inevitably affects the use of space and how space is created and maintained. In low-context environments, space is characterized as having many boundaries: individualized and private areas are important, and there is less sharing of personal property. In a high-context environment, space is characterized as communal: privacy is less important and personal property is shared. A lab setting may produce either a low- or high-context environment. However, when lab environments were discussed during the PMPS interviews, respondents' language suggested a tendency toward multicontextual lab environments that value privacy and individual interaction with faculty, but also the opportunity to be a part of a community in which peer mentoring is utilized.

Table 3, Space, presents evidence that suggests a multicontextual approach to space is valued by PMPS participants. While a majority of students noted the importance of privacy and the ability to meet with faculty one-on-one, over half of the students preferred working in groups to working alone, and a majority noted that being a part of a community is important. In the family-like communities discussed previously, a team approach to mentoring develops organically.

Although faculty mentors play a leadership role and have frequent contact with their PMPS undergraduates, they often employ the help of graduate students to teach the students procedures and get them up to date on experiments. Here, a professor of medicine discusses how he utilizes peer mentoring in his lab:

> So, you can couple students together to get them to share their experiences and have a better opportunity and better chance to do

TABLE 3. Space

Interaction	Description Space is communal	Practice Lab (not one-on-one); study groups; diverse environments		
Percentage:		**Disagree**	**Neutral**	**Agree**
PMPS provided me an opportunity to be a part of a community.		4.71	21.76	73.53
Being part of a campus community is important to me.		8.33	13.64	78.03
I prefer open, direct communication.		1.52	2.27	96.21
I prefer to work with a group of students, rather than by myself.		9.16	36.64	54.2
I prefer meeting with faculty one-on-one.		4.55	18.94	76.52
Having privacy is important to me.		3.12	15.62	81.25

> what they want to do. Many of these students have a vision, and some of them feel like they can't achieve what they're trying to get at because they don't have somebody in the family or somebody that is going to give them a path. If you help them get a path, many of them can do it.

An associate professor of psychology noted how this co-mentoring environment also benefits the advanced students who are on the mentor end of the relationship in terms of self-confidence and a sense of belonging to the lab environment, "New students come in and now they can show the other students how things are done. They gain a lot of confidence. . . . That boosts their confidence and also makes them feel that that they belong to a lab. This is somewhere where they've acquired some mastery."

PMPS students described their relationships with their faculty mentors in very positive terms (16). The most common descriptions of mentors used terms such as "awesome" and called mentors very supportive, experienced, and accessible. A junior in the life sciences discussed how working with someone she sees as experienced and caring toward undergraduates inspired her to want to "be like him" in the future. Another student, a junior in physics, described how the supportive and kind relationship she developed with her faculty mentor made her change her view of professors:

> Something really valuable I found with them is a support kind of community, maybe. Because they [faculty mentor and graduate

> student mentor] were really friendly people, both of them. . . . I always thought professors were kind of scary or prejudiced or really busy. But these people gave me their time to teach me something. That's really valuable and you really appreciate that when someone does that, when you start building some of that confidence, I realized that they took that time out of their busy lives to help an undergrad.

The interactions described by both students and faculty highlight the importance of checking in on emotions and creating a space where they are valued within the STEM environment. Not only does this help the student feel part of a community, but it also influences their self-confidence and motivation to continue. Aside from a sense of community in the labs, students were attracted to being a part of a diverse community on campus, especially one in which they were surrounded by other students of similar backgrounds (19). One student wrote:

> I was surprised that the PMPS officers, like [name], she's Hispanic. And [name], she's from Peru. Stuff like that. [Another name] is Spanish, or part-Spanish. All these people are from different cultures. I feel like, "cool." I felt very accepted coming in. I guess that's something that I really appreciate about PMPS, because I've also worked in research in the physics department and it's quite different there. You don't see any Hispanics . . . and [smiling] I'm probably the only Hispanic female in physics.

Students referred to the diversity of the communities in a variety of ways, including having a female faculty mentor in their lab research (when many of their university class instructors were male), working with other students from underrepresented backgrounds, being in environments where they felt comfortable speaking Spanish, and being around people from other disciplines. Nearly one-third of the students mentioned that they enjoyed being around students and faculty from other disciplines and learning their perspectives on common research problems.

Being exposed to a diverse community of scholars was comforting to the underrepresented students who participated in PMPS. It let them know that they were not alone, and that they belonged in the academic environment where everyone was smart and capable, regardless of their skin color. A senior in biology noted:

> Being with PMPS, it's nice to know that there are lots of minorities out there, but they are just as smart. They are just as good as everybody else, regardless of skin color. They have so much more to contribute. And it's nice to be part of that community.

ASSOCIATION: ATTRACTING UNDERREPRESENTED STUDENTS TO STEM ENVIRONMENTS

In multicontext theory, the concept of association refers to the degree to which individuals are personally connected to people and the world around them and how individuals deal with success in their professional lives. In a low-context environment, personal commitment among community members is low. Being nice to others and the development of personal relationships is not as important as the job at hand or advancing one's career. Success means being recognized and seeking public praise; standing out in order to "get ahead" is highly valuable. In contrast, personal commitment to people is high in a high-context environment. It is important to build trusting relationships that are long-term and stable. Success in a high-context environment means being unobtrusive; talking about accomplishments can be seen as boastful and humility is valued. In higher education, a low-context approach to association is clearly valued and rewarded; high-context association is seen as passive and weak.

However, we found evidence to support a multicontextual approach to association in the PMPS interviews and survey data, as shown in Table 4, Association. This evidence emerged as students found ways that their PMPS research and work benefited people and communities around them, or had an "altruistic" purpose. Students also learned to value self-promotion through presenting their altruistic work. A large majority (88 percent) of students who completed the online survey noted that it was important that their research might improve the world around them.

During interviews, students mentioned being attracted to the research projects that their faculty mentors were working on because they saw that the work could help communities around them (21). Here, a senior in geology discusses how her initial reluctance to become involved in serious research was displaced by feeling the need to help a community:

TABLE 4. Association

Interaction	Description	Practice		
	Commitment to People	Altruistic Research		
Percentage:		**Disagree**	**Neutral**	**Agree**
It is important that my research improve the world around me.		1.52	10.61	87.88
I enjoy praise for my academic accomplishments.		7.81	28.12	64.06

> I was like, "Oh, my God, I don't want to do this." But I feel that I have to. There is a community living there. This research is going to help what happens in the future here—the future generation. I link it to that because I want to help people at the same time I am doing science. I don't want to do science . . . without people who make use of it. . . . Believing [in] the problem, [is] believing in the solution. Believe that you will get there, because it's better for our society. That's what I believe.

Another student discussed the uncertainty she felt about the value of the research that her faculty mentor was working on, until he encouraged her to learn about the problem by watching a popular movie about how the problem affects real people. This allowed her to connect personally to the issue. "I was like, 'Oh, this is an actual problem.' So that's where I started my research. It might be so simple to watch a movie, but it actually helped connect what I'm doing." Some students even mentioned that they had decided to forego their premedical studies to do academic research because they saw research as a place where they could affect more people and have a larger impact on the world around them. One senior in engineering wrote:

> Well, I'm from a third-world country, so the reason I wanted to be a doctor is because I wanted to help people. But it's not enough. Doctors help, but if they don't solve healthcare problems, technology by itself won't do it. So we need to provide tools and stuff to doctors to do their job.

Hands-on experiences with high-level work and the opportunity to participate at an advanced level contributed to students' increased confidence in themselves and their own capabilities. Here, a senior engineering student discusses how she now thinks about people doubting her abilities. "Actually, sometimes I [think], if people don't believe in us, look who I am, look where I am standing, look where I am going to be, and once I get my PhD no one can ever tell me something that I cannot do."

Some students were initially confused at why faculty chose them to work in their labs. Over the course of their PMPS experience, they were able to gain the confidence that they were capable of doing this type of academic work. A junior in chemistry wrote:

> I would say when I first started, I thought the man [faculty mentor] was crazy, because I had no idea what was going on. But now when I think about science and math and everything, I understand it to the point where I'm helping others, I'm teaching others. I didn't think I would ever have that understanding, but people actually come to me, fellow classmates come to me.

Many other students mentioned having confidence in their plans as a result of the skills they developed during their PMPS funded experience, often a result of the hands-on research in which they participated.

LEARNING:
HANDS-ON, HIGH-LEVEL RESEARCH

The concept of learning in multicontext theory is broad. It addresses how knowledge is acquired, what types of thinking are important, and which learning styles are valued. In a low-context environment, knowledge is based on reasoning, and analytical thinking is valued. Learning is focused on the individual, and often involves following directions. In a high-context environment, knowledge is contextual and comprehensive thinking is important. Learning is group-oriented and interactive, often through demonstration.

Table 5, Learning, suggests that participants in PMPS value multicontextual learning environments. A large majority of students noted that they learn best when they apply material hands-on (93 percent), or after seeing a demonstration (87 percent). However, over half the students (66 percent) agreed that they learn well from reading a set of instructions, which is low-context learning. However, results from our interviews suggest that the hands-on, realistic research that students participated in through PMPS was one of the activities that attracted them to STEM and one of those they valued most.

TABLE 5. Learning

Interaction	Description Hands-on through demonstration; group oriented	Practice Hands-on research; research teams; peer mentoring		
Percentage:		**Disagree**	**Neutral**	**Agree**
I learn best through reading and memorization.		40.63	25.78	33.60
I learn best by applying material in a hands-on way (lab experiments, etc.)		1.56	5.47	92.97
I learn best when a list of instructions is given to me to follow.		12.50	21.09	66.41
I learn best after seeing a demonstration from an instructor.		2.36	10.24	87.40
When I work, I have a set schedule that I stick to.		13.28	25.00	61.72

Most students mentioned that the opportunity to learn and participate "hands-on" real-world research (22) was fun (15) and felt that it drew them into the experience. A junior in chemistry wrote:

> The one thing that caught my interest was . . . researching. It was a whole new environment. . . . I grew up in a low-income family, and in school we didn't have those opportunities. We were given textbooks, and that was our research. So just being able to go into a lab caught my interest, because I never had that opportunity. So I was like, "Yeah, I would love to do this hands-on."

All of the students who were involved in faculty-led research, hands-on and at a high-level, mentioned advanced research as the most significant experience they had with PMPS. Students were able to work with faculty on projects funded by large organizations such as NASA, the National Institutes of Health, and the National Science Foundation.

Many students and faculty described PMPS research as a "more realistic" experience with doing science than what they were exposed to in their traditional university STEM courses. A professor of biochemistry noted that, "[PMPS students] are doing research, they are really doing research, okay? I mean they are doing things that nobody has done before. It is original research." Another faculty mentor, an associate professor of physics and astronomy, noted the fundamental differences between a PMPS project and STEM study in a traditional classroom, referring to the formulaic nature of the latter:

> You're not going to duplicate the experience in an actual research lab in a lab class. . . . [In the PMPS lab] you're exposed to a much more focused area of science. So the students have to learn in detail about some area, whereas the lab classes are generally trying to cover a broad area of science [and] skills that are broadly applicable. This [PMPS research] is what scientific research is like. . . . They're not going to get that experience just from classes.

This realistic research experience also helps students to make informed decisions about what they want to do after they graduate. According to faculty, this informed decision may not happen if they have only classroom experiences. The students' experience in PMPS-funded research environments are described by faculty as more realistic than what students are exposed to in a traditional academic environment. Students' experience of real academic research encourages them to think about whether or not they want to pursue this type of work. Thus, students enter graduate school with less risk of departure because they have a realistic idea of the type of work they are getting into. It also gives student participants an advantage as they apply for graduate school, as admissions committees increasingly look for solid research experiences to minimize the risk of graduate student departure. Faculty respondents noted that this exposure does not occur in a typical STEM classroom.

MULTICONTEXTUAL SYSTEMS: CREATING OPPORTUNITIES TO BECOME ENGAGED

The final aspect of multicontext theory to emerge from our empirical work focused on multicontextual systems. A low-context system, so far as STEM is concerned, can be characterized as a traditional scientific field in which context is not important and teaching is technical. Analyses are focused on large-scale quantitative data, and scientific thinking is emphasized. A high-context system is characterized by disciplines that are more directly involved with contextual thinking, for example, research about living organisms and people. Practical thinking is valued and teaching is personal. Evidence from our study suggests that PMPS can create multicontextual learning environments (see Table 6, Systems).

A majority (nearly 74 percent) of students who responded to our survey noted that what they do in a traditional classroom at their institutions is very different from what they do in PMPS, and our interview data highlight these differences. In comparison to the hands-on research supported by PMPS, typical classroom environments that include labs were described as formulaic. An associate professor of chemistry and biochemistry noted how he saw these two environments as "fundamentally different":

> This (PMPS-supported research) is fundamentally different . . .
> in a classroom setting, the outcome is clear so they [students] go
> in there, they have like a cooking instruction on a sheet. They do

TABLE 6. Systems

Interaction	Description	Practice		
	Disciplines: traditional scientific; thinking is practical and personal	STEM LC; applied research; develop connections to research problems		
Percentage:		**Disagree**	**Neutral**	**Agree**
What I do with my PMPS research is different from what I do in a typical class at my college.		8.83	17.65	73.53

> their thing and then at the end of one or two or three sessions, [it's] done. That's fundamentally different from the [PMPS faculty] lab where we give them projects that are open-ended.

A student who had recently graduated and started a master's degree program in life sciences agreed that her PMPS experience had prepared her for a more realistic view of the world of science by requiring hard work, independence, and patience. These skills, she noted, were important as she entered the next stage of her professional career to working on other research projects:

> Being in the lab in a class is so much easier. They're holding your hand. But conducting research, it's not all black and white. There are so many grey areas and I think working with Dr. [*redacted*] really taught me that . . . he pushed me to understand that it's not going to be easy. I think that's helped me with my other research projects outside of lab.

Students described what they do in a traditional classroom environment as general and formulaic. In these settings, they were not granted opportunities to work independently or engage creatively by setting up their own research protocols. Since the outcome of classroom lab work is pre-established, students are not given the opportunity to understand that in science things do not always go as planned. In the PMPS-supported environments, they are exposed to this aspect of science and given the opportunity to troubleshoot and find solutions when something does not go right. They are able to learn all of this relatively independently in comparison to the classroom environment, where protocols are pre-set and the lab instructor "holds your hand" through the experiment until all goes as planned.

MULTICONTEXT THEORY IN PRACTICE IN PMPS: A CONCLUSION

In undertaking this project, we attempted to determine whether an assimilationist model of student retention (Tinto 1993) that seeks to identify specific barriers that underrepresented minority students (URM) in STEM face and subsequently helps students assimilate into a dominant academic culture is still viable, or whether an alternative multicontext theoretical framework (called Context Diversity; see Ibarra 2001, 2005) that has proven useful in understanding the process of change in institutional culture is a better explanatory framework.

The study revealed that a multicontextual theoretical framework (Ibarra 2001) was an important element in attracting and developing URM students to pursue STEM-related research in graduate school. The interviews suggested that elements of a Context Diversity model were indeed evident when the PMPS program and mentors changed the context of academic culture in teaching undergraduate students to become scientists.

> Rather than recruit and retain populations, Context Diversity strives to create a learning community replete with myriad ways to *attract* diverse populations and have them *thrive* in an academic or workplace environment. Results are measured not only by how well we attract them, but also by how well we enhance campus cultures to improve upon the academic and work performance for *all* students, faculty, and staff. Rather than strive to increase diversity using just structural [affirmative action programs] or multicultural [ethnic studies] models, the focus is on finding ways to study, apply, and eventually build diversity *into* the higher education system, if you will, *into* the context of our learning communities and beyond (Ibarra 2005, 7).

The findings in this article suggest that major concepts in multicontext theory have emerged over time within one highly successful program and are associated with student success in that program. This new model has the potential to reframe academic departments and institutions in order to promote systemic institutional success in increasing the number of underrepresented minority students in STEM, rather than forever focusing on changing a student to fit into an imbalanced system. These include a multicontextual approach to interaction, space, association, learning, and systems in STEM education.

STEM fields and higher education institutions would increase their ability to serve underrepresented minority students by focusing on creating STEM communities where lab environments support the development of close-knit, diverse communities in which students feel comfortable working with their peers and their faculty. Faculty members can facilitate this community by checking in on the emotional needs of their students, embracing racial and ethnic differences, and seeing these differences as an asset to their team. STEM fields will have better luck attracting underrepresented minority students if they highlight how STEM research can be altruistic in nature and positively affect the lives of individuals in the world around them. It is important to not separate the context and importance of STEM research from ideals of humanism and altruism. By emphasizing the humanistic components of STEM research, individuals will not only be attracted to those fields, but will thrive through personal motivation to remain in the field to make a difference.

In our survey and interviews, learning within traditional low-context STEM environments (including traditional classrooms and labs) was described as formulaic, unrealistic and "general." The learning environments developed through PMPS were described as hands-on, team-oriented, applied, and realistic: students were able to connect their work to real problems in the world. This generated excitement among students and a desire to stay within the field. A majority of faculty and students noted that this multicontextual learning program was more of an exception within their PMPS environments rather than the rule at their institutions. Individuals and institutions interested in improving STEM education and minority retention in STEM fields will be well served by reimagining their learning environments in ways that espouse multicontextual learning, rather than supporting the traditional low-context practices that define the field today.

With regard to the focus on cultural assimilation of URMs in higher education today, there is evidence that students, especially Latinos, seem not only reluctant but resistant to this kind of social pressure to conform (Ibarra 2001). The interviews with PMPS participants revealed a tendency for student participants to respond well to faculty mentors when mentors acted to facilitate their process of learning to become scientists, and when students were welcomed into their labs and recognized for their contributions to the research. The interviews did not reveal any problems derived from cultural differences between mentors and students or the need to "remediate" their students to help them fit into the cultural fabric of their STEM labs. In fact, faculty mentors frequently mentioned how they appreciated learning from their PMPS students, and offered that their best advice to other mentors was to spend time listening carefully to their PMPS students to learn more about their rich cultural backgrounds.

Identity formation—here, we mean learning to become a scientist via PMPS mentors—can be perceived as a form of cultural assimilation, but in this program, the mentors are not attempting to replace someone's racial or ethnic identity with the professional identity of a research scientist. It was observed that the process of helping students to become good research scientists included no mention of cultural differences causing dissonance in student/mentor relationships. In fact, many students mentioned the cultural diversity of faculty mentors as a benefit of the program, and faculty mentors noted the importance of recognizing and valuing the diverse backgrounds of their students. Whether or not changes occurred in roles and relationships, the process of acculturating students into the occupational or professional role of a scientist in specific academic cultures was clearly evident. The program had a positive effect on both students and faculty, with the emphasis on inclusion rather than assimilation.

It is clear that students are attracted to "realistic research experiences" that go beyond the context of classroom or classroom-based lab experiences. Students frequently cited the positive attributes of the program, and mentioned that they had thrived on the ability to be creative, the freedom to make mistakes, and the unexpected approachability of lab directors and staff—all components of community building within the construct of the Context Diversity model. In our analysis, there is evidence to project that assimilationist models are no longer capable of explaining how and why programs such as these are successful. However, the facts gathered so far indicate that the PMPS is on the cutting edge of a new paradigm for diversity in higher education, and more importantly, that it is successful in preparing and encouraging more and more underrepresented students to pursue advanced degrees in important STEM fields.

The future of affirmative action policies and the expansion of more authentic diversity initiatives are intertwined with the ability to understand how to develop integrated identities for all students in higher education. Integrated identities not only benefit students, who will be more academically successful, but also promote the institution in terms of student success and happiness and degree completion. This reciprocal benefit can propel the development of diverse student bodies at all levels in the academic pipeline, even in post affirmative action political environments. Context Diversity models, which focus on policies that foster inclusion and diversity beyond personal characteristics (race, class, gender difference), may be seen more favorably than current policies of access and retention that focus on distributing resources based on individualized racial classifications (Epperson 2011). Documenting the benefits of alternative, diverse spaces on campus and speculating about the effects of the removal of affirmative action programs, like the ones discussed in this study, can play an important role in the future of diversity initiatives in higher education.

REFERENCES

Austin, A. E. 2002. "Preparing the Next Generation of Faculty: Graduate School as Socialization to the Academic Career." *Journal of Higher Education* 73:1, 94–122.

Berger, J. B., and J. F. Milem. 2000. "Organizational Behavior in Higher Education and Student Outcomes." In *Higher Education: Handbook of Theory and Research,* edited by J. C. Smart, Vol. 15, 268–338. New York: Agathon.

Bourdieu, P. 1973. "Cultural Reproduction and Social Reproduction." In *Knowledge, Education and Cultural Change,* edited by R. Brown, 56-68. London: Tavistock.

Brickhouse, N. W. 2001. "Embodying Science: A Feminist Perspective on Learning." *Journal of Research in Science Teaching* 38:3, 282–295.

Carter, P. 2005. *Keepin' It Real: School Success Beyond Black and White*. New York: Oxford University Press.

Castañeda, A. 1974. *Cultural Democracy, Bicognitive Development, and Education*. New York: Academic Press.

Chen, R. 2012. "Institutional Characteristics and College Student Dropout Risks: A Multilevel Event History Analysis." *Research in Higher Education* 53:5, 487–505.

Clewell B. C., and P. B. Campbell. 2002. "Taking Stock: Where We've Been, Where We Are, Where We're Going." *Journal of Women and Minorities in Science and Engineering* 8:3-4, 255–284.

Clewell, B., C. Cohen, L. Tsui, and N. Deterding, 2006. "Revitalizing the Nation's Talent Pool in STEM: Science, Technology, Engineering and Mathematics." Washington, DC: Urban Institute-National Science Foundation.

Coleman, J. S. 1990. *Equality and Achievement in Education*, 63–126. Boulder: Westview Press.

_____. 1988. "Social Capital and the Creation of Human Capital." *American Journal of Sociology* 94, 95–120.

Epperson, L. 2011. "New Legal Perspectives: Implications for Diversity in the Post-Grutter Era." *Diversity in Higher Education: Toward a More Comprehensive Approach*, edited by L. M. Stulberg and S. L. Weinberg. New York: Routledge.

Espinosa, L. L. 2011. "Pipelines and Pathways: Women of Color in Undergraduate STEM Majors and the College Experiences that Contribute to Persistence." *Harvard Educational Review* 81, 209–240.

Floor, C. E., S. E. Walden, and D. A. Trytten. 2007. "I Wish that I Belonged More in this Whole Engineering Group: Achieving Individual Diversity." *Journal of Engineering Education* 96:2, 103–115.

Hall, E.T., and M.R. Hall. 1990. *Hidden Differences: Doing Business with the Japanese*. 2nd edition, New York: Anchor.

Ibarra, R. A. 2005. "A Place to Belong: The Library as Prototype for Context Diversity," in H. Thompson (ed.), *Currents and Convergence: Navigating the Rivers of Change* (pp. 1-18). Proceedings of the 12th Annual National Conference of the Association of College and Research Libraries. Chicago: American Association of Libraries.

_____. 2001. *Beyond Affirmative Action: Reframing the Context of Higher Education*. Madison: University of Wisconsin Press.

Johnson, A. 2007. "Unintended Consequences: How Science Professors Discourage Women of Color." *Science Education* 91:5, 805–821.

Lovitts, B. 2001. *Leaving the Ivory Tower: The Causes and Consequences of Departure from Doctoral Study*. Lanham, MD: Rowman and Littlefield.

Malone, K. R., and G. Barabino. 2009. "Narration of Race in Science, Technology, Engineering and Math: Identity Formation and Its Discontents." *Science Education* 93:3, 485–510.

Moorehead, R., and R. G. Barrios. n.d. *External Evaluation Report of the Western Alliance to Expand Student Opportunities*. Louis Stokes Alliances for Minority Participation. Final report submitted to the National Science Foundation. Unpublished.

National Science Foundation. 2010. *Science and Engineering Indicators, 2010*. Arlington, VA: National Science Foundation.

Ong, M., C. Wright, L. L. Espinosa, and G. Orfield. 2011. "Inside the double bind: A synthesis of empirical research on undergraduate and graduate women of color in science, technology, engineering and mathematics." *Harvard Educational Review*, (81)2, 178-208.

Ramírez III, M. 1999. *Multicultural Psychotherapy: An Approach to Individual and Cultural Differences*, 2nd ed. Boston: Allyn and Bacon.

Tierney, W., and E. Bensimon. 1996. *Promotion and Tenure: Community and Socialization in Academe*. Albany: State University of New York (SUNY) Press.

Tinto, V. 1993. *Leaving College: Rethinking the Causes and Cures of Student Attrition*, 2nd ed. Chicago: University of Chicago Press.

Weidman, J. C. 1989. "Undergraduate Socialization: A Conceptual Approach." In *Higher Education: Handbook of Theory and Research*, edited by J. C. Smart. Vol. 5, 289–322. New York: Agathon.

Weidman, J. C., D. J. Twale, and E. L. Stein. 2001. *Socialization of Graduate and Professional Students in Higher Education: A Perilous Passage?* ASHE–ERIC Higher Education Report 28:3. 3. San Francisco: Jossey-Bass.

A State of Neglect

LATINO EDUCATIONAL ATTAINMENT

Blanca Rincón, Belinda De La Rosa, and Jorge Chapa

Dedicated to Jorge Chapa, in memoriam:
May his scholarship and activism live on.

Data from the US Census Bureau and the National Center for Education Statistics indicate that Latinos continue to lag behind non-Latinos in education and other socioeconomic characteristics. The three sections of this article open up that statement to explore Latino population and educational attainment in detail. The first documents how the US Latino population has changed in the past 25 years in terms of size, age, and geographic distribution. The second analyzes Latinos' educational attainment over time, and examines contemporary measures of educational attainment in detail. The third presents salient socio-demographic characteristics for Latinos that are highly correlated with educational outcomes, including family type and size, economic status, occupation, and language use.

THE US LATINO POPULATION

Who are US Latinos? In this article, we use the term to refer to the traditional heterogeneous mix that comprises that population in the United States, regardless of gender, age, sexual orientation, or immigration status. Among US Latinos, the following major subgroups are represented: Mexicans (63.9%), Puerto Ricans (9.5%), Cubans (3.7%), and all others of Latino origin (22.9%). Data cited is the latest available from the US Bureau of the Census.

TABLE 1. Percentage distribution of the Latino population by origin, 1990, 2000, 2010, and 2014

	1990 (%)	2000 (%)	2010 (%)	2014 (%)
All Latinos	100	100	100	100
Mexican	60.4	58.5	63.0	63.9
Puerto Rican	12.2	9.6	9.2	9.5
Cuban	4.7	3.5	3.5	3.7
Other Latino	22.8	28.4	24.3	22.9
Latinos as a percentage of total US population	9.0	12.5	16.3	17.3

Sources: Chapa and De La Rosa (2004); US Census Bureau (2011, 2015).

In 2014, Latinos comprised 17.3% of the US population. The Census Bureau documents an increase in the US Mexican population from 60.4% in 1990 to 63.9% in 2014. In comparison, the Puerto Rican and Cuban populations have decreased in size, from 12.2% to 9.5% and 4.7% to 3.7%, respectively (see Table 1). The percentage of other Latinos stayed essentially the same, varying only one tenth of a percent (22.8% to 22.9%) between 1990 and 2014. The Pew Research Center noted a change in the total population (September 2015): "In 1965, 84% of Americans were non-Hispanic whites. By 2015, that share had declined to 62%. Meanwhile, the Hispanic share of the US population rose from 4% in 1965 to 18% in 2015."

Both immigration and US birth rates contribute to the number of Latinos in the United States. Latinos have more children than other ethnic groups: in 2010, they had the highest fertility rate (2.4) of all racial groups. In comparison, Blacks' fertility rate was 2.1 and both Asian and White fertility rates were 1.8 (Passel, Livingston, and Cohn 2012). In part, relative age fuels the higher fertility rates. Prime childbearing years for women are 20 to 35 (Parker et. al. 2013, 1); Latinos tend to be younger than whites. The median age for all Latinos in 2014 was 28.4, which is in the bracket of prime childbearing age. In contrast, the median age for Whites was 43.1, well above the upper limit of 35 years (see Table 2). The comparatively young median age of Latinos masks important differences between subgroups. For example, the median age of Mexican-origin Latinos (26.6) is approximately 15 years lower than the median for Cuban-origin Latinos (40.8). Indeed, the age distribution of the Cuban

TABLE 2. Percentage of population by age for Latino subgroups and White Non-Latinos, 2014

	Median Age	<5	18–24	65 Plus
US Total	37.7	6.2	9.9	14.5
White, Non-Latino	43.1	5.0	8.8	18.3
All Latinos	28.4	9.2	12.1	6.4
Mexican	26.6	9.8	12.4	5.2
Puerto Rican	28.9	9.0	11.7	7.9
Cuban	40.8	5.9	8.2	16.8
Central American	29.8	9.1	11.7	4.4
South American	35.6	6.6	10.7	8.9

Source: US Census Bureau (2015).

population is more similar to Whites than to Mexicans, Puerto Ricans, and Central Americans.

In the coming years, a much larger proportion of the Latino population will be entering various points of the educational system, including preschool and college, than will other groups. Hayes-Bautista, Schink, and Chapa (1988) accurately predict the population predominance of Latinos (33), noting that "The first [trend] is that the Baby Boom bulges its way upwards, until, in the year 2015, its earliest cohort has fully passed into the retirement age of 65. At that point, the young, working-age population becomes increasingly composed of Latinos and other minorities."

Geographic Distribution

Traditionally, Latinos have been widely dispersed throughout the United States, but in a rather specific pattern. Table 3 illustrates that they continue to be concentrated in the Southwestern United States. Since 1980, California has had the largest concentration of Latinos, with substantial but lesser populations in Texas, New York, Florida, and Illinois. Column 7 shows that 66% of Latinos were concentrated in these five states in 2014.

TABLE 3. States with the largest Latino populations in 1980, 1990, 2000, 2010, and 2014 (in thousands)

	1980	1990	2000	2010	2014	2014 % of US Pop.	2014 Cum. % of US Latino Pop.
US Total	14,609	22,379	35,306	50,478	55,279	100	100
California	4,544	7,704	10,967	14,014	14,989	27	27
Texas	2,986	4,340	6,670	9,461	10,408	19	46
New York	1,659	2,214	2,868	3,417	3,670	7	53
Florida	858	1,574	2,683	4,224	4,789	9	62
Illinois	636	904	1,530	2,028	2,152	4	66
Arizona	447	688	1,296	1,895	2,056	4	70
New Jersey	485	748	1,117	1,555	1,729	3	73
New Mexico	482	579	765	953	994	2	75
Colorado	341	424	736	1,038	1,135	2	77

Sources: Chapa and De La Rosa (2004); US Census Bureau (2011, 2015).

Table 4 identifies metropolitan areas with total population greater than 1 million whose Latino population constituted at least 10 percent of the total in 2014, further illustrating that Latinos are concentrated in large metropolitan areas. The San Antonio-New Braunfels metro area in Texas had a population of 2.3 million, of whom 1.2 million (54.7%) were Latino residents. The Riverside-San Bernardino-Ontario metro area in California, with 4.4 million residents of whom roughly 2 million (49.4%) are Latinos, follows closely behind San Antonio-New Braunfels. Of the Los Angeles-Long Beach-Santa Ana metro area's total population of 13.2 million, 45.1% (or 5.9 million) were Latinos. Even states not in the Southwest attract concentrations of Latinos. Salt Lake City had a total population of 1.1 million in 2014; Latinos comprised 17.5% of that population (201,578 residents). And Utah is not the only state outside the Southwest that is attracting concentrations of Latinos.

The increase in the percentage of Latinos moving to non-Southwestern states was higher in 1990–2000, as shown in Table 5, than in 2000-2010. Despite the slowdown during the second decade, South Carolina, Alabama, Tennessee, Kentucky, Arkansas, North Carolina, Mississippi, and South

TABLE 4. Population data for metro areas over one million that are at least 10% Latino (2014)

	US Pop.	Latino Pop.	(%) Latino	Cum. % US Latino
New York-Northern New Jersey-Long Island, NY-NJ-PA	20,092,883	4,785,019	23.8	9
Los Angeles-Long Beach-Santa Ana, CA	13,262,220	5,978,066	45.1	20
Chicago-Joliet-Naperville, IL-IN-WI	9,553,810	2,072,324	21.7	24
Dallas-Fort Worth-Arlington, TX	6,954,003	1,962,628	28.2	27
Houston-Sugar Land-Baytown, TX	6,490,180	2,356,245	36.3	31
Washington-Arlington-Alexandria, DC-VA-MD-WV	6,032,744	910,166	15.1	33
Miami-Fort Lauderdale-Pompano Beach, FL	5,929,819	2,567,076	43.3	38
Atlanta-Sandy Springs-Marietta, GA	5,611,829	584,904	10.4	39
Boston-Cambridge-Newton, MA-NH	4,732,161	484,812	10.2	40
San Francisco-Oakland-Fremont, CA	4,594,060	1,008,334	21.9	41
Phoenix-Mesa-Glendale, AZ	4,489,109	1,355,233	30.2	44
Riverside-San Bernardino-Ontario, CA	4,441,890	2,196,198	49.4	48
San Diego-Carlsbad-San Marcos, CA	3,263,431	1,083,028	33.2	50
Tampa-St. Petersburg-Clearwater, FL	2,915,582	517,432	17.7	51
Denver-Aurora-Broomfield, CO	2,754,258	628,890	22.8	52
Portland-Vancouver-Hillsboro, OR-WA	2,347,127	270,453	11.5	52
San Antonio-New Braunfels, TX	2,326,665	1,272,595	54.7	55
Orlando-Kissimmee-Sanford, FL	2,321,418	648,259	27.9	56
Sacramento-Arden-Arcade-Roseville, CA	2,244,397	472,302	21.0	57
Las Vegas-Paradise, NV	2,069,681	627,310	30.3	58
San Jose-Sunnyvale-Santa Clara, CA	1,952,872	537,055	27.5	59
Austin-Round Rock, TX	1,943,299	622,658	32.0	60
Providence-Warwick, RI-MA	1,609,367	186,596	11.6	60
Milwaukee-Waukesha-West Allis, WI	1,572,245	160,750	10.2	61
Oklahoma City, OK	1,336,767	163,578	12.2	61
Raleigh, NC	1,242,974	129,007	10.4	61
Hartford-West Hartford-East Hartford, CT	1,214,295	169,558	14.0	61
Salt Lake City, UT	1,153,340	201,578	17.5	62
Tucson, AZ	1,004,516	362,438	36.1	62

Source: US Census Bureau (2015).

TABLE 5. Latino population growth of more than 100 percent during 1990–2000 and 2000–2010

	1990 Latino Pop.	2000 Latino Pop.	(%) Increase 1990-2000	Latino Pop. 2010	(%) Increase 2000-2010	(%) Latino State Pop. 2010
South Carolina	30,500	95,076	212	235,682	148	5.9
Alabama	24,629	75,830	208	185,602	145	4.2
Tennessee	32,742	123,838	278	290,059	134	5.1
Kentucky	22,005	59,939	172	132,836	122	3.3
Arkansas	19,876	86,866	337	186,050	114	7.0
North Carolina	76,745	378,963	394	800,120	111	9.9
Mississippi	15,998	39,569	147	81,481	106	2.9
South Dakota	5,252	10,903	108	22,119	103	2.9
Delaware	15,824	37,277	136	73,221	96	9.3
Georgia	108,933	435,227	300	853,689	96	10.4
Virginia	160,403	329,540	105	631,825	92	8.9
Oklahoma	86,162	179,304	108	332,007	85	9.6
Iowa	32,643	82,473	153	151,544	84	5.2
Nevada	124,408	393,970	217	716,501	82	35.9
Indiana	98,789	214,536	117	389,707	82	6.4
Utah	84,597	201,559	138	358,340	78	16
Nebraska	36,969	94,425	155	167,405	77	9.8
Minnesota	53,888	143,382	166	250,258	75	5.1
Wisconsin	93,232	192,921	107	336,056	74	6.3
Washington	214,568	441,509	106	755,790	71	12.8
Oregon	112,708	275,314	144	450,062	63	13.2
Kansas	93,671	188,252	101	300,042	59	11.2

Sources: Chapa and De La Rosa (2004); US Census Bureau (2003); US Census Bureau (2011).

Dakota more than doubled their Latino populations between 2000 and 2010. Even states with less than a 100% increase had considerable Latino populations. Georgia had 853,689 Latinos in 2010, which represented 10.4% of the total state population. From 2000 to 2010, Georgia had a 96% increase in its Latino population. Nevada is another example: its 716,501 Latinos in 2010 represented 35.9% of its total population, an 82% increase over the period of the last two censuses.

Educational Attainment

Educational attainment continues to elude Latinos and has serious implications for the economic growth of the United States. Table 6 illustrates overall enrollment rates, Latino enrollment rates, and the change (as percentage)

TABLE 6. Fall education enrollment by level and race, 2000 and 2013

	2000		2013		2000–2013
	Number	(%)	Number	(%)	% Change
All Students					
US Total	15,312,289	100.0	20,375,789	100.0	33
White	10,462,099	68.3	11,590,717	56.9	11
Black	1,730,318	11.3	2,872,126	14.1	66
Latino	1,461,806	9.5	3,091,112	15.2	111
Asian/Pacific Islander	978,224	6.4	1,259,598	6.2	29
Native/American Indian	151,150	1.0	162,563	0.8	8
Nonresident	528,692	3.5	840,311	4.1	59
Two-Year					
Total	5,948,431	100.0	6,968,739	100.0	17
White	3,804,055	64.0	3,636,111	52.2	-4
Black	734,875	12.4	1,073,066	15.4	46
Latino	843,914	14.2	1,491,224	21.4	77
Asian/Pacific Islander	401,930	6.8	415,729	6.0	3
Native/American Indian	74,677	1.3	70,975	1.0	-5
Nonresident	8,898	0.1	9,203	0.1	3
Four-Year					
Total	9,363,858	100.0	13,407,050	100.0	43
White	6,658,044	71.1	7,954,606	59.3	19
Black	995,443	10.6	1,799,060	13.4	81
Latino	617,892	6.6	1,599,888	11.9	159
Asian/Pacific Islander	576,294	6.2	843,869	6.3	46
Native/American Indian	76,473	0.8	91,588	0.7	20
Nonresident	439,712	4.7	748,281	5.6	70
Graduate					
Total	2,156,896	100.0	2,900,954	100.0	34
White	1,478,644	68.6	1,691,549	58.3	14
Black	181,425	8.4	367,312	12.7	102
Latino	110,781	5.1	220,962	7.6	99
Asian/Pacific Islander	132,679	6.2	195,239	6.7	47
Native/American Indian	12,644	0.6	14,797	0.5	17
Nonresident	240,723	11.2	356,907	12.3	48

Source: US Department of Education (2014).

in each from 2000 to 2013. The percentage of Latinos enrolled in higher education rose 111%. Although the number of Latinos enrolled, a little over 3 million, represented only 15.2% of all enrollments in Fall 2013, the percentage of increase was the largest among all racial groups. Despite these gains, differences among the types of educational institutions in which Latinos are enrolled suggest large disparities.

Latinos are overrepresented at two-year institutions, where they comprise 1.5 million (21.4%) of the student population. Since 2010, Latino enrollment at two-year institutions has increased by 77%, while the rate of enrollment for Whites decreased by 4% during the same period. At four-year institutions, Whites are overrepresented (59.3%) when compared to Latinos (11.9%) and Blacks (13.4%). The education gap widens at the graduate level, with Whites comprising the largest percentage (58.3%) and number (1.6 million) of student enrollments. Blacks outpace Latinos with 367,312 graduate students, or 12.7% of enrollments. Nonresidents surpassed Latinos with 356,907 students, or 12.3% of enrollments. Latinos ranked fourth highest in enrollments, with 220,962 students, or 7.6%. Despite their continued underrepresentation, Latino enrollments at the graduate level have doubled since 2010.

Degree completions continue to be an issue for Latinos (see Table 7). As the table shows, 34.7% of Latinos age 25 or older had less than a high school education in 2014, but only 11.2% of Whites were in the same status. High school graduation rates were almost identical for Latinos

TABLE 7. Distribution of educational attainment for Latinos 25 and over, by subgroup and in comparison to Non-Latino Whites (2014)

	US Total	Latino	White, Non-Latino	Mexican	Puerto Rican	Cuban	Central American	South American
Total	100	100	100	100	100	100	100	100
Less than high school diploma	13.1	34.7	11.2	40.1	22.6	20.1	44.1	15.0
High school graduate	27.7	27.2	28.0	27.3	29.7	29.6	25.0	25.1
Some college or associate degree	29.2	32.3	29.4	22.2	30.0	25.0	18.9	28.0
Bachelor's degree	18.7	9.9	19.5	7.6	11.6	15.9	8.4	20.5
Graduate or professional degree	11.4	4.5	11.8	2.9	6.1	9.3	3.5	11.4

Source: US Census Bureau (2015).

(27.2%) and Whites (28%). The data indicates that slightly more Latinos (32.3%) are gaining access to college in comparison to Whites (29.4%). However, when it comes to completing a bachelor's degree, Latinos (9.9%) still lag considerably behind Whites (19.5%). The gap increases for graduate and professional school completions, with Latinos at 4.5% and Whites at 11.5%. The educational disparities are even more striking when looking at Latino subgroups. Mexicans fair much worse than any other Latino subgroup. Only 7.6% complete bachelor's degrees and 2.9% complete graduate or professional school degrees. All other Latino subgroups exceed those percentages.

The educational inequity manifests itself most at the upper end of the educational pipeline. The professoriate includes very few Latinos and Blacks, as Table 8 illustrates. Among all minorities in the professoriate, Latinos comprise the smallest percentage of professors at the levels of full (3.1%), associate (4.1%), assistant (4.1%) and instructor (5.8%). At the lowest level, lecturer, Latinos (5.8%) slightly outpaced Blacks (5%). This table also illustrates the gender gap among minorities in the professoriate. At all levels of the professoriate, except the full professor level, women outnumber their colleagues. Among Latinos and Asians, women at the associate level do not outnumber their male colleagues. Asian females are also below parity at the assistant professor level.

TABLE 8. Full-time minority faculty in degree-granting institutions by gender (2013)

Academic Rank	Black		Asian		Latino	
	(%) of Total	(%) Female	(%) of Total	(%) Female	(%) of Total	(%) Female
Full Professor	3.7	39.7	8.5	22.9	3.1	34.5
Associate Professor	5.7	51.0	10.2	37.4	4.1	44.6
Assistant Professor	6.1	60.5	10.6	46.3	4.1	50.8
Instructors	6.8	63.6	4.8	56.0	5.8	54.4
Lecturers	5.0	56.0	7.1	59.3	5.8	58.6

Source: US Department of Education (2015).

Socioeconomic Status

Family types and sizes contribute to the overall socioeconomic status of the US population. Table 9 documents the change in family type for US total population and Latinos, in both 2005 and 2014. Overall, the percent-

TABLE 9. Distribution of family type, US total population and Latinos, 2005 and 2014

	US Total (%)		Latino (%)	
Family type	2005	2014	2005	2014
Married couple	49.7	47.9	49.4	47.3
Male head of household	4.6	4.9	9.3	9.0
Female head of household	12.6	13.0	18.9	20.2

Source: US Census Bureau (2006, 2015).

age of married couples in the United States declined from 49.7% to 47.9%. This trend also manifested itself among Latinos. In 2005, married couples were 49.4% of the Latino population, declining to 47.3% in 2014. The percentages of male and female heads of household increased slightly in the United States as a whole, from 4.6% to 4.9% and 12.6% to 13.0%, respectively. Among Latinos, the trend for male heads of household slightly declined from 9.3% to 9.0%. Female heads of households increased from 18.9% to 20.2%, which was higher than the national average.

The average Latino family size tends to be larger than that of others in the United States, as shown in Table 10. It illustrates that for the years 2000 and 2010, the average family size of all families in the United States has stayed constant at 3.1. However, White families have decreased slightly in size, from 3 to 2.9, while Latino families have stayed steady at 3.9. Mexican, Puerto Rican, and South American families decreased slightly in size from 2000 to 2010.

TABLE 10. Average family size, Non-Latino Whites, Latinos, and Latino subgroups, 2000 and 2010

	2000	2010
US Total	3.1	3.1
White, Non-Latino	3.0	2.9
All Latinos	3.9	3.9
Mexican	4.2	4.1
Puerto Rican	3.5	3.4
Cuban	3.2	3.3
Central American	4.0	4.0
South American	3.6	3.5

Source: US Census Bureau (2001, 2011).

TABLE 11. Poverty characteristics, total US population and Latino subgroups, 2006 and 2014

	US Total (%)		Latino (%)		Mexican (%)		Puerto Rican (%)		Cuban (%)	
	2006	2014	2006	2014	2006	2014	2006	2014	2006	2014
All persons below poverty level	13.3	15.5	21.5	24.1	23.0	25.4	24.6	26.2	14.6	18.8
Children under 18 below poverty level	18.3	21.7	28.0	32.1	29.7	33.6	31.5	33.4	15.6	20.8

Source: US Census Bureau (2007, 2015).

Latinos are more likely to live in poverty than the US average in the United States, as shown in Table 11. Between 2006 and 2014, the percentage of all persons in the United States living below the poverty level rose from 13.3% to 15.5%. However, the 21.5% of Latinos living in poverty in 2006 rose to 24.1% in 2014. The percentage of children under the age of 18 living in poverty also rose in the United States overall, from 18.3% in 2006 to 21.7% in 2014. Again, Latinos outpaced that, rising from 28% in 2006 to 32.1% in 2014. Among Latino subgroups, Mexican and Puerto Rican children grow up in poverty at much higher rates than Cuban children, 33.6%, 33.4%, and 20.8% respectively.

Occupation has a great effect on poverty rates. Table 12 shows the occupational distribution for non-Latino Whites, Latinos, and Latino subgroups 16 years old or greater in 2014 and indicates that the majority of US individuals participate in the labor force, at the rate of 63.3%. However, Latinos participate at a higher rate, 67.1%, in comparison to Whites at 63.1%. While Latinos participate at a higher rate, the work they perform is indicative of their socioeconomic status. Latinos work mostly in service occupations, at a rate of 26.1%. In contrast, Whites have a service-sector occupation rate of 15%; among all individuals in the US labor force it is 18.2%. Sales and office occupations are the next highest category for Latinos in the labor force, at 21.8%, relatively close to the 23.7% in those occupations for the entire labor force and the 24.2% figure for Whites considered separately. The next most likely occupations for Latinos are management, business, science, and the arts, at a total 20.4%. Whites participate in these occupations at double that rate, 41.4%, higher than the national average of 36.9%.

Latinos participate in greater proportion in higher-risk occupations involving production, transportation, and material moving, at 16.4% in contrast to Whites at 11% and the US overall at 12.3%. Similarly, Latinos

TABLE 12. Occupational distribution for population 16 years and over, Non-Latino Whites, Latinos, and Latino subgroups, 2014

	US Total (%)	White, Non-Latino (%)	Latino (%)	Mexican (%)	Puerto Rican (%)	Cuban (%)	Central American (%)	South American (%)
In labor force	63.3	63.1	67.1	67.2	62.4	62.5	73.7	71.0
Unemployed	7.2	6.1	5.6	5.6	7.2	4.5	5.4	4.9
Management, business, science, and arts	36.9	41.4	20.4	17.4	28.1	31.3	14.6	31.5
Service	18.2	15.0	26.1	26.1	23.4	20.7	32.1	24.2
Sales and office	23.7	24.2	21.8	21.2	27.4	24.6	17.2	22.8
Natural resources, construction, and maintenance	8.9	8.5	15.4	17.6	7.4	9.7	19.6	9.6
Production, transportation, and material moving	12.3	11.0	16.4	17.7	13.7	13.7	16.5	11.8

Source: US Census Bureau (2015).

participate in the occupations of natural resources, construction, and maintenance occupations at higher rates (15.4%) than Whites (8.5%).

Another factor related to socioeconomic status is the acquisition of English language. Table 13 shows the language spoken at home and the ability to speak English for the population 5 years and older, and illustrates that Latinos are more likely to speak another language more often than English only. Of the total US population, 78.9% speak only English; for Latinos the rate is 26.5%. Of the entire US population, 8.9% reported that they speak English less than "very well"; among Latinos it was 31.7%—a very marked difference. Also telling is that 21% of the total US population speaks a language other than English, whereas 74% of Latinos speak more than one language. Individuals speaking more than one language are viewed as having greater social capital in all industrialized nations with the exception of the United States. As Valenzuela and Maxcy (2011) have noted:

> Subtractive cultural assimilation refers to a schooling process that divests youth of their culture and language in an assimilationist fashion. Rather than promoting bilingualism and biliteracy, most US schooling subtracts children's bilingual and bicultural competencies. (38)

TABLE 13. Language spoken at home and ability to speak English for the population 5 years and older, 2014

	US Total (%)	All Latinos (%)	Mexican (%)	Puerto Rican (%)	Cuban (%)	Central American (%)	South American (%)
Ages 5 and older speaks:							
Only English	78.9	26.5	26.5	38.8	20.3	13.8	16.5
English less than "very well"	8.9	31.7	31.6	17.3	40.0	47.6	36.9
Language other than English	21.0	74.0	73.5	61.2	79.7	86.2	83.5

Source: US Census Bureau (2015).

Conclusion

Despite the Latino population constituting 18% of the overall population in the United States as of 2015, educational and other inequities persist. Mexicans continue to be the largest subgroup among Latinos. Both immigration and US birth rates contribute to the number of Latinos in the United States. Latinos are younger and thus more prolific. Their larger numbers at younger ages leads to their higher participation in the labor force. This has many implications for the economic growth of the country and the long-term support of the Social Security system. Latinos continue to settle in the Southwest but increasingly spread to other areas of the country. The number of Latinos more than doubled in such states as South Carolina, Alabama, Tennessee, Kentucky, Arkansas, North Carolina, Mississippi, and South Dakota between 2000 and 2010. Educational inequality continues to persist in the Latino population.

The upward trend in the number of Latinos enrolled in higher education has not translated into significantly higher numbers of Latinos graduating from these institutions. Latino enrollments still total only a third of White enrollments. The educational gap increases at the graduate and professional school levels and manifests itself in the professoriate. Among all minorities in the professoriate, Latinos comprise the smallest percentage of participants at all levels, with the exception of lecturers.

Latinos tend to have larger families and higher poverty rates. The percentage of Latinos living in poverty was higher in 2014 than in previous years, as was the percentage of Latino children under the age of 18 living in poverty. The percentage of Latino male heads and Latina female heads of households is almost twice that of Whites. Latinos participate in the labor force at higher rates than the national average. However, Latinos work primarily in the service sector and are more often in hazardous jobs than are Whites. Latinos are also more likely to speak another language in addition to English.

No country can ignore its labor force. All segments of the population should achieve the highest educational goals they desire. The shift from a manufacturing base to a technology base that encompasses not only a national but an international economy makes it vital that every segment of society is educated to its full potential. Latino educational attainment can no longer be neglected.

REFERENCES

Chapa, Jorge, and Belinda De La Rosa. 2004. "Latino Population Growth, Socioeconomic and Demographic Characteristics, and Implications for Educational Attainment." *Education and Urban Society* 36:2, 130–150.

Hayes-Bautista, David, Werner O. Schink, and Jorge Chapa. 1988. *Burden of Support: Young Latinos in an Aging Society*. Stanford: Stanford University Press.

National Science Foundation. 2013. "Women, Minorities, and Persons with Disabilities in Science and Engineering." Arlington: National Center for Science and Engineering Statistics, http://www.nsf.gov/statistics/wmpd/2013/race.cfm.

Parker, Jennifer, Amy Branum, Daniel Axelrad, and Jonathan Cohen. 2013. "Adjusting National Health and Nutrition Examination Survey Sample Weights for Women of Childbearing Age." *Vital Health Statistics* 2, 1–29.

Passel, J. S., G. Livingston, and D'Vera Cohn. 2012. *Explaining Why Minority Births Outnumber White Births*. Washington, DC: Pew Research Center, http://www.pewsocialtrends.org/2012/05/17/explaining-why-minority-births-now-outnumber-white-births/

Pew Research Center. 2015. *Modern Immigration Wave Brings 59 Million to US, Driving Population Growth and Change Through 2065: View of Immigration's Impact on US Society Mixed*. Washington, DC: Pew Research Center.

US Bureau of the Census. 2015. "Age and Sex." *2014 American Community Survey 1-Year Estimates*, http://factfinder2.census.gov. [All US Bureau of the Census publications cited in the following references can be found at this site.]

_____. "Average Family Size (White Alone, Not Hispanic or Latino)." 2000 Census Summary File 1.

_____. "Educational Attainment." *2014 American Community Survey 1-Year Estimates*.

_____. "Sex by Educational Attainment for the Population 25 Years and Over (White Alone)." *2014 American Community Survey 1-Year Estimates*.

_____. "Geography-United States: Profile of General Population and Housing Characteristics: 2010." *2010 Census Summary File 1*.

_____. "Households and Families." *2005 American Community Survey 1-Year Estimates*.

_____. "Households and Families." *2014 American Community Survey 1-Year Estimates*.

_____. "Hispanic or Latino Origin by Specific Origin." *2014 American Community Survey 1-Year Estimates.*

_____. "Language Spoken at Home by Ability to Speak English for the Population 5 Years and Over (Hispanic or Latino)." *2014 American Community Survey 1-Year Estimates.*

_____. "Median Age by Sex (Hispanic or Latino)." *2014 American Community Survey 1-Year Estimates.*

_____. "Median Age by Sex (White Alone, Not Hispanic or Latino)." *2014 American Community Survey 1-Year Estimates.*

_____. "Selected Population Profile in the United States." *2010 American Community Survey 1-Year Estimates.*

_____. "Selected Population Profile in the United States." *2014 American Community Survey 1-Year Estimates.*

_____. "Sex by Age." *2014 American Community Survey 1-Year Estimates.*

_____. "Sex by Age (Hispanic or Latino)." *2014 American Community Survey 1-Year Estimates.*

_____. "Sex by Age (White Alone, Not Hispanic or Latino)." *2014 American Community Survey 1-Year Estimates.*

_____. "Sex by Educational Attainment for the Population 25 Years and Over (Hispanic or Latino)." *2014 American Community Survey 1-Year Estimates.*

_____. "Sex by Educational Attainment for the Population 25 Years and Over (White Alone)." *2014 American Community Survey 1-Year Estimates.*

US Department of Education. "Total Fall Enrollment in Degree-Granting Institutions by Level of Enrollment, Sex, Attendance Status, and Race/Ethnicity of Student: Selected Years, 1976 through 2013. *Digest of Educational Statistics, 2013.*" Washington, DC: US Department of Education, National Center for Education Statistics, https://nces.ed.gov/programs/digest/d13/tables/dt13_306.20.asp.

_____. "Full-time Faculty in Degree-Granting Institutions, by Race/Ethnicity, Sex, and Academic Rank: Fall 2009, Fall 2011, and Fall 2013." *Digest of Educational Statistics, 2014.* Washington, DC: US Department of Education, National Center for Education Statistics. https://nces.ed.gov/programs/digest/d14/tables/dt14_315.20.asp.

Valenzuela, Angela, and Brendan Maxcy. 2011. "Limited English Proficient Youth and Accountability: All Children (Who Are Tested) Count." In David L. Leal and Kenneth J. Meier, eds., *The Politics of Latino Education.* New York: Teachers College Press, 23-42.

Five Design Principles for Equity and Excellence in Hispanic-Serving Institutions

Lindsey E. Malcom-Piqueux and Estela Mara Bensimón

In this article, we offer and describe five design principles for equity and excellence that can be used to assess the extent to which HSIs (Hispanic-Serving Institutions) truly serve Latino/a students. Many higher education researchers, policymakers, educational advocates, institutional leaders, and educational practitioners have called for extensive dialogue on what it means to be truly Hispanic-serving. Due in part to a lack of consensus, HSIs lack guidance on assessing how well they serve Latino/a students.

HSIs shoulder unique responsibilities, including the education of post-traditional student populations, while facing distinct resource-related challenges. Any efforts to assess the performance of HSIs must be done with these facts in mind. Our aim is to help make the "Hispanic-serving" designation more meaningful to students and their families, higher education practitioners, institutional leaders, and policymakers, and to inform ongoing dialogue on what it means to be authentically Hispanic-serving.

THE FIVE DESIGN PRINCIPLES

Principle 1. Hispanic-serving designation is reflected in the institutional identity, mission, and priorities, as well as in the goals of campus divisions, departments, and units.

Principle 2. Latino/a student success is a shared value among institutional leadership, faculty, and staff.

Principle 3. Examining equity in educational outcomes for Latino/a students is central to institutional assessment processes and practices.

Principle 4. Promoting Latino/a student success and ensuring equity in outcomes is a subject of ongoing reflection and action by institutional leadership and individual practitioners.

Principle 5. Engaging Latino/a students with culturally sustaining practices is central to promoting and supporting Latino/a student success.

The "Hispanic-serving" designation was established during the 1992 reauthorization of the Higher Education Act (HEA). With increasing levels of college access across a growing and more geographically dispersed Latino/a population, the number of Hispanic-Serving Institutions (HSIs) continues to rise. In the two ensuing decades after passage of the HEA, the number of HSIs increased from 189 institutions in 1994-95 to 370 institutions in 2012-13 (*Excelencia* in Education 2014). These 370 HSIs enroll a disproportionately high share of Latino/a college students: though they constitute just 11 percent of US postsecondary institutions, they educate 59 percent of all Latino/a undergraduates (Calderón Galdeano and Santiago 2014). At present, an additional 277 two- and four-year institutions are "emerging" HSIs; they are approaching the 25-percent Latino/a full-time equivalent undergraduate enrollment threshold necessary to attain HSI status (Calderón Galdeano and Santiago 2014).

Given the growth in HSIs and the large numbers of Latino/a students they enroll, these institutions have become critical to increasing educational opportunity and attainment among the Latino/a diaspora. Though an HSI is designated as such based on its enrollment, many have argued that truly *serving* Latino/a students requires that HSIs focus on facilitating academic success, and not merely on providing educational access (see, for example, Santiago, Andrade, and Brown 2004; Contreras, Malcom, and Bensimón 2008; Malcom, Bensimón, and Davila 2010; and Núñez 2014).

While external accountability schemes such as performance-funding models and college rating systems provide metrics for assessing institutional performance, these traditional measures are inappropriate for HSIs, given the communities that they serve and the lack of resources with which they grapple (Jones 2014; Núñez 2014; and Núñez and Elizondo, in press). For example, graduation rates may not be an accurate characterization of institutional performance due to disparate levels in the academic preparation of HSI student populations and because graduation rates exclude transfer students, who are disproportionately Latino/a (Jones 2014; Núñez 2014; and Núñez and Elizondo, in press). Further, because these accountability schemes are heavily outcome-driven and lack process benchmarks (Dowd 2005; Jones 2014), they neither aid HSIs in understanding *how* current practices serve (or do not serve) Latino/a students nor provide direction on how to improve educational practice. The above criticisms of traditional performance metrics underscore the need for a framework to facilitate institutional self-assessment for HSIs.

HSIs shoulder unique responsibilities, including the education of post-traditional student populations, while facing distinct resource-related challenges. Any efforts to assess the performance of HSIs must be done with these facts in mind. In this brief, we offer design principles for equity and excellence at HSIs that can be used to assess the extent to which these institutions truly serve Latino/a students. These design principles, along with the tools we offer to implement them, draw upon the work of the Center for Urban Education (CUE), based at the University of Southern California. Established in 1999, the mission of the Center for Urban Education is to lead socially conscious research and develop tools for institutions of higher education to produce equity in student outcomes. Particularly relevant are the Equity Scorecard and the STEM Toolkit, available at http://cue.usc.edu/tools/stem/. Our aim is to help make the "Hispanic-serving" designation more meaningful to students and their families, higher education practitioners, institutional leaders, and policymakers, and to inform ongoing dialogue on what it means to be authentically Hispanic-serving. To that end, we address each of the design principles defined at the beginning of this article.

Design Principle 1

Hispanic-serving designation is reflected in the institutional identity, mission, and priorities, as well as in the goals of campus divisions, departments, and other units.

Scholars of organizational cultures view mission statements as the embodiment of an institution's values, commitment, and purpose (Contreras, Bensimón, and Malcom 2008). Mission statements guide strategic planning efforts (Gioia and Thomas 1996), and campus participants typically spend a great deal of time deliberating their content. Mission statements and other formal documents guide long-term change efforts, reminding decision makers of institutional values and goals. Mission statements influence what campus leaders and practitioners value, prioritize, and focus on. Therefore, the presence or absence of HSI identity in an institution's mission statement may influence how much attention its leaders pay to it. Speaking of the University of Houston, Professor Michael Olivas observes that reminders of the university's aspirations to be recognized as a Tier 1 institution are everywhere, but references to its HSI identity are nowhere to be found. He says, "Not a publication comes out that does not highlight the Tier One status claimed by UH . . . [but] I cannot find a reference to the University of Houston's HSI status in a single online article or website" (Olivas 2015, x). An examination of the mission statements of ten two- and four- year HSIs in California, Colorado, New Mexico, New York, and Texas revealed that none explicitly mentioned their HSI designation (Contreras, Bensimón, and Malcom 2008). More recently, we searched the mission statements, strategic plans, and accreditation self-studies of 103 HSIs in California; likewise, none made specific reference to HSI status in their mission statements.

Recognizing that mission statements may be older than an institution's acquired HSI status, we decided that strategic plans and accreditation self-studies might be more likely to incorporate the HSI identity. We examined these documents to determine whether they made mention of the HSI designation, formally stated the importance of promoting Latino/a student success; and/or provided specific data on Latino/a outcomes, either by student census or by outcomes reported by departments or fields of study. Among the 103 institutions, a small number mentioned their HSI identity in their plans and accreditation documents. For example, California State University at Fresno in its accreditation self-study indicated that the university is a designated HSI. California State University, Fullerton, explicitly addresses the importance of promoting Hispanic student success throughout its main website and includes quick facts (for example, "Fall 2014: 36% Hispanic Enrollment," and "Number 1 in California and tenth in the nation among top universities awarding bachelor's degrees to Hispanics"). East Los Angeles Community College's strategic plan refers to the many ways in which the college is Hispanic-serving, as well as its commitment to serving the Hispanic community in light of the demographic changes in its service community and in the state of California as a whole.

Overall, however, an HSI designation did not seem to play a prominent role in the core content of the institutions' strategic plans or self-studies. We did not find evidence that strategic plans or self-studies were vehicles for critical reflection on the goals and indicators of performance implied in the label "Hispanic-serving." Notably, many of the institutions whose documents were examined are recipients of Developing Hispanic-Serving Institutions Program funding (Title V), which means they have submitted proposals that required them to elaborate on the needs of Latino/a students and set forth improvement goals. However, the goals articulated in Title V proposals seem to exist in a vacuum, failing to make their way into the institutional documents that will presumably guide decisions about curriculum, programs, resource distribution, and evaluation.

We are aware that leaving out or acknowledging HSI identity in official institutional documents is not an assurance of conscious and intentional responsiveness to the needs and success of Latino/a students. Written documents cannot compensate or substitute for the absence of leadership actions (Schein 1985). However, mission statements, strategic plans, and accreditation self-studies are cultural artifacts (Schein 1985) that communicate institutional values, commitment, and purpose (Caruthers and Lott 1981; Chaffee and Tierney 1988; and Peeke 1994) and, if well understood and taken seriously, can be a guide for change, consensus-building, and accountability (Contreras, Malcom, and Bensimón 2008). The presence and absence of HSI identity in institutional documents can be illustrated in this way:

GENERAL MISSION STATEMENT, WITH EXAMPLE	
Includes general language such as "Prepare students for a changing multicultural world" or "Promote access and success for underserved students"	*We are a comprehensive, regional university with a global outlook located in a technologically rich and culturally vibrant metropolitan area. Our expertise and diversity serve as a distinctive resource and catalyst for partnerships with public and private organizations. We strive to be a center of activity essential to*
Indistinguishable from those of predominantly white institutions	*the intellectual, cultural, and economic development of our region*

MISSION STATEMENT RECOGNIZING HSI IDENTITY, WITH EXAMPLE	
Identifies institution as Hispanic-serving	*We are a comprehensive, regional Hispanic-serving university with an educational outlook based on values of equity, excellence, and inclusiveness. More*
Includes statements affirming the institution's HSI status and such elements as a commitment to an excellent educational experience for first-generation Latino and Latinas	*college-educated Latinos and Latinas are imperative for the economic and social well-being of California. Nevertheless, we have a long way to go in order to achieve a Latino/a college-educated population that is proportional to their representation in California. As a Hispanic-serving university, we hold ourselves accountable for increasing college-educated Latinos and Latinas.*

Many factors may contribute to institutions' silence about their HSI identity. Some may fear of making students from other groups uncomfortable or discouraging them from enrolling. Understandably, an HSI that barely meets the 25-percent Latino/a enrollment criterion may not feel as strongly about its HSI status as one that is predominantly Latino/a. Another factor that may contribute to a weak HSI identity is that institutions often acquire it accidentally as a result of demographic changes within their geographic area, changes over which they have no control.

Even though the majority of HSI institutions did not obtain their status by choice, they can nonetheless be intentional about recognizing and implementing their identity. In fact, as a nation, we need HSIs to be successful. Clearly, the success or failure of HSIs in educating Latinos/as has national consequences. Hence, it is important that the leaders, administrators, faculty, and staff of HSIs be intentional about expressing the HSI identity. This process can be facilitated by a document review protocol such as one used by CUE's institutional partners (see Table 1).

TABLE 1. Assessing the recognition of HSI identity in institutional artifacts

FORM FOR IDENTIFYING HSI RECOGNITION IN INSTITUTIONAL ARTIFACTS		
Title of Document:		
Name of Reviewer:		
Are the following Hispanic-serving characteristics present in this document?	Does the document reflect the corresponding characteristic in the first column?	How could the document be changed to reflect HSI identity? Who should be involved?
HSI designation is clearly stated	○ Yes ○ No ○ Somewhat If Yes or Somewhat, how?	Possible steps:
Stated goals are explicitly informed by HSI identity	○ Yes ○ No ○ Somewhat If Yes or Somewhat, how?	Possible steps:
Importance of HSI identity in history, language, and community empowerment is clear	○ Yes ○ No ○ Somewhat If Yes or Somewhat, how?	Possible steps:
Commitment to equity in student outcomes is evident	○ Yes ○ No ○ Somewhat If Yes or Somewhat, how?	Possible steps:

Design Principle 2

Latino/a student success is a shared value among institutional leadership, faculty, and staff.

Student learning and success are core values of the nation's higher education institutions. On any given college campus, institutional leadership, faculty, and academic and student affairs practitioners talk of "student success" as a central and uncontroversial goal. HSIs undoubtedly share this general commitment to fostering student learning and success, however that "success" might best be defined for their unique population of students (Santiago, Andrade, and Brown 2004; Núñez 2014; and Núñez and Elizondo, in press). Yet in spite of the well-meaning rhetoric surrounding student success, national and institutional data illustrate that many higher-education institutions continue to fall short in producing positive outcomes for a significant proportion of their students. And, at many HSIs, Latino/a students—the very students that these institutions purport to serve—experience inequities in educational outcomes, including persistence, degree completion, and participation in high-demand fields (Contreras, Malcom, and Bensimón 2008; Malcom-Piqueux, Suro, Bensimón, and Fischer 2013)[1].

The US Department of Education has tasked HSIs with "increasing educational opportunity and attainment among Latinos/as" (US DoE, no date). Our second principle for equity and excellence is that Latino/a student success has to be a shared value among institutional leadership, faculty, and staff. This principle calls for HSIs to move beyond a general commitment to student success to a specific commitment to Latino/a student success. That is, leaders of Hispanic-Serving Institutions and their administrations ought to acknowledge the importance of Latino/a student success explicitly, and how this value ought to be embedded into the shared understanding of their overarching mission and day-to-day practices.

Why is it important that HSIs value Latino/a student success? According to organizational theorists, values are central to the work of an organization or institution. Values are embedded within institutional communities (Lavé and Wenger 1991) and provide tacit instruction about an institution's purpose—and, by extension, the areas to which organizational actors direct their efforts (Tierney 2008). Spoken or unspoken, the shared values of an

---

1. Non-HSIs also fall short in producing equity in educational outcomes for Latino/a students, and steps ought to be taken to redress these inequities. See Witham, Malcom-Piqueux, Dowd, and Bensimón (2015) for an in-depth discussion of how equity ought to drive higher education reforms at all institutions.

institution drive what it does and where it directs its resources. Institutional values also signal to new faculty and staff that this is "what we are about," and ensures that they, too, align their actions to work toward that goal (Tierney 2008).

Institutional leaders, faculty, and staff who value Latino/a student success are more likely to think about their own practices in relation to producing positive educational outcomes for those students (Dowd and Bensimón 2015). Valuing Latino/a student success does not mean that an HSI is not concerned with facilitating success among all students, nor does it suggest that it concentrates on Latino/a students to the detriment of other student populations. It does, however, mean that the institutional community, practitioners in particular, recognizes its responsibility to Latino/a students and considers whether Latino/a students are benefitting from the educational resources HSIs employ to support persistence, course completion (across all disciplines), and degree attainment (Bensimón 2012).

As already mentioned, our examination of the websites, strategic plans, and other organizational artifacts of California's 103 HSIs revealed that they refer generally to their commitment to supporting student success and learning, without mentioning Latinos/as or any other specific student populations. In Table 2, we share the description of the Office of Undergraduate Education listed on the website of a four-year public Hispanic-serving university. This is the information that greets Latino/a students and their families when they click Academics on the institutional homepage. While the office's commitment to "student success" is stated, a commitment to Latino/a student success is not. This HSI does have an Office of Chicano Student Programs dedicated to supporting academic success among Latino/a students. However, the absence of any mention of Latino/a student success elsewhere on the institutional website suggests that this value may not be shared across the entire institutional community. By contrast, at another four-year public HSI in California, there was evidence (also shown in Table 2) that the institutional value of Latino/a student success informed the redesign of the academic advising model that would be used throughout the entire campus.

Design Principle 3

Examining equity in educational outcomes for Latino/a students is central to institutional assessment processes and practices.

TABLE 2. Evidence of Latino/a student success as a shared value

GENERIC COMMITMENT TO STUDENT SUCCESS	EXAMPLE OF GENERIC COMMITMENT
Institutional leadership, faculty, and staff speak generally about promoting student success and learning, but rarely acknowledge their responsibility to serve Latino/a students explicitly. Practitioners who *do* articulate the importance of promoting Latino/a student success do so in their roles within ad hoc offices tasked with dealing with these issues (for example, Title V office or Minority Student Affairs).	The Office of Undergraduate Education is committed to student success and the creation of a supportive educational environment at [Public 4-Year HSI]. The office oversees the development of programs designed to support student learning, research and experiential opportunities. Visit our offices to learn about the support programs that can help you be more competitive in the job market and in the pursuit of graduate and professional education.
EXAMPLE: GENERIC COMMITMENT	**EXAMPLE: LATINO SUCCESS AS SHARED VALUE**
Institutional leadership, faculty and staff openly state the importance of promoting Latino/a student success and understand Latino/a student success to be a shared responsibility. Latino/a student success is discussed in a manner that does not pit the duty to serve Latino/a students against promoting success of other student populations. Leadership, faculty and staff recognize that the efforts undertaken to promote Latino/a student success will benefit all students.	At a public, 4-year comprehensive Hispanic-serving university in California, the final institutional proposal to revamp the academic advising model to an integrated one incorporates several strategies and practices demonstrated in the higher education literature to promote Latino/a student success. The proposal states the need to employ such strategies to support its Latino/a student population and notes that all students would benefit from these practices.

As indicated in the second design principle, one of the most effective ways leaders communicate what is important to internal and external constituencies is by what they pay attention to systematically—what they notice and comment on and what they measure, reward, and control, as well as their casual remarks and the questions they ask (Schein 1985). Table 3 illustrates this theme.

HSI leaders, including presidents, vice presidents, deans, department chairs, and directors of divisions and programs, can demonstrate that they are paying attention to student success by engaging systematically in the following practices:

TABLE 3. Presence/absence of disaggregated data and goals with example

GENERIC DATA PRACTICES	HSI DATA PRACTICE MODEL
Data are not disaggregated by race and ethnicity. Goals for student success are not measurable.	Data are disaggregated by race and ethnicity. Equity metrics for Latinos/as (and all other groups) are routinely reported. Performance benchmarks are set for Latinos/as (and all other groups).
EXAMPLE: GENERIC DATA PRACTICE	EXAMPLE: HSI DATA PRACTICE
An HSI university creates a new initiative to involve more undergraduates in research activities with faculty. At the end of the first year, the program is praised as an exemplary "high impact" practice, but there is no information on how many Latinos/as participated.	A HSI community college produces an annual report on the state of equity and excellence and provides data to assess student outcomes by race and ethnicity. The institution has identified high-risk courses for Latinos/as and monitors their performance systematically.

1. Insisting that all data on educational outcomes be disaggregated by race and ethnicity to enable continuous monitoring of students' progress.
2. Adopting specific metrics of equity and applying them to disaggregated student outcomes (see Figures 1 and 2).
3. Engaging in performance benchmarking to set equity goals in specific outcomes to monitor Latino/a student success (see Figures 3 and 4).
4. Modeling the practices of equity-minded data interpretation.

The first three data practices represent essential aspects of paying attention to the success of all students, including Latinos/as. HSI presidents need to have answers to questions like these: "Is the rate of admission for Latinos/as equal to their representation in the college-age population within the college's service area?" and "Are Latinos/as completing the minimum number of credits required for on-time graduation?" A dean of engineering would need to have answers to such questions as "Is the proportion of Latinos/as majoring in engineering equal to their share of all undergraduates?" and "What are the high-risk engineering prerequisite courses for Latinos/as?"

　　At a minimum, HSIs should monitor equity for Latinos/as in basic indicators of access, academic progress, and excellence. In the examples below, we represent equity as proportionality based on overall enrollment. Figure 1 shows that Latinos/as have a 46 percent share of the

FIGURE 1. Indicators of equity in student outcomes (example)

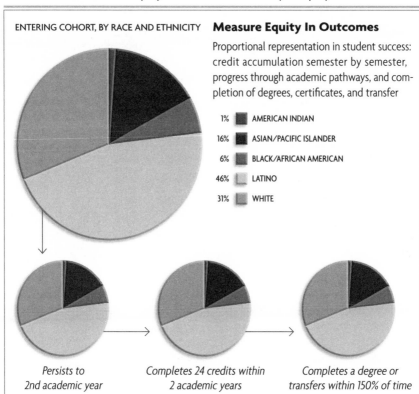

ENTERING COHORT, BY RACE AND ETHNICITY

Measure Equity In Outcomes

Proportional representation in student success: credit accumulation semester by semester, progress through academic pathways, and completion of degrees, certificates, and transfer

1% AMERICAN INDIAN

16% ASIAN/PACIFIC ISLANDER

6% BLACK/AFRICAN AMERICAN

46% LATINO

31% WHITE

Persists to 2nd academic year

Completes 24 credits within 2 academic years

Completes a degree or transfers within 150% of time

EQUITY IN STUDENT PROGRESS AND SUCCESS

undergraduate enrollment pie. Therefore, equity in academic progress for Latinos/as would be met if they constitute 46 percent of all the students who are retained after the first year; have completed 24 credits within two years (if they are part-time community college students); and have completed a degree or transferred within three years. In our definition, equity means maintaining a consistent share of the pie on key indicators of student success.

Figure 2 provides indicators of excellence that measure equity in the participation of Latinos/as in high-value and high-priority fields such as science and engineering. The kinds of data provided in Figures 1 and 2 are necessary to set performance benchmarks for increasing Latino/a success. As simple as these data may appear, most colleges do not follow cohort progress routinely for Latinos/as or any other group.

FIGURE 2. Sample indicators of equity in excellence

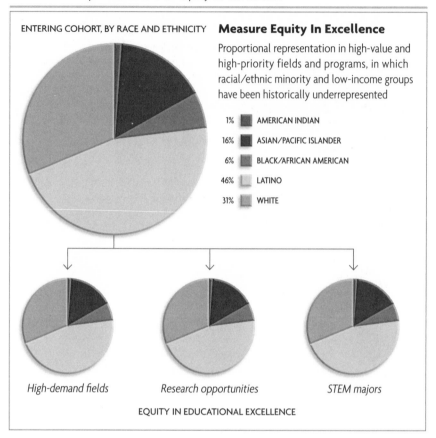

ENTERING COHORT, BY RACE AND ETHNICITY   **Measure Equity In Excellence**

Proportional representation in high-value and high-priority fields and programs, in which racial/ethnic minority and low-income groups have been historically underrepresented

1% AMERICAN INDIAN
16% ASIAN/PACIFIC ISLANDER
6% BLACK/AFRICAN AMERICAN
46% LATINO
31% WHITE

High-demand fields   *Research opportunities*   *STEM majors*

EQUITY IN EDUCATIONAL EXCELLENCE

Or if they do, the information conveyed in data reports goes unused because colleges lack a structured process to help practitioners make sense of the data.

Earlier in this article, we indicated that equity is defined by each group's share of a defined population, for example, total enrollment, total majors in engineering, and total number of students in a particular course. Figures 3 and 4 provide an example of how to use the kind of data represented in Figures 1 and 2 to set measurable goals to improve outcomes. Figure 3 shows that Latinos/as represent 46 percent of the full-time student population at HSI Community College (hypothetical), even though they represent only 29.3 percent of the students who graduated and/or transferred within three years. Latinos/as are 16.7 percentage points below equity. Figure 4 shows that Latinos/as' degree attainment

FIGURE 3. Latino/a share of students who earned the associate degree and/or transferred to a four-year college within three years of enrolling at HSI community college

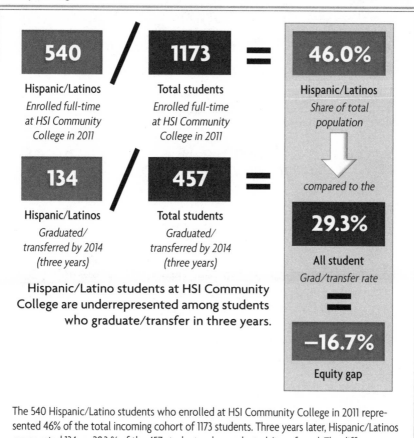

The 540 Hispanic/Latino students who enrolled at HSI Community College in 2011 represented 46% of the total incoming cohort of 1173 students. Three years later, Hispanic/Latinos represented 134, or 29.3 % of the 457 students who graduated/transferred. The difference between 29.4% and 46% reveals a −16.7 percentage point equity gap.

and/or transfer would be proportional to their share of total enrollment if 76 additional Latinos/as attained one or both of these goals.[2]

Goal setting that is as specific as the illustration in Figure 4 should be a routine practice of all institutions of higher education for all students,

---

2. The calculation in this example assumes that the share of Latinos/as would remain constant at 46 percent. We realize that this is unlikely but use that figure here for the sake of simplicity. Institutions can also benchmark to the highest performing group or to an aspirational goal.

FIGURE 4. Projection for Latino/a student equity in successful completion/transfer

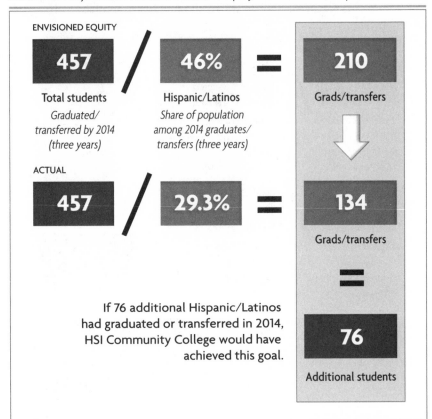

all of the time. Unless higher education institutions focus on outcomes deeply and discretely, equity will remain America's unmet promise (Witham, Malcom-Piqueux, Dowd, and Bensimón 2015). It is important that equity goals meet these criteria:

1. Basis in specific indicators, for example, graduation within four years of enrollment, participation in undergraduate research, completion of basic skills courses within the first two semesters.
2. Capable of being expressed in both percentages and numerically.
3. Organized so that they can be represented clearly in both graphics and writing, with goals that are broadly accessible and transparent.

While Figures 3 and 4 may seem very elementary to the experienced institutional researcher, their format is very appealing to leaders, faculty, and staff precisely because their simplicity provides a goal that is clear, measurable, and achievable.

The data HSIs need to develop clear goals and benchmarks can easily be extracted from student records. Yet few institutions, including HSIs, organize their data systematically, as shown in Figures 1 through 4. Why not? The most probable reason is that leaders have not made it clear that they want these kinds of data and that they want it in a format that is accessible. It may also be that leaders are fearful that the disaggregation of data by race and ethnicity violates affirmative action policies. However, affirmative action regulations apply only to admissions and do not preclude colleges from setting completion goals by race and ethnicity.

Goal setting is the first step toward greater accountability for student outcomes, but by itself is insufficient. Ideally, numeric data, particularly those that show unequal outcomes, should cause feelings of discomfort and distress, so much so that they have the power to mobilize institutional actors to take action. But the power of numeric data as a catalyst for critical examination of service to Hispanic students in regard to outcomes depends on the mindsets of institutional participants. Disaggregating data by race and ethnicity is essential, but embedding a culture of truly serving Hispanic students requires that leaders and practitioners shift their interpretation of the data from the student to institutional practices, structures, and policies.

Instead of rationalizing unequal outcomes on the basis of student deficiencies—for example, under-preparedness, underdeveloped study habits, unwillingness to seek help, economic disadvantaged, and high-risk environments (Rendón, Nora, and Kanagala 2014; Bensimón and Malcom 2012), the focus should be on analyzing how institutional practices might be failing Latino/a students. Practitioners and scholars typically respond to evidence of low rates of college completion by asking questions that focus attention on the student: Are these students academically integrated? Do these students exhibit particular behavioral patterns? Do these students exert as much effort as another group you might oppose them to? Do these students have social capital? How do the aspirations of high-performing students compare to low performers? Are they engaged? Are they involved? Are they motivated? Are they prepared?

However, leaders, from the president to the department chair, need to model for others how to reframe unequal outcomes as a problem of practice, rather than one of student deficiencies. Equity-minded interpretations require that the quality of practices be doubted rather than the capabilities, characteristics, attitudes, behaviors, predispositions, and motivation of students. Examples of equity-minded data interpretations include the following:

- Instead of declaring, "We have state-of-the-art resources on this campus, but students do not use them," institutional leaders and practitioners could be more proactive, asking such questions as "Why are our resources not reaching Latinos/as?" "How do Latinos/as experience the resources we offer?" "Are the resources we offer responsive to the actual needs of Latinos/as?"

- Instead of complaining ("I tell them to see me during office hours, but they just do not come"), instructors can reflect on questions such as, "What might prevent students from taking advantage of office hours?" "How is the purpose of office hours communicated to students?" "How could office hours be integrated into course requirements?"

- Instructors can improve their practices by understanding that help-seeking is a cultural competency that comes more naturally to those who feel entitled to receive assistance.

Design Principle 4

Promoting Latino/a student success and ensuring equity in outcomes is a subject of ongoing reflection and action by institutional leadership and individual practitioners.

The principle of promoting equity and excellence at HSIs emphasizes both reflection and action by leaders and practitioners. Faculty, administrators, and staff at HSIs must be willing to examine how their practices and language contribute to the problem of inequitable rates of Latino/a student success (Dowd and Bensimón 2015). Inquiry using institutional data, as described in the previous principle, not only makes leaders, faculty, and staff aware of inequities that Latino/a students might be experiencing but also leads them to question how existing policies and practices might be creating inequitable outcomes. For example, do the admissions criteria for the honors program at a HSI create inequities between working and non-working students? Do faculty who wish to involve undergraduates in research projects inadvertently hinder the participation of commuter students, compared to residential students? This type of reflective practice creates new knowledge and motivates practitioners to change their own practices as well as those institutional policies within their control (Bensimón 2007; Bensimón and Malcom 2012; Dowd and Bensimón 2015).

Armed with the knowledge and insight gained from reflective practice, practitioners can act as institutional agents to advocate for and provide resources and opportunities for historically underserved students (Stanton-Salazar 2011). Institutional agents are individuals in positions of power within organizations and institutions who use their human, social, and cultural capital to transmit resources, opportunities, and services to historically underserved and marginalized students (Stanton-Salazar 2011). Any practitioner at a HSI who occupies a high-status position and knows how to access high-value resources, navigate complex systems, and take effective action has the potential to be a transformative institutional agent (Bensimón and Dowd 2012; Dowd and Bensimón 2015; Dowd, Pak, and Bensimón 2013).

In Table 4, we outline the characteristics of practitioners and leaders at HSIs who act as transformative agents to promote Latino/a student success and those who, however well intentioned, do not. Following the table, we provide an example that illustrates how one science faculty member acted as an institutional agent to promote the success of Latinos/as in STEM fields, and one did not (example drawn from CUE research on STEM education at HSIs).

Though the previous examples of action by two different institutional agents showcase faculty members, transformative agents do not have to interact directly with students to transmit opportunities, privileges, and services to them. Faculty and administrators who work at the system and campus levels of HSIs to generate increased opportunities for Latino/a students are also institutional agents (Bensimón and Dowd 2012; Dowd and Bensimón 2015). Institutional agents go beyond what is typically expected of faculty and staff to pursue change at their institutions. At HSIs, transformative agents mobilize the resources to which they have access to promote Latino/a student success. Finally, we note that transformative agents cannot pursue the goal of Latino/a student success in isolation. To have a meaningful and lasting impact on educational outcomes of Latino/a students at their institutions, transformative agents require the support of leaders within their departments, divisions, and institution (Bensimón and Dowd 2012).

Developing transformative agents. Some practitioners act as transformative agents out of a personal understanding or identification with the challenges that Latino/a students face. However, transformative agents can and must be purposefully developed by HSIs. Below, we offer specific actions that leaders, faculty, and staff at HSIs can take to create transfor-

TABLE 4. Distinctive characteristics of transformative agents

INSTITUTIONAL AGENTS IN GENERAL	TRANSFORMATIVE AGENTS
Treat all students as though they are the same, failing to recognize that students enter college with vastly different aspirations, life experiences, ways of engaging in learning and participating in college, and identities as students.	Understand how the administrative policies and organizational cultures of colleges present greater obstacles to minority students than to others.
View existing policies and practices as rigid and believe all students should adapt to them; unwilling to examine how their own practices contribute to inequity.	Reflect on whether seemingly "neutral" institutional policies and practices create or contribute to inequitable outcomes experienced by Latino/a students.
Attribute problems of retention and completion to student deficits.	Approach problems of retention and completion as structural or systemic problems and work to reform policies, "remediate" practice, and change organizational culture.

INSTITUTIONAL AGENT: EXAMPLE	TRANSFORMATIVE AGENT: EXAMPLE
Professor Jones is on the science faculty at a four-year HSI. When asked about intra-institutional inequities experienced by Latino/a students, he responded: "A lot of our kids come here, again, especially if they don't have anybody in the family that's gone to college, not really realizing how much work they have to put in . . . We've been trying to [help the students] simply by telling them that what they're doing is not right and telling them you know this is the way you should be doing it. I don't think we really have the time to try to think through what more effective ways there might be to help them change their habits."	Professor Ramírez teaches math at a four-year HSI in the Southwest. Alarmed by the small number of Latinos/as in STEM fields at his institution and their persistent under-representation in STEM professions and among STEM faculty nationally, he took action to increase Latino/a student participation. The interdisciplinary program gives students a head start by providing the opportunity to learn lab skills prior to enrolling in a lab course.
When asked by a CUE researcher what he does to let students know he is available to them, he replied, "I just make comments . . . in class about how I'm available and I'd like to talk to them if they want. I've heard of programs where the professors actually call students and try to get them engaged. I just never felt like I had the time to go out hunting through all those different students trying to get them to come through."	He shared this: "When students get into a lab, they don't really have the skills to work in the lab. So the faculty gets frustrated because they have to spend a lot of time teaching those students. So I started a summer boot camp: for three weeks, they're going to be in the lab, and they're going to learn how to do cells."
	Ramírez also spoke of the importance of building relationships with his students and helping to connect them with individuals who could act as mentors: "I think that connecting with the students makes a big difference. I cannot connect with the hundreds of students in my mathematics class that I teach, but I can connect with my students in my STEM support program."

mative agents and become such agents themselves. CUE's STEM Toolkit includes a self-assessment instrument that helps faculty members identify how their actions fit within the framework of being a transformative agent. A sample item from the self-assessment reads:

Over the past semester . . .

STATEMENT	FREQUENCY		
For a significant number of my students, I've actively served as a human "bridge" to key faculty members, college/university personnel, authority figures, and gatekeepers who I know are supportive of students.	NEVER **1**	SOMETIMES **3**	FREQUENTLY **5**
How do you do this?			
What are the challenges?			
To what extent have you done this specifically for Latina/o students?			

The lists below consist of recommendations for developing HSI administrators and faculty (Bensimón and Dowd 2012, 11–13).

RECOMMENDATIONS FOR DEVELOPING HSI ADMINISTRATORS

- Engage faculty in an examination of departmental culture and interrogate how it supports Latino/a student success.

- Give priority in faculty hiring to individuals whose backgrounds, experiences, values, and aspirations make them identifiable as institutional agents.

- Reward (materially or symbolically) and recognize faculty who act as transformative agents in support of Latino/a students and other students from historically underserved groups outside of the classroom. Provide released time or other kinds of support to encourage writing grant applications for special programs; provide programmatic funds to encourage faculty members to offer academic support through social gatherings to Latino/a students.

- Use transformative agent characteristics as criteria for faculty performance assessment and evaluation.

- Use the Center for Urban Education (http://cue.usc.edu) tools to help teams and individuals reflect on how their own actions and behaviors, as well as institutional practices and resources, affect Latino/a student success.

RECOMMENDATIONS FOR FACULTY DIRECTIONS AT HSIs

- Reflect on the actions associated with transformative agent roles and enact them.

- Identify Latino/a students and become familiar with their life histories; provide them with the resources and experiences to develop their identities as students and learners.

- Become familiar with federally funded programs to support Latino/a student success, and collaborate with other faculty members to write grant applications.

- Participate in faculty search committees and develop methods to identify individuals who are knowledgeable about Latino/a students and possess the characteristics of transformative agents.

Design Principle 5

Engaging Latino/a students with culturally sustaining practices is central to promoting and supporting Latino/a student success.

The growing number of HSIs and "emerging" HSIs (*Excelencia* in Education 2014) reflects broad changes in the college student population. College campuses are increasingly diverse, though we note that longstanding patterns of stratification in college access remain (Witham et al. 2015). The shifting demographics of colleges have sparked criticism that higher education practice has failed to evolve with the students that postsecondary institutions serve (see for example Danowitz and Tuitt 2011; and Dowd and Bensimón 2015). Current policies and practices have not mitigated the inequities in educational experiences nor the outcomes of racial and ethnic minority, first-generation, and low-income students. And, there is increasing recognition that in order to achieve "inclusive excellence" (Williams, Berger, and McClendon 2005), institutions and their practitioners must alter their approaches to teaching, curriculum, student learning, assessment, and other institutional functions. We argue that for all higher education institutions, but particularly for HSIs, engaging Latino/a students with culturally inclusive practices is necessary for excellence.

Culturally inclusive practice—sometimes called culturally relevant practice (Ladson-Billings 1995), culturally responsive, or more recently, culturally sustaining practice (Paris 2012)—refers to educational practice that promotes students' academic success while supporting the maintenance of their cultures and communities and raising critical consciousness of social inequality (Ladson-Billings 1995; Paris 2012). Culturally inclusive practices affirm and validate minoritized students by "building on their cultural, linguistic, and community-based knowledge" (Valenzuela 1999, 62). It is in this manner that culturally inclusive practice is distinct from dominant "race-neutral" educational approaches, which disconnect practice from students' cultures, communities, and lived experiences (Dowd and Bensimón 2015). Though typically discussed in the context of K-12 education (Ladson-Billings 1995), culturally inclusive practice is increasingly advocated for in undergraduate (Harper and Hurtado 2011; Hurtado et al. 2012; Museus and Quaye 2009) and graduate education (Danowitz and Tuitt 2011) as a means to increasing belonging and learning among college students of color.

Given their Hispanic-serving mission and their role in advancing educational opportunity and attainment for Latino/a students, HSIs must engage in culturally responsive practices inside and outside the classroom. Efforts to be "culturally inclusive" cannot be limited to faculty in disciplines that are "the usual suspects" for critical pedagogy, for example, Chicano studies or sociology. Much has been written about how the full range of disciplines can be more culturally inclusive. Math faculty members at HSIs, for instance, might teach mathematical concepts and their application in ways that enhance Latino/a students' understanding of their own communities (Rubel 2010; Rubel, Chu, and Shookhoff 2011).

In Table 5, we outline the characteristics of culturally inclusive educational practice in the context of higher education as described in Dowd and Bensimón (2015), and contrast it with more dominant "race-neutral/color-blind" approaches. We also offer examples to illustrate the distinction between these practices.

As the preceding examples illustrate, being culturally inclusive requires that HSI faculty be aware of and knowledgeable about the students that they teach. They must also be willing to move their practices into alignment with the needs of Latino/a students. Staff and administrators must also strive to become more culturally inclusive in their own practices. Academic advisers and counselors could achieve this by employing practices that account for and seek to understand disparate patterns of help-seeking by Latinos/as and other students of color. Academic support staff can be more culturally inclusive by supporting the collectivist cultures of many communities of color (Guiffrida, Kiyama, Waterman, and Museus 2012) and leveraging them to promote Latino/a student success. Practitioners can

TABLE 5. Examples of color-blind and color-conscious practices

"RACE-NEUTRAL" EDUCATIONAL PRACTICE	CULTURALLY INCLUSIVE EDUCATIONAL PRACTICE
Presumes that Latino/a students are deficient and require "remediation"	Assumes that all students, regardless of their background, are capable of excelling academically
Makes students solely responsible for their learning and developing relationships with faculty	Makes instructors responsible for students' learning and for maintaining equitable relationships with all students
Considers students solely responsible for identifying and acquiring resources needed to excel academically	Demands that institutions be responsible for providing resources and information needed to meet high expectations
Sees the knowledge and experiences that students bring into the classroom as tangential to academic content and detracting from learning	Expects practitioners to hear, value, and engage the knowledge and experience that students bring into the classroom in meaningful ways
Views the development of students' capacities to act as social change agents as unrelated to the purposes of college	Foster students' capacities to act as social change agents to address racial inequities

"RACE-NEUTRAL" EXAMPLE	CULTURALLY INCLUSIVE EXAMPLE
Asked what it means to teach at a HSI and how it is "different" during an interview with a CUE researcher, a philosophy instructor was at first surprised. He responded that he had not thought about it, and he did not think it would be right to do anything different for Latino/a students. The question prompted him to share that he had recently added to his reading list the work of Gloria Anzaldúa and noticed that Latinas in his class, typically not very actively involved, were suddenly quite lively.	Professor Maria Tuttle at Los Medanos College (LMC) in California designed her syllabus to be culturally inclusive. A picture on the first page prominently displayed Latino/a LMC students holding tee shirts bearing the names of four-year institutions to which they had transferred. The syllabus, which is formatted as a newsletter, includes detailed information on academic resources and support (for example, the tutoring center), describes the benefits of utilizing these resources, and provides clear statements of how to succeed.
The faculty member was clearly dedicated, serious, and creative; however, he had never before considered how he might alter his teaching practices in light of his presence at an HSI. Nor had he been invited to consider this question by the leaders, deans, or department chair at this institution.	The instructor also includes step-by-step directions for using the course Blackboard site and sets a welcoming and supportive tone: "Communication with your instructors and your counselor will help you feel supported by the program. You can count on us to help you work it out. No problem is too big or too small."
	Finally, assigned readings are culturally relevant and include Rudolfo Anaya's *Bless Me, Ultima* and *The Latino Reader* (Augenbraum and Fernández Olmos, Mariner Books, 1997).

also design programs that intentionally engage students in experiences that raise consciousness about issues of social justice and inequality.

Nurturing culturally inclusive educational practice. HSIs must take steps to reflect on, and if necessary change, their current approach to educational practice. Leaders at HSIs must challenge faculty and staff to think about what it means to be Hispanic-serving, and support and encourage practitioners to be more culturally inclusive. We offer the following specific recommendations for faculty:

- Use tools, such as those developed by CUE, to review course syllabi and other instructional documents to determine whether they are culturally inclusive.
- Use language that is supportive, welcoming, and affirming when interacting with students inside and outside of the classroom.
- Assess teaching practices against standards of culturally responsive teaching.

A self-assessment survey, titled "How Culturally and Linguistically Responsive is My Teaching?" was developed by Professors Ana María Villegas and Tamara Lucas of Montclair State University and provides items faculty can use for assessment:

_____ I use pertinent examples and analogies from students' lives to introduce or clarify new concepts.

_____ I use instructional materials that not only promote the learning goals but are also relevant to my students' experiences.

_____ I frequently use community resources (both human and otherwise) in my teaching.

_____ I often help students examine the curriculum to determine whose voices are heard and whose voices are excluded.

_____ I often work with other teachers in my school to make the curriculum, instruction, and testing practices we use more supportive of all students.

_____ I consistently advocate for individual students in my class, when such advocacy is needed.

Incorporating cultural inclusivity into hiring practices. Leaders and faculty should review faculty search practices and incorporate culturally inclusive competencies into interview questions and hiring criteria. The following are sample interview questions from CUE's STEM Toolkit. The questions are designed to emphasize the unique skills and motivation a candidate should possess (or seek to develop) in order to successfully instruct and mentor Latino/a students in STEM fields.

SAMPLE INTERVIEW QUESTIONS TO ASSESS COMPETENCIES TO WORK IN HSI

1. Briefly describe your previous roles or experiences (committee, classroom, etc.) as they relate to Latina/o students in STEM fields.
   - How are you involved with Latina/o students in STEM fields?
   - How did you get involved?
   - What motivates you to be involved with Latina/o students in STEM fields?

2. Can you talk about three students you have helped in particular ways?
   - Are any of these students Latina/o? Transfer students? STEM majors?
   - Describe the steps that you took to help these students.

3. Based on your knowledge of the academic culture of STEM fields, what would a Latina/o transfer student in STEM need to know in order to succeed?
   - How would you help students learn what they need to know?
   - How would you assess a student's current knowledge and experience?

CONCLUSION

Making Latino/a student success a shared value will not happen overnight. There are, however, specific actions that can aid in its adoption and institutionalization. Institutional leaders embed specific values into their higher education organizations through what they measure, talk about, and reward (Bensimón 2012). Thus, HSI leadership plays a central role in making Latino/a student success a value shared by the institutional community.

- Talk often to both campus and community audiences about the importance of Latino/a student success to fulfilling the Hispanic-serving mission.
- Reassure faculty and staff that institutional practices intended to support Latino/a students will benefit the entire student body. Latino/a

student success does not come at the detriment of success for other students. If the institution is a recipient of Title V funding, point out that all students benefit from the resources it makes available.

- Measure, disseminate, and discuss Latino/a student outcomes within academic programs, departments, and across the institution.

- Encourage faculty and staff to examine how Latino/a students are faring on appropriate measures of academic success in their own classrooms and programs.

Developing an HSI identity requires a structure that involves the campus community in a process that leads to change from within. Drawing on the action research methods employed by CUE to help institutions develop a culture of equity, we recommend that as a first step campus leaders create a process that engages the campus in a collaborative self- assessment. The assessment can be begun by framing some central questions, such as:

- In what ways do our institutional artifacts (for example, the website, official documents, board of trustee meetings, presidents' speeches, strategic plans) reflect our HSI identity?

- In what ways do our data practices help us learn how we are performing as an HSI?

- In what ways is the HSI identity incorporated into the curriculum, pedagogical practices, and evaluation?

- In what ways do we communicate and develop the competencies that are essential to be a successful practitioner at a HSI?

Evidence from CUE's action research projects shows that the engagement of practitioners in inquiry is a catalyst to questioning familiar and taken-for-granted practices and reflecting on whether they are appropriate. Inquiry into how artifacts and practices reflect a commitment to Hispanic-serving values is a concrete activity toward self-transformation.

REFERENCES

Bensimón, E. M. 2007. "The Underestimated Significance of Practitioner Knowledge in the Scholarship of Student Success." *Review of Higher Education* 30:4, 441–469.

_____. 2012. Statement on Latino/a College Completion, Town hall before Assembly Member Das Williams, Chair of the Assembly Higher Education Committee, and Senator Hannah-Beth Johnson. Sacramento, CA.

Bensimón, E. M., and A. C. Dowd. 2012. *Developing the Capacity of Faculty to Become Institutional Agents for Latino/as in STEM.* Los Angeles: University of Southern California.

Bensimón, E. M., and L. E. Malcom, eds. 2012. *Confronting Equity Issues On Campus: Implementing the Equity Scorecard in Theory and Practice.* Sterling, VA: Stylus Publishing.

Calderón Galdeano, E. and D. A. Santiago. 2014. *Hispanic-Serving Institutions (HSIs) Fact Sheet: 2012-13.* Washington, DC: *Excelencia* in Education. Retrieved from http://www.edexcelencia.org/hsi-cp2/research/hispanic-serving-institutions -hsis-fact-sheet-2012-13.

Caruthers, J. K., and G. B. Lott. 1981. *Mission Review: Foundation for Strategic Planning.* Boulder, CO: National Center for Higher Education Management Systems.

Chaffee, E. E., and W. G. Tierney. 1988. *Collegiate Culture and Leadership Strategies.* New York: American Council on Education and Macmillan Publishing.

Contreras, F. E., L. E. Malcom, and E. M. Bensimón. 2008. "Hispanic-Serving Institutions: Closeted Identity and the Production of Equitable Outcomes for Latino/a Students." In *Interdisciplinary approaches to understanding Minority Serving Institutions,* edited by M. Gasman, B. Baez, and C. Turner, 71–90. Albany: SUNY Press.

Danowitz, M. A., and F. Tuitt. 2011. "Enacting Inclusivity through Engaged Pedagogy: A Higher Education Perspective." *Equity and Excellence in Education* 44:1, 40–56.

Dowd, A. C. 2005. *Data Don't Drive: Building a Practitioner-Driven Culture of Inquiry to Assess Community College Performance.* Indianapolis: Lumina Foundation for Education, Research Report.

Dowd, A. C., and E. M. Bensimón. 2015. *Engaging the Race Question: Accountability and Equity in U.S. Higher Education.* New York: Teachers College Press.

Dowd, A. C., J. H. Pak, and E. M. Bensimón. 2013. "The Role of Institutional Agents in Promoting Transfer Access." *Education Policy Analysis Archives* 21:15, 1–44.

Excelencia in Education. 2014. *Hispanic-Serving Institutions: HSI Origin Timeline.* Washington, DC: *Excelencia* in Education. Retrieved from: http://www.edexcelencia.org/hsi-cp2/hsis-101/hsi-timelines/origin-timeline

Gioia, D. A., and J. B. Thomas. 1996. "Identity, Image and Issue Interpretation: Sensemaking During Strategic Change in Academia." *Administrative Science Quarterly* 41:3, 370–403.

Guiffrida, D. A., J. M. Kiyama, S. J. Waterman, and S. D. Museus. 2012. "Moving from Cultures of Individualism to Cultures of Collectivism in Support of Students of Color." In *Creating Campus Cultures: Fostering Success Among Racially Diverse Student Populations,* edited by S. D. Museus and U. M. Jayakumar, 68–87. New York: Routledge.

Jones, T. 2014. *Performance Funding MSIs: Considerations and Possible Measures for Public Minority-Serving Institutions.* Southern Education Foundation: Atlanta.

Harper, S. R., and S. Hurtado. 2011. "Nine Themes in Campus Racial Climates and Implications for Institutional Transformation." In *Racial and Ethnic Diversity in Higher Education,* ASHE Reader Series, edited by S. R. Harper and S. Hurtado, Vol. 2, 204–216. Boston: Pearson.

Hurtado, S., C. L. Álvarez, C. Guillermo-Wann, M. Cuellar, and L. Arellano. 2012. "A Model for Diverse Learning Environments: The Scholarship on Creating and Assessing Conditions for Student Success." In *Handbook of Higher Education,* edited by J. C. Smart, Vol. 27, 41–122. New York: Springer Publishing.

Ladson-Billings, G. 1995. "Toward a Theory of Culturally Relevant Pedagogy." *American Educational Research Journal* 32:3, 465–491.

Lave, J., and E. Wenger. 1991. *Situated Learning: Legitimate Peripheral Participation.* New York: Cambridge University Press.

Malcom, L. E., E. M. Bensimón, and B. Davila. 2010. *(Re)Constructing Hispanic-Serving Institutions: Moving Beyond Numbers Towards Student Success.* Ames: Iowa State University.

Malcom-Piqueux, L. E., R. Suro, E. M. Bensimón, and A. Fischer. 2012. *Addressing Latino/a Outcomes at California's Hispanic-Serving Institutions.* Los Angeles: Center for Urban Education and Tomás Rivera Policy Institute, University of Southern California.

Museus, S. D., and S. J. Quaye. 2009. "Toward an Intercultural Perspective of Racial and Ethnic Minority College Student Persistence." *Review of Higher Education* 33:1, 67–94.

Núñez, A.-M. 2014. *Counting What Counts for Latinas/os and Hispanic-Serving Institutions: A Federal Ratings System and Postsecondary Access, Affordability, and Success.* A knowledge essay commissioned by the President's Advisory Commission on Educational Excellence for Hispanics and presented at the Postsecondary Access and Completion for All: Latinas/os in America's Future Symposium, New York.

Núñez, A.-M.,and D. Elizondo. (2015). "Institutional Diversity among Hispanic-Serving Institutions." In *Hispanic-Serving Institutions: Advancing Research and Transformative Practice,* edited by A-M. Núñez, S. Hurtado, and E. Calderón Galdeano. New York: Routledge.

Olivas, M. H. 2015. "Foreword: Then and Now." In *Hispanic-Serving Institutions: Advancing Research and Transformative Practice,* edited by A-M. Núñez, S. Hurtado, and E. Calderón Galdeano. New York: Routledge.

Paris, D. C. 2012. "Culturally Sustaining Pedagogy: A Needed Change in Stance, Terminology, and Practice." *Educational Researcher* 41:3, 93–97.

Peeke, G. 1994. *Mission and Change: Institutional Mission and Its Application to the Management and Further of Higher Education.* Buckingham, England: Open University Press.

Rendón, L. I., A. Nora, and V. Kanagala. 2014. *Ventajas/Assets y Conocimientos/Knowledge: Leveraging Latin@ Strengths to Foster Student Success.* San Antonio: Center for Research and Policy in Education, University of Texas at San Antonio.

Rubel, L. H. 2010. "Centering the Teaching of Mathematics on Urban Youth: Equity Pedagogy in Action." In *Mathematics Teaching and Learning in K-12: Equity and Professional Development,* edited by M. Q. Foote, 25–40. New York: Palgrave Macmillan.

Rubel, L. H., H. Chu, and L. Shookhoff. 2011. "Learning to Map and Mapping to Learn Our Students' Worlds." *Mathematics Teacher* 104:8, 586–591.

Santiago, D. A., S. J. Andrade, and S. E. Brown. 2004. *Latino/a Student Success at Hispanic-Serving Institutions: Findings from a Demonstration Project.* Washington, DC: *Excelencia* in Education.

Schein, E. H. 1985. "Understanding Culture Change in the Context of Organizational Change." *Organizational Culture and Leadership,* 244–310.

Stanton-Salazar, R. D. 2011. "A Social Capital Framework for the Study of Institutional Agents and Their Role in the Empowerment of Low-Status Youth." *Youth and Society* 43:3, 1066–1109.

Tierney, W. G. 2008. *The Impact of Culture On Organizational Decision Making: Theory and Practice in Higher Education.* Sterling, VA: Stylus Publishing.

US Department of Education. Undated. *Developing Hispanic-Serving Institutions Program—Title V.* Retrieved from http://www2.ed.gov/programs/idueshsi/index.html.

Valenzuela, A. 1999. *Subtractive Schooling.* New York: SUNY Press.

Williams, D. A., J. B. Berger, and S. A. McClendon. 2005. *Toward a Model of Inclusive Excellence and Change in Postsecondary Institutions.* Washington, DC: Association of American Colleges and Universities.

Witham, K., L. E. Malcom-Piqueux, A. C. Dowd, and E. M. Bensimón. 2015. *America's Unmet Promise: The Imperative for Equity in Higher Education.* Washington, DC: Association of American Colleges and Universities.

From Student to Professor

HOW HISPANICS ARE FARING AS
FACULTY IN HIGHER EDUCATION

Melissa A. Martínez

In the early years of the twenty-first century, US demographics have come to reflect greater diversity, particularly given the rapidly growing Hispanic[1] population. In 2000, the total US Hispanic population was 35,204,480, or 12.5% of the population; by 2011, the Hispanic population had risen to 51,927,158, representing 16.7% of the nation (Motel and Patten 2013). As of 2011, Hispanics comprised about a quarter of all K-12 public school enrollment, and the number of 18-to-24-year-old Hispanics enrolled in college reached an all-time high, comprising 16.5% of all college enrollments (Fry and López 2012). Despite the latter gains, there are still too few Hispanics over 25 with a bachelor's degree or higher when considering the size of the Hispanic population and comparing the gains to those of other racial/ethnic groups.

During the years 2006 to 2010, only 8.9% of Hispanics had a bachelor's degree and 4.1% had a graduate or professional degree (Ogunwole, Drewery, and Rios-Vargas 2012). In comparison, 18.5% of whites, 11.6% of blacks or African Americans, 8.7% of American Indians and Alaska Natives, 30.0% of Asians, and 10.4% of Native Hawaiians and other Pacific Islanders attained a bachelor's degree during this period (Ogunwole, Drewery, and Rios-Vargas 2012). Further, almost all other racial and ethnic groups, except for Native Hawaiian and other Pacific Islanders, had more 25-year-olds or older with a graduate or professional degree than did Hispanics: 10.8% for whites, 6.1% for blacks or African Americans, 4.4% for American Indians and Alaska Natives, and 20.3% for Asians (Ogunwole, Drewery, and

---

1. The terms *Hispanic* and *Latina/o* are used interchangeably in this article and in accordance with the literature cited.

Rios-Vargas 2012). Thus, there remains a need to improve the educational outcomes for Hispanics to help ensure their social and economic mobility and increase their representation in particular fields and careers, including as faculty in higher education.

Recruiting and retaining more Hispanic faculty, and other faculty of color, in higher education has been an increasing concern nationwide (Castellanos and Jones 2003; Delgado-Romero et al. 2003; Diggs et al. 2009; Ibarra 2003; Ponjuan 2012; Turner, González, and Wood 2008). This article contributes to previous work in this area by providing a look at the current state of Hispanic faculty in higher education. The first part of the article draws on the most recent data from the National Center for Education Statistics to determine the level of representation of Hispanic faculty in comparison to faculty from other racial/ethnic backgrounds. Next comes a brief overview of research that has focused on the experiences of Hispanic faculty, presented to consider the ways in which Hispanic faculty are being supported or challenged within academia. Finally, the article will close with insights from 18 Hispanic faculty members on the tenure-track as they share advice with future generations of Latina/o faculty and other faculty of color.

In considering Hispanic faculty representation over the last 15 years, it is clear that there is much room for improvement. Between the fall of 2001 and fall of 2011 the percentage of Hispanic faculty (whose race and ethnicity was known) in full- and part-time positions in all public and private two-year and four-year institutions rose only one percentage point, from 3.3% to 4.3% (see Table 1). The largest increase in Hispanic faculty representation between these two points in time was at two-year private institutions, which showed a 4% increase, from 4.3 to 8.3%. It is also important to note that Hispanic faculty were represented in greater numbers in part-time positions than full-time positions: in fall 2001, 3.6% were part-time, compared to 3.0% full-time. In fall 2011, those figures had risen to 4.5% and 4.1%, respectively (Snyder and Dillow 2015; Snyder, Tan, and Hoffman 2004).

TABLE 1. Percentage of Hispanic faculty, Fall 2001 and Fall 2011

	ALL FACULTY, ALL INSTITUTIONS	FULL-TIME, ALL INSTITUTIONS	PART-TIME ALL INSTITUTIONS	PUBLIC 4-YEAR	PRIVATE 4-YEAR	PUBLIC 2-YEAR	PRIVATE 2-YEAR
2001	3.3	3.0	3.6	3.0	2.4	4.6	4.3
2011	4.3	4.1	4.5	4.2	3.5	5.0	8.3

Source: Snyder and Dillow 2015; Snyder, Tan, and Hoffman 2004

To be more precise, in fall 2011 there were 32,243 Hispanic female faculty (including part-time and full-time) working within degree-granting postsecondary institutions; they comprised 22.0% of all female faculty of color and 4.3% of all female faculty (Snyder and Dillow 2015). In comparison, black females comprised 8.3%, Asian females 5.4%, American Indian/Alaska Native females 0.5%, and white females 73.4% of all female faculty (Snyder and Dillow 2015). Slightly more Hispanic male faculty (33,028) were employed at degree-granting postsecondary institutions in the fall of 2011 than Hispanic female faculty (Snyder and Dillow 2015). However, Hispanic males comprised a slightly larger proportion among male faculty of color (24.0%) but about the same proportion among all male faculty (4.2%), when compared to Hispanic female faculty. Black male faculty (5.5%), Asian male faculty (6.8%), and white male faculty (74.2%) all comprised larger proportions of the male faculty population than did Hispanic males, while Pacific Islander male faculty (0.2%) and American Indian/Alaska Native (0.4%) male faculty comprised a smaller proportion (Snyder and Dillow 2015).

Also noteworthy is the degree to which Hispanics in faculty positions are in tenured and tenure-track roles. Among full-time Hispanic faculty in degree-granting institutions, fewer hold the ranks of full or associate professor and they are more often represented in the non-tenure track roles of instructors and lecturers (see Table 2). This trend was evident in fall of 2011 and continued in a later study, in fall 2013 (Aud et al. 2013; Kena et al. 2015). Moreover, the percentage of Hispanics in full, associate, assistant, instructor, and lecturer positions remained the same during these two years (Aud et al. 2013; Kena et al. 2015).

Data from 2009 and 2011 on degree-granting postsecondary institutions (see Table 3) also indicates that while the number of full-time tenured and tenure-track Hispanic faculty has increased minimally over this time span, from 16,855 to 18,751, a gender gap remains in the representation of female and male Hispanic full-time faculty (Snyder and Dillow 2015). There were almost twice as many Hispanic males as females in the associate and full professor ranks in 2009, 6,305 compared to 3,761 (Snyder

TABLE 2. Percent of Hispanic full-time faculty, Fall 2011 and Fall 2013

	TOTAL	FULL PROFESSORS	ASSOCIATE PROFESSORS	ASSISTANT PROFESSORS	INSTRUCTORS	LECTURERS
2011	4	3	4	5	7	6
2013	5	3	4	5	7	6

Source: Aud et al. 2014; Kena et al. 2015

and Dillow 2015). In 2011, this gender gap lessened but remained, with 6,936 Hispanic males at the associate and full professor ranks compared to 4,387 Hispanic females at the same levels (Snyder and Dillow 2015). The number of Hispanic male and female assistant professors was comparable in both these years, with 3,367 females and 3,422 males in 2009, and 3,736 females and 3,692 males in 2011. However, Hispanic females outnumbered males in the lower, non-tenure track ranks of instructors and lecturers in these two years. In 2009, there were 4,432 female instructors and lecturers, and 3,728 male instructors and lecturers. In 2011, this gender gap increased with 4,793 female and 3,886 male instructors and lecturers (Snyder and Dillow 2015).

It is also important to consider the fields in which Hispanic faculty are most and least represented in higher education. Data from the most recent National Study of Postsecondary Faculty indicates that as of fall 2003 Hispanics were most represented in the humanities (4.4%), social sciences (4.0%), and education (3.3%), and least represented in business (1.9%), fine arts (2.2%), and engineering (2.4%), when compared to full-time faculty and instructors of all other races and ethnicities at all institutions (Forrest Cataldi, Fahimi, and Bradburn 2005). This trend was similar among all part-time faculty and instructional staff: Hispanics were most represented in the humanities (4.6%) and education (3.7%), and least represented in business (1.3%) and engineering (1.3%) (Forrest Cataldi, Fahimi, and Bradburn 2005).

Overall, Hispanic faculty representation in higher education remains minimal in comparison to that of other racial and ethnic groups, and given the overall growth of the Hispanic population nationwide. In regard to the differences in representation among female and male Hispanic faculty in

TABLE 3. Full-time Hispanic faculty in degree-granting postsecondary institutions, 2009 and 2011

	PROFESSOR	ASSOCIATE	ASSISTANT	INSTRUCTOR	LECTURER
2009					
Females	1,474	2,287	3,367	3,499	933
Males	3,209	3,096	3,422	3,078	650
2011					
Females	1,681	2,706	3,736	3,773	1,020
Males	3,499	3,437	3,692	3,133	753

Source: Snyder and Dillow 2015

tenured, tenure-track, and non-tenure track positions, statistics suggest that the intersectionality of race and gender likely play a factor in this gender gap. Examining current literature on the experiences of Hispanic faculty within higher education can provide a more holistic picture of the factors contributing to Hispanics' underrepresentation.

HISPANIC FACULTY EXPERIENCES

Much of what is known about Hispanic faculty's experiences in higher education has been revealed through the more general literature on the experiences of faculty of color (Aguirre, Martinez, and Hernández 1993; Antonio 2002; Baez 2000; Bower 2002; Chang et al. 2013; Delgado Bernal and Villalpando 2002; Diggs et al. 2009; Fenelon 2003; Johnsrud and Sadao 1998; Padilla 1994; Sadao 2003; Stanley 2006; Sue et al. 2011; Thompson 2008; Tuitt et al. 2009; Turner 2003; Turner, González, and Wood 2008). On one hand, research has found that many faculty of color find teaching rewarding, and find service particularly worthwhile when they are able to engage in work that is meaningful to communities of color (Baez 2000).

Positive relationships with colleagues, strong allies and networks, student and faculty diversity, professional development opportunities, and research/teaching enhancement programs, and a supportive administration have also tended to contribute to a positive work environment for faculty of color (Turner, González, and Wood 2008). Yet they also note experiences with racism, sexism, classism, tokenism, and cultural taxation, particularly at predominantly white institutions (Aguirre 2000; Delgado Bernal and Villalpando 2002; Diggs et al. 2009; Padilla 1994; Stanley 2006; Turner 2003). Such experiences have resulted in some faculty of color feeling isolated (Stanley 2006) and somewhat dissatisfied with faculty life (Aguirre 2000). Additionally, some have dealt with resistance, including hostility, from students who doubted their professional credibility (Johnsrud and Sadao 1998) and faculty colleagues who have questioned and challenged their research interests, methods, or theoretical frameworks (Delgado-Bernal and Villalpando 2002). Some have come forward to describe the challenge of maintaining their cultural integrity and personal identity while developing their academic identity (Chang et al. 2013; Diggs et al. 2009; Sadao 2003).

Within the last 15 years, the nuanced experiences of Hispanic faculty in particular have been examined in a limited number of studies. However, findings from these studies mirror many of those in earlier work on faculty of color in general, and Hispanic/Latina/o faculty specifically (Aguirre and Martinez 1993; Garza 1992, 1993; Guerrero 1998; Verdugo 1992, 1995). They confirm that some Latina/os continue to contend with micro-aggressions, discrimination, and a devaluing of their research and service if it is ethnically focused or deals with diversity (Arredondo and Castellanos 2003; Cuádraz 2011; Delgado-Romero et al. 2003; Delgado-Romero et al. 2007; De Luca and Escoto 2012; Ek, Quijada Cerecer, Alanís, and Rodríguez 2010; Guanipa, Santa Cruz, and Chao 2003; Ibarra 2003; Nuñez and Murakami-Ramalho 2011; Padilla 2003; Ponjuan 2012; Segura 2003; Urrieta and Chávez 2010; Verdugo 2003). Due to their limited numbers in academia, some Latina/os also experience feelings of isolation, marginalization and encounter tokenism (De Luca and Escoto 2012; Urrieta and Chávez 2010).

Many of the challenges that Latina/os face are attributed to the dissonance between their own cultural backgrounds, which tend to be more collectivistic in nature, and the individualistic and achievement-oriented culture of academia (Delgado-Romero et al. 2003; De Luca and Escoto 2012; Ibarra 2003). Given this, some scholars suggest there is a need to consider the unique multicontextual backgrounds (Ibarra 2003) of Latina/os, and the intersectionality of their identities (Nuñez and Murakami-Ramalho 2011) in order to uncover and validate the diversity among faculty that identify as Latina/o/Hispanic (Delgado-Romero et al. 2007). This approach provides for greater understanding of the challenges that Latinas/os face in the hiring, tenure, and promotion process, as is the case for those who experience double or triple minority status (for example female and Latina, or female, lesbian, and Latina).

A growing body of work focuses on the experiences of female Latinas and Chicanas in the professoriate (Arredondo and Castellanos 2003; Cuádraz 2011; Ek, Quijada Cerecer, Alanís, and Rodríguez 2010; Segura 2003; Nuñez and Murakami-Ramalho 2011). This scholarship particularly highlights how female Latinas/Chicanas develop their identities as professors, and how they continue to utilize their agency and resistance to find success within academia.

Segura's 2003 case study of four Chicana faculty provides an example:

> [They] entered the academy with a multidimensional mission: to challenge hegemonic discourse in their respective disciplines, articulate the needs of their diverse communities mindful of the danger of false representation, serve as role models for members of historically disenfranchised groups, and to contest racially gendered limitations imposed on their communities (47).

Yet other Latina/o subgroups have not gotten as much attention, including Latina/o faculty who identify as a part of the lesbian, gay, bisexual, transgendered, and questioning or queer (LGBTQ) community

(Delgado-Romero et al. 2007). There are also the foreign-born, recently emigrated Latina/o faculty, and Latina/o faculty working in particular types of higher education institutions, including community colleges and minority-serving institutions.

Consequently, strategies to recruit and retain Latina/o faculty have focused on restructuring and expanding promotion and tenure policies and practices so that they are more inclusive of collaborative work and ethnic and diversity-focused scholarship and service (De Luca and Escoto 2012). Providing various mentoring and social networking opportunities for Latina/o faculty, and respecting and understanding the diversity within the Latina/o community, have also been suggested (Delgado-Romero 2007; Ibarra 2003). The latter is particularly important in the hiring process so that search committees become educated on the needs and potential contributions of Latina/o faculty and faculty from diverse backgrounds (Ponjuan 2012). For institutions with few Latina/os or faculty of color in general, cluster hiring is also advocated to ensure there is at least a potential network of support within the institution (Ek, Quijada Cerecer, Alanís, and Rodríguez 2010). Once hired, protecting untenured Latina/o faculty from excessive committee or service work is also vital to their retention so that they do not burn out, as is reallocating resources within a department to support the scholarship and professional development of junior faculty of color (Ponjuan, 2012).

Insights from Hispanic Faculty on the Tenure-Track

Eighteen Hispanic tenure-track faculty members (11 females, 7 males) working in different disciplines at four-year public and private universities across the country provide additional insight. The author, along with a team of four other females of color working in academia in Texas, Georgia, Illinois, and Wyoming (three tenure-track assistant professors and one postdoctoral research assistant at the time), collaborated to design and conduct a larger nationwide qualitative study to examine the experiences of 56 tenure-track assistant professors of color. Data for the larger project was collected in 2012-13 and included semi-structured interviews that lasted approximately an hour and were conducted either in person or via video call. The tenure-track assistant professors in the larger study self-identified as Latina/o/Hispanic, African American/black, Asian or Pacific Islander, and/or Native American/Indigenous.

Faculty Participants. Faculty participants were recruited through the research team's extended professional networks and through snowball sampling (Creswell 2013). They were asked about their journeys to and within the professoriate, challenges and successes they had experienced along the way, and supports that were instrumental to them. Other questions asked how they perceived their experiences in comparison to those of their Latina/o and non-Latina/o counterparts and elicited advice they might give to Latina/o students, and other students of color who are considering or seeking to join the professoriate.

Several data sets previously drawn from the larger project for particular study resulted in publications, but none examined the voices of all 18 of the Latina/o faculty members who were interviewed. For one publication, the research team drew on the *testimonios* (personal testimony) of six of the Latina/o faculty members to illuminate how they drew on their *cultura* and sense of *comunidad* to navigate the professoriate; the team members then wove their own stories of resistance into the piece (Cortez et al. 2015). In another study, data gathered about female faculty of color were examined to explore how the women had made sense of their new academic identities and how they had enacted agency as academicians (Chang et al. 2013). Martinez and Welton (2017) focused their study on 12 participants who had worked in educational leadership programs, to shed light on the experiences of assistant professors of color in this field. Additionally, Martinez, Chang, and Welton (2017) utilized another subset of data from 16 faculty participants (six of them Latina/o) to explore how they drew on their community cultural wealth to navigate academia (Yosso 2005).

All 18 Latina/o faculty participants had at least one year of experience on the tenure-track, and given their various journeys to and in the professoriate at the time of their interviews, each had insightful advice to share with future generations of Latina/o faculty, and other faculty of color (see Table 4 for additional participant information). Their advice centered on three areas:

- Understanding what academia entails
- Preparing for academia
- Learning to navigate academia as a scholar of color

Understanding what academia entails. A number of faculty participants stressed the need for Latina/o students, and other students of color, interested in academia to first understand what the job entails. Blanca suggested that interested students shadow a professor, and "meet with them, talk to them" to get a sense of the job. Similarly, Marisa felt interested students need to be "cognizant of what the tenure-track life is like." To do this, she too spoke to the need "to talk to people" in academia to gain varying

TABLE 4. Disciplines and institutions of Latino/a faculty research participants, 2012-13

NAME	ACADEMIC DISCIPLINE	INSTITUTION TYPE	STATE
Sara	Anthropology	Private, liberal arts	Texas
Rosa	Communication disorders	Public, comprehensive, Hispanic-serving	Texas
Petra	Music	Public, comprehensive, Hispanic-serving	Texas
Carol	Journalism	Public, comprehensive, Hispanic-serving	Texas
Blanca	Educational leadership	Public, comprehensive, Hispanic-serving	California
Alisa	Anthropology	Public, research intensive	Texas
Esther	Education-student affairs	Public, research intensive	Maryland
Gloria	Educational leadership	Public, comprehensive, Hispanic-serving	Texas
Beatriz	Environmental health science	Public, research intensive	Arizona
Marisa	Educational leadership	Public, comprehensive, Hispanic-serving	Texas
Crystal	Teacher education	Public, research intensive	Wyoming
Robert	Educational leadership	Public, research intensive, Hispanic-serving	New Mexico
Vince	Educational leadership	Public, research intensive	Texas
Steven	Higher ed. administration	Public, research intensive	Texas
Cruz	Biology	Public, comprehensive, Hispanic-serving	Texas
Nathan	Education policy studies	Public, research intensive	Arizona
Pablo	Mathematics	Public, research intensive	Illinois
Mark	Middle Secondary Education	Public, comprehensive	Georgia

Source: Tenure-track assistant professors of color qualitative research project, 2012-13

perspectives and understand the expectations of the profession. Crystal expanded on this sentiment, saying that she would ask first "Do you like to write alone a lot?" and then explained: "Because you're going to be doing a lot of that." She stressed that students need to be "good with that solitariness," and admitted to being just as realistic with her students about what being a professor means. Crystal's advice reflects the individualistic nature of the academy, and how it can stand in contrast to cultural norms that tend to be more collaborative and communal (De Luca and Escoto 2012; Garrison-Wade et al. 2012).

Crystal also spoke about students needing to take into account whether their personal and familial goals aligned with the expectations and lifestyle of academia. As a single Latina without children, Crystal spoke of the advice she gives to female students of color who say, "I want to do this, but I also want to get married and have a family." Crystal affirms their hopes but also refers them to others who can speak to this experience. "You can do that, but don't talk to me about what that's like . . . because I don't know what that's like. You need to talk to people that are mothers and spouses." She admitted that she "encourage[s] them, but I also give them at least what I see as a realistic sense of what to expect."

Other scholars like Rosa, Steven, and Cruz talked about how interested students of color need to have a passion and love for the work in academia—a degree of certainty that this path is for them. "You should be enjoying what you do," Rosa explained, "It shouldn't be like, 'Oh, I have to go to work today.'" Steven shared a similar perspective: "I think you have to continually ask yourself if this is a pathway for you as a young professional." In his own mentorship of students of color he admitted, "I never assume that any student wants to be an academic. I recognize that it is not for everybody, and nor should it be, nor should it be the barometer. It should be like option A or something, it should be just an option." Cruz, who was a faculty member in Biology, was also very up front with interested students of color:

> The first thing I'm going to ingrain . . . is that you put 400 percent of your effort or get out of here. . . . First, give them the choice: . . . if you think in this field you're just going to get by, this is not a field where you can get by. Because there are many jobs where you can just get by. . . . But in here it's . . . either you are in or you are not. . . . You really have to love it. I mean you really have to [have]—I don't know if this is the right word—lust for science. If you don't have that, it's going to be so hard because it's always going to be just like you're forcing it. So you have to ask yourself if that's really what you want.

Esther spoke to how students of color need to be aware that they will likely have to work harder than their white academic peers because faculty of color can often be judged by a higher standard. If they are committed to racial and ethnically focused research, she added, publishing can be difficult. She explained, "Your work is always going to have to be great . . . you really have to be able to do work that is meaningful and rigorous." This is in part because, "you don't want anyone to ever question your work." Esther referred to the politics and various forms of oppression that can exist within academia, and how some "methodologies that are not statistical enough" can be viewed as less than acceptable, and how "publishing houses and their reviewers tend to privilege new methodologies" or "traditional, objective methodology or perspectives."

Preparing for academia. Latina/o scholars also shared their advice for those Latina/o students who were confident about wanting to pursue a life in academia. Taking advantage of opportunities to explore research interests and engage in and publish research while in graduate school is key, according to Nathan, Rosa, and Robert. Nathan reflected on some of his student mentees of color, and how he stressed to them that they "have a direction in graduate school, but also flexibility."

> What I mean by that is there are research opportunities that will come up that may be slightly tangential to what you are doing, what you are really and truly interested in. Those are still valuable experiences, both from learning how to do research, getting published, rounding out a skill set . . . I see too many students of color coming through, who are like, "Okay, I'm going to study the racial experiences of Black men on a college campus." And it's like anything that slightly deviates from that [is] irrelevant. Which is weird, because, you know, in order to understand that, you need to understand things about the campus racial climate, gender identity, racial identity, you know, structural inequality. And you can do a lot of different things along those lines.

In the same respect, Nathan warned against graduate students of color getting "caught up" in the "issue of publish or perish." While he felt students should keep this in mind, he found that "students get so caught up in that, especially during graduate school, that they're putting out really crappy work." Instead, he suggested students "value the experiences of graduate school to be able to really hone your focus, to be able to actually go through the process of creating peer reviewed articles that are really sound—methodologically, empirically. Because that's going to be your currency moving ahead."

Nathan offered advice that he feels male students of color particularly need to heed if they are interested in academia. He described how he often saw students of color, and young men in particular, who are very impatient with the publishing process, and resistant to mentorship because it threatens their masculinity. He said they might say something like "You know my ideas are valuable, I've read critical race theory and I have the experiential knowledge of the community, that's where I come from." But he would tell them, "It's like, great. But you haven't yet learned how to put it all together in a peer-reviewed article."

Nathan continued:

> All too often as men of color in the academy we resist opportunities for mentorship. We do not accept influence, we don't, we would prefer in class, even in social situations, to act like

professors, even if we're not. 'I'm professing truth, here's my argumentation. I'm the man.' All that stuff. Not realizing that some of the most successful people who I have met along this crazy journey are willing to admit publicly when they don't know . . . admit they are incomplete and don't have all the answers. They have a very specific expertise, and it's okay to be incomplete. Because the way that we construct how it is to be a man is the opposite. 'I have to know, I have to be in control, I have to . . . You know, all this stuff. I mean, that's the whole idea of 'the man.' And I feel that we are losing a whole generation of young men because they are spending all of their time trying to be 'the man' instead of just trying to be really good at what they do for all they've got.

Considering students who are confident about wanting to join the professoriate, a number of scholars like Sara, Marisa, and Gloria find it imperative that they determine the right university and the program that is a good fit for them. "I would say really do your homework when it comes to picking your program," Sarah explained. Gloria agreed, "I would say this to people: 'What is your outcome? What do you want to do? Where do you want to end up?' " This means first knowing the general differences in expectations for professors at different types of postsecondary institutions, whether it be four-year, two-year, public, private, research-intensive, comprehensive, or teaching institutions. Expectations vary by field, program, and department as well, so it is key for students to devote time to familiarizing themselves with such variances and coming to terms with their own preferences in terms of work environment.

It is true that differences between programs and departments at varying institutions are not always apparent, and cannot always be determined prior to applying to a faculty position. However, relying on mentors and reaching out to faculty search committee chairs can often help a student determine whether a program or department might be a good fit. Geographic location and the diversity among the existing faculty in the program or university can also be factors to consider, if these are of particular importance to the student.

Some students may have varied work experiences and degrees in multiple disciplines that allow them the flexibility to apply to multiple programs and departments within their field of study. This was the case for Marisa, who could "fit into multiple programs" within the field of education given her previous experience as a K-12 teacher and counselor, her doctoral studies in educational administration, and her research interests, which centered on college access. Thus, for students in similar circumstances, she stressed that they think about "which one [program or department] really would be a better fit."

Navigating academia as a scholar of color. Once hired as a tenure-track faculty member, there are a number of things that the project participants suggested that Latina/o and other students of color keep in mind. Of particular importance is the need to stay connected with supportive colleagues, mentors, and one's community members, family, and friends. This was a key piece of advice shared by Sara, Robert, Esther, Carol, Gloria, Steven, and Vince. "Make sure you have those networks, those connections, those support systems with colleagues," stressed Robert. Esther described the process of finding "your crew," as she did:

> I found my dissertation crew and we would work together and talk about our challenges . . . Know that you can get different types of mentors who are going to help you at different points of your life that you may not necessarily think of right now, but it's going to be vital . . . It's the only reason I survive: a crew that I research with and write with. . . . Well, I think about that when I look at older senior scholars of color; I mean they have these relationships with people that they've had since grad school. I mean that's us; we're the next generation, you know. It is really exciting!

Carol, Gloria, and Steven expanded on the need to find a multitude of mentors, both mentors of color and white allies. Gloria believed this was vital to a scholar of color in learning "about the implicit culture" of higher education." Steven continued this thought: "You have to understand there are certain unwritten rules about any line of work. You have to find people that can help you make sense of it, because no one can do it themselves." Carol shared her perspective as a Latina originally from Mexico whose native tongue was Spanish:

> In my case, my main mentor is not a Latino. But it is very important that they also find a color mentor [sic]. It is super important because there are going to be certain things that I didn't—that I have to realize by myself because those were the things that he never mentioned because he never experienced those. He didn't have a language obstacle, culture obstacle, citizenship obstacle, which I did.

"One of the best pieces of advice" that Vince had received from colleagues in his field was, "*No te quedes solo*—don't stay by yourself, don't stay disconnected." As a faculty member of color with four years of experience, he now understands this piece of advice. "We have to stay in contact. If you're an emerging scholar, and you're a young faculty member, you have to stay connected." He admitted, "Sometimes I have to swallow my pride and ask for help . . . I don't like to do that," but without supportive relationships he feels he would likely succumb to feelings of isolation, particularly as he is one of few faculty of color on his campus. Vince also visited his family as often as he could, because they were "a huge support" for him. Even so, he emphasized that "To make it in academia professionally you can't be alone. It is so isolating; it is very individualistic; it's not a collective effort and . . . I do feel alone sometimes and I have to fight that."

More general in nature was the advice of a few of the scholars regarding the need to balance work and one's personal life, to schedule time for writing, and to stay true to one's self by doing academia "on your terms." The latter advice came from Alisa, who expanded on this notion:

> I would say, actually to all students, to do it on your terms; I think another thing I've been surprised at is that everybody just talks about what's expected, what's expected, and sometimes you go in limiting yourself already. I got to [University] just expecting I could never propose a very different kind of course; I could never take a leave in my second year, you know. I've been surprised when I've asked and I've been lucky, but you can do a lot more than you think. But I think it's important to do it on your terms.

Mark also spoke to the need for students of color to stay true to who they are within academia. He urged students of color to "be wise, and open, and be real."

REFLECTIONS

This article has provided an up-to-date perspective on the state of Hispanics in the professoriate. The data provides a clear indication that there is a continued need to recruit and retain more Hispanics in the field of academia, despite incremental but slow gains made over the past several decades. This need is more critical now than ever before, given the increasingly diverse college-going student population in the United States that could benefit from working with and being mentored by a more diverse faculty. The advice offered to future generations of Latina/o faculty by the 18 Latina/o tenure-track assistant professors introduced in this article underscores the truth that higher education institutions must do more not only to recruit Latina/o faculty and other faculty of color, but to offer the necessary supports and to make the vital changes to the culture of academia to support and retain them. Thus, in the words of Mark, one of the Latina/o faculty participants, we must continue to "fight the fight, stay with the struggle" if Latina/o faculty are to achieve greater representation in the professoriate.

REFERENCES

Aguirre Jr., Adalberto. 2000. *Women and Minority Faculty in the Academic Workplace: Recruitment, Retention, and Academic Culture.* ASHE-ERIC Higher Education Report 27:6. Washington, DC: Office of Educational Research Improvement.

Aguirre, Jr., Adalberto and Rubén Martínez. 1993. *Chicanos in Higher Education: Issues and Dilemmas for the 21st Century.* ASHE-ERIC Higher Education, No. 3. Washington, DC: George Washington University Press.

Aguirre, Jr., Adalberto, Rubén Martínez, and Anthony Hernández. 2002. "Majority and Minority Faculty Perceptions in Academe." *Research in Higher Education* 34:3, 371–385.

Antonio, Anthony L. 2002. "Faculty of Color Reconsidered: Reassessing Contributions to Scholarship." *Journal of Higher Education* 73:5, 582–602.

Arredondo, Patricia, and Jeanett Castellanos. 2003. "Latinas and the Professoriate: An Interview with Patricia Arredondo." In *The Majority in the Minority. Expanding the Representation of Latina/o Faculty, Administrators and Students in Higher Education,* edited by Jeanett Castellanos and Lee Jones, 221–240. Sterling, VA: Stylus.

Aud, Susan, Sidney Wilkinson-Flicker, Paul Kristapovich, Amy Rathbun, Xiaolei Wang, and Jijun Zhang. 2013. *The Condition of Education 2013* (NCES 2013–037). Washington, DC: US Department of Education, National Center for Education Statistics.

Baez, Benjamin. 2000. "Race-Related Service and Faculty of Color: Conceptualizing Critical Agency in Academe." *Higher Education* 39:3, 363–391.

Bower, Beverly L. 2002. "Campus Life for Faculty of Color: Still Strangers after All These Years?" *New Directions for Community Colleges* 118, 79–87.

Chang, Aurora, Anjalé D. Welton, Melissa A. Martinez, and Laura J. Cortez. 2013. "Becoming Academicians: An Ethnographic Analysis of the Figured Worlds of Racially Underrepresented Female Faculty." *Negro Educational Review* 64:1-4, 97–118.

Cortez, Laura J., Melissa A. Martinez, Danielle Alsandor, and Aurora Chang. 2015. "Nuestras Raíces Ground Us: Reflecting Comunidad and Cultura in Who We Are as Latin@ Faculty." In *Abriendo Puertas, Cerrando Heridas (Opening Doors, Closing Wounds,* edited by Frank Hernandez, Elizabeth Murakami, and Gloria Rodríguez, 173–182. Charlotte, NC: Information Age Publishing.

Creswell, John W. 2013. *Qualitative Inquiry and Research Design: Choosing among Five Approaches,* 3rd ed. Thousand Oaks, CA: Sage Publications.

Cuádraz, Gloria H. 2011. "From Doctoral Students to Faculty: Chicanas' Articulation with Trauma in Academe." In *Women of Color in Higher Education: Turbulent Past, Promising Future,* edited by Jean-Marie Gaëtane and Brenda Lloyd-Jones, 195–216. United Kingdom: Emerald Group Publishing Limited.

Delgado Bernal, Dolores, and Octavio Villalpando. 2002. "An Apartheid of Knowledge in Academia: The Struggle over the 'Legitimate' Knowledge of Faculty of Color." *Equity & Excellence in Education* 35:2, 169–180.

Delgado-Romero, Edward A., Lisa Y. Flores, Alberta M. Gloria, Patricia Arredondo, and Jeanett Castellanos. 2003. "Developmental Career Challenges for Latina/o Faculty in Higher Education." In *The Majority in the Minority. Expanding the Representation of Latina/o Faculty, Administrators and Students in Higher Education*, edited by Jeanett Castellanos and Lee Jones, 257–284. Sterling, VA: Stylus.

Delgado-Romero, Edward A., Angela Nichols Manlove, Joshua D. Manlove, and Carlos A. Hernández. 2007. "Controversial Issues in the Recruitment and Retention of Latina/o Faculty." *Journal of Hispanic Higher Education* 6:1, 34–51.

De Luca, Susan M., and Ernesto R. Escoto. 2012. "The Recruitment and Support of Latino Faculty for Tenure and Promotion." *Journal of Hispanic Higher Education* 11:1, 29–40.

Diggs, Gregory A., Dorothy F. Garrison-Wade, Diane Estrada, and Rene Galindo. 2009. "Smiling Faces and Colored Spaces: The Experiences of Faculty of Color Pursuing Tenure in the Academy." *Urban Review* 41:4, 312–333.

Ek, Lucila D., Patricia Quijada Cerecer, Iliana Alanís, and Mariela A. Rodríguez, A. 2010. " 'I don't belong here': Chicanas/Latinas at a Hispanic Serving Institution Creating Community Through Muxerista Mentoring." *Equity & Excellence in Education* 43:4, 539–553.

Fenelon, James. 2003. "Race, Research, and Tenure: Institutional Credibility and the Incorporation of African, Latino, and American Indian Faculty." *Journal of Black Studies* 34:1, 87–100.

Forrest Cataldi, Emily, Mansour Fahimi, and Ellen M. Bradburn. 2005. *2004 National Study of Postsecondary Faculty (NSOPF:4) Report on Faculty and Instructional Staff in Fall 2003* (NCES 2005–172). Washington, DC: US Department of Education, National Center for Education Statistics.

Garza, Hisauro. 1993. "Second-Class Academics: Chicano/Latino Faculty in U.S. Universities." *New Directions for Teaching and Learning* 53, 33–41.

_____. 1992. "Dilemmas of Chicano and Latino Professors in U.S. Universities." *Journal of the Association of Mexican American Educators*, 6–22.

Guanipa, Carmen, Rafaela M. Santa Cruz, and Grace Chao. 2003. "Retention, Tenure, and Promotion of Hispanic Faculty in Colleges of Education: Working toward Success within the Higher Education System." *Journal of Hispanic Higher Education* 2:2, 187–202.

Guerrero, Janis K. 1998. *Latino Faculty at Research Institutions in the Southwestern United States*. Charles A. Dana Center: University of Texas at Austin.

Ibarra, Roberto A. 2003. "Latina/o Faculty and the Tenure process in Cultural Context." In *The Majority in the Minority. Expanding the Representation of Latina/o Faculty, Administrators and Students in Higher Education*, edited by Jeanett Castellanos and Lee Jones, 207–220. Sterling, VA: Stylus

Johnsrud, Linda K., and Kathleen C. Sadao. 1998. "The Common Experience of "Otherness": Ethnic and Racial Minority Faculty." *Review of Higher Education* 21:4, 315–342.

Kena, Grace, Lauren Musu-Gillette, Jennifer Robinson, Xiaolei Wang, Amy Rathbun, Jijun Zhang, Sidney Wilkinson-Flicker, Amy Barmer, and Erin Dunlop Velez. 2015. *The Condition of Education 2015* (NCES 2015-144). Washington, DC: U.S. Department of Education, National Center for Education Statistics.

Martinez, Melissa A., Aurora Chang, and Anjalé D. Welton. 2017. "Assistant Professors of Color Confront the Inequitable Terrain of the Academy: A Community Cultural Wealth Perspective." *Race Ethnicity and Education* 20:5, 697-710.

Martinez, Melissa A., and Anjalé D. Welton. 2017. "Straddling Cultures, Identities, and Inconsistencies: Voices of Pre-tenure Faculty of Color in Educational Leadership." *Journal of Research on Leadership Education.* 12: 2, 122–142.

Motel, Seth, and Eileen Patten. 2015. *Statistical Portrait of Hispanics in the United States, 2011.* Washington, DC: Pew Research Center, 2013, http://www.pewhispanic .org/2013/02/15/statistical-portrait-of-hispanics-in-the-united-states-2011/

Nuñez, Anne-Marie, and Elizabeth Murakami-Ramalho. 2011. "Advocacy in the Hyphen: Perspectives from Latina Junior Faculty at a Hispanic-Serving Institution." *Diversity in Higher Education* 9, 171–194.

Ogunwole, Stella U., Malcolm P. Drewery Jr., and Merarys Rios-Vargas. 2012. *The Population with a Bachelor's Degree or Higher by Race and Hispanic Origin: 2006–2010.* Washington, DC: US Department of Commerce, US Census Bureau.

Padilla, Amado M. 1994. "Ethnic Minority Scholars, Research, and Mentoring: Current and Future Issues." *Educational Researcher* 23:4, 24–27.

Padilla, Raymond V. 2003. "Barriers to Accessing the Professoriate." In *The Majority in the Minority. Expanding the Representation of Latina/o Faculty, Administrators and Students in Higher Education*, edited by Jeanett Castellanos and Lee Jones, 179–206. Sterling, VA: Stylus.

Ponjuan, Luis. 2011. "Recruiting and Retaining Latino Faculty Members: The Missing Piece to Latino Student Success." *Thought & Action*, 99-110.

Sadao, Kathleen C. 2003. "Living in Two Worlds: Success and the Bicultural Faculty of Color." *Review of Higher Education* 26:4, 397–418.

Segura, Denise A. 2003. "Navigating between Two Worlds: The Labyrinth of Chicana Intellectual Production in the Academy." *Journal of Black Studies* 34:1, 28–51.

Snyder, Thomas D., and Sally A. Dillow. 2015. *Digest of Education Statistics 2013* (NCES 2015-011). Washington, DC: National Center for Education Statistics, Institute of Education Sciences, U.S. Department of Education.

Snyder, Thomas D., Alexandra G. Tan, and Charlene M. Hoffman. 2004. *Digest of Education Statistics 2003* (NCES 2005–025). Washington, DC: National Center for Education Statistics, US Department of Education.

Stanley, Christine A. 2006. *Faculty of Color: Teaching in Predominately White Colleges and Universities.* Bolton, MA: Anker Publishing Company, Inc.

Sue, Derald Wing, David P. Rivera, Nicole L. Watkins, Rachel H. Kim, Suah Kim, and Chantea D. Williams. 2011. "Racial Dialogues: Challenges Faculty of Color Face in the Classroom." *Cultural Diversity and Ethnic Minority Psychology* 17:3, 331–340.

Thompson, Chasity Q. 2008. "Recruitment, Retention, and Mentoring Faculty of Color: The Chronicle Continues." *New Directions for Higher Education* 143, 47–54.

Tuitt, Frank, Michele Hanna, Lisa M. Martínez, María del Carmen Salazar, and Rachel Griffin. 2009. "Teaching in the Line of Fire: Faculty of Color in the Academy." *Thought & Action*, 65–74.

Turner, Caroline S. 2003. "Incorporation and Marginalization in the Academy from Border toward Center for Faculty of Color?" *Journal of Black Studies* 34:1, 112–125.

Turner, Caroline Sotello Viernes, Juan Carlos González, and J. Luke Wood. 2008. "Faculty of Color in Academe: What 20 Years of Literature Tells Us." *Journal of Diversity in Higher Education* 1:3, 139–168.

Urrieta, Jr., Luis, and Rudolfo Chávez Chávez. 2010. "Latin@ faculty in Academe-landia. In *Handbook of Latinos and Education: Theory, Research, and Practice*, edited by Enrique G. Murrillo Jr., Sofia A. Villenas, Ruth Trinidad Galván, Juan Sánchez Muñoz, Corinne Martínez, and Margarita Machado-Casas, 219–231. New York: Routledge.

Verdugo, Richard R. 2003. "Discrimination and Merit in Higher Education: The Hispanic Professoriate." In *The Majority in the Minority. Expanding the Representation of Latina/o Faculty, Administrators and Students in Higher Education*, edited by Jeanett Castellanos and Lee Jones, 241–256. Sterling, VA: Stylus.

_____. 1995. "Racial Stratification and the Use of Hispanic Faculty As Role Models: Theory, Policy, and Practice." *Journal of Higher Education* 66:6, 669–685.

_____. 1992. "Analysis of Tenure Among Hispanic Higher Education Faculty." *Journal of the Association of Mexican American Educators*, 23–30.

Yosso, Tara. 2005. "Whose Culture Has Capital? A Critical Race Theory Discussion of Community Cultural Wealth." *Race Ethnicity and Education* 8:1, 69–91.

PART

academic
preparation

"That's Just Like Here, at Our College"

TRACKING LATINA/O INEQUALITY FROM HIGH SCHOOL PROGRAMS TO HONORS COLLEGES

Gilda L. Ochoa

Whereas politicians and pundits emphasize academic achievement gaps, this article shifts the focus to other, more important gaps—opportunity, social, racial/ethnic, and economic.[1] Focusing in particular on the practice of curriculum tracking—the placement of students into different academic programs and paths—this article looks at how our K-16 educational system reproduces a practice that is exclusionary in its origins, justifications, and manifestations, yet persists largely unquestioned. Its continuation normalizes an accumulation of privilege, to the detriment of students and communities who are underrepresented in higher education, including first-generation students and Latinas/os.

Years after I graduated from high school, I returned to a Southern California school (referred to in this article as SCHS) as a researcher.[2] For 18 months, with a group of students from the Claremont Colleges, I interviewed hundreds of students, educators, and parents. I also sat in on classes, rallies, assemblies, and club meetings. Across tables, gathered around benches, and sitting in circles, I listened to the school's predominantly working-class Mexican American and upper-middle-class Asian American students with

---

1. Throughout this article, I use the terms "racial/ethnic" and "race/ethnicity," not to conflate them or to assume that they are biological, cultural, or static categories, but instead to acknowledge that they are interrelated systems and social-political-economic-cultural constructs that influence life chances and perspectives.

2. As is the norm in social science research, the names of the high school and all of participants have been changed. The name changes were selected to approximate participants' names by gender and race/ethnicity.

families from Hong Kong and Taiwan talk about their experiences at their relatively well-resourced school.[3]

"Smart and stupid—they're smart; we're stupid." These words rang loudly as Latinas/os described themselves in relation to their Asian American schoolmates. The frequency with which many used these labels revealed how these descriptions were part of the campus culture and permeated students' experiences. Underlying students' narratives were the ways that school practices, prevailing beliefs, and everyday dynamics reinforced racial/ethnic and class inequalities.

During my twenty years of college teaching, many first-generation Latina/o college students have shared similar feelings. In college, they question their abilities, wonder if they belong, talk about not being fully supported, and critique the burden of disproving people's stereotypes.[4] While some internalize these feelings and blame themselves, others attribute them to unequal K-12 schooling that has disparately prepared them for college relative to wealthier classmates.

Much has been written about the schooling conditions that fuel these feelings in both high school and college for Latinas/os.[5] However, despite the continuity of these experiences and calls for greater integration, educational reforms and academic scholarship still often focus on either K-12 schooling *or* higher education, as though these educational systems and students' experiences are unrelated.[6] This division is also reflected in the limited

3. I use the pan-ethnic categories Asian American, Latina/o, white, and black or African American to be inclusive. However, most of the students interviewed at SCHS identify as Asian, Mexican, or Mexican American, and many of the Asian students are the children of Chinese and Korean immigrants.

4. Gilda L. Ochoa, *Learning from Latino Teachers* (San Francisco: Jossey-Bass, 2007); Gilda L. Ochoa and Daniela Pineda, "Deconstructing Power, Privilege, and Silence in the Classroom," *Radical History Review* 102 (2008): 54–62.

5. See Angela Valenzuela, *Subtractive Schooling: U.S.-Mexican Youth and the Politics of Caring* (Albany: State University of New York Press, 1999); Julie Bettie, *Women without Class: Girls, Race, and Identity* (Berkeley: University of California Press, 2003); Nancy López, *Hopeful Girls, Troubled Boys: Race and Gender Disparity in Urban Education* (New York: Routledge, 2003); Patricia Gándara and Frances Contreras, *The Latino Education Crisis: The Consequences of Failed Social Policies* (Cambridge: Harvard University Press, 2009); and Gilda L. Ochoa, *Academic Profiling: Latinos, Asian Americans and the Achievement Gap* (Minneapolis: University of Minnesota Press, 2013).

6. For some exceptions, see Clifford Adelman, *Answers in the Tool Box: Academic Intensity, Attendance Patterns, and Bachelor's Degree Attainment* (Washington, DC: US Department of Education, 1999); Tara Yosso, *Critical Race Counterstories along the Chicana/Chicano Educational Pipeline* (New York: Routledge, 2006); and Andrea Venezia, Michael W. Kirst, and Anthony L. Antonio, "Betraying the College Dream: How Disconnected K-12 and Postsecondary Education Systems Undermine Student Aspirations" (Palo Alto: Stanford Institute for Higher Education Research, 2003).

interaction between K-12 teachers and college professors: most have little to no contact.

This divide reinforces an artificial approach to schooling wherein students' educational lives and their schooling are bracketed as either "high school" or "college." Such segmentation hurts students' transition from high school to college. It mystifies college, especially for first generation and other underrepresented students.[7] At the college level, it hinders a holistic approach to working with students, one in which emphasis is placed on the whole person and the multiple factors influencing students' educations, including their pre-college experiences. As such, this divide fuels false beliefs that high schools and colleges are completely distinct and have nothing to learn from one another. When the contexts that precede students' college lives are overlooked, this disconnect may also perpetuate misperceptions that there is a level playing field and that individual students or communities are to blame for unequal educational outcomes.

Drawing on an extensive qualitative study at SCHS that resulted in *Academic Profiling: Latinos, Asian Americans, and the Achievement Gap* (2013), this article uses a case-study approach to explore how the lessons learned at one high school can be used to explore the dynamics at colleges and universities. While the overall demographics at SCHS and institutions of higher education differ, making connections between what is happening in high schools and dynamics in colleges provides an integrated framework for understanding educational outcomes. It also addresses some of the contemporary calls for a K-16 perspective.[8] Making connections between high school and college also facilitates shifting college cultures and enhancing Latina/o opportunities throughout the educational pipeline.

THE UNEQUAL SORTING, SELECTING, AND SEPARATING OF STUDENTS

> There's the honor, AP [Advanced Placement], IB [International Baccalaureate] courses, and then there's the rest . . . I think almost all of them now are designated college prep.
>
> —*Mark Durand, Southern California High School (SCHS) teacher*

Like most US schools, students at SCHS are funneled through a system of curriculum tracking that places them into distinct classes and academic programs with labels such as advanced, honors, or college prep. This system

---

7. Venezia, Kirst, and Antonio, "Betraying the College Dream," 8.

8. Ibid., 14.

of sorting and selecting students into different courses based on perceived capabilities can be traced to the changing demographics at the turn of the twentieth century and is rooted in historical practices of school segregation.[9] Its ramifications are felt today in the reproduction of racial/ethnic and class inequality. Tracking emerged at a time when access to public schooling was increasing and growing numbers of poor, immigrant, and second-generation children from southern and eastern Europe were entering US schools.[10] Characterized as the most efficient way to educate a mass citizenry, it was justified by Social-Darwinian assumptions about the biological superiority of white Anglo-Saxon protestants, cultural-deficiency perspectives advocating Americanization programs for immigrants, and scientific management-based models of the factory.[11] Historically, Mexican American students were channeled into slow-learner ability tracks and vocational courses in so-called Mexican classrooms and Mexican schools.[12]

Despite decades of research exposing the fallacies behind tracking and the racist myths undergirding it, the practice and assumptions persist. Today, the belief that some populations are more academically adept and geared toward success than others is embodied in the model minority myth. This myth characterizes Asian Americans as innately and culturally predisposed to academic excellence and Latinas/os as not valuing education.[13] These assumptions persist, despite studies indicating that Latina/o students have greater aspirations to go to college than do students from the general population and that 94 percent of Latina/o parents say they expect their children to attend college.[14] At SCHS, everyday comments by students and educators perpetuate stereotypes. Sandra Wu, a senior enrolled

---

9. Jennie Oakes, *Keeping Track: How Schools Structure Inequality* (New Haven: Yale University Press, 1985); Gilbert G. González, *Chicano Education in the Era of Segregation* (Philadelphia: Balch Institute Press, 1990).

10. Oakes, Keeping Track, 25.

11. Ibid., 27.

12. See González, *Chicano Education in the Era of Segregation;* and Gilda L. Ochoa, *Becoming Neighbors in A Mexican American Community: Power, Conflict, and Solidarity* (Austin: University of Texas Press, 2004).

13. Stacey J. Lee, *Unraveling the "Minority Myth" Stereotype: Listening to Asian American Youth* (New York: Teachers College, 1996); Vivian Louie, *Compelled to Excel: Immigration, Education, and Opportunity among Chinese Americans* (Stanford: Stanford University Press, 2004).

14. Concha Delgado-Gaitán, "School Matters in the Mexican American Home: Socializing Children to Education," *American Educational Research* 29:3 (1992): 495–513; Grace Kao, "Group Images and Possible Selves among Adolescents: Linking Stereotypes to Expectations by Race and Ethnicity," *Sociological Forum* 15:3 (2000): 407–430; Pew Hispanic Foundation/Kaiser Family Foundation, *National Survey of Latinos: Education* (Washington, D.C., 2004): 10.

in the school's most prestigious program espouses a recurring assumption at the school: "The approach to education might be like an Asian tradition. Since back for thousands of years, education has been the thing for like millions of years. Chinese dinosaurs probably took school seriously."

Initially, Sandra's comment may appear more humorous than harmful. However, her statement that Asian Americans are biologically and culturally predisposed to education reflects an assumption held even by some SCHS educators. Teacher Anthony Castro's comments are illustrative: "The Asians seem to be motivated and driven. The Latinos don't seem to value education in the same way. [Their] parents don't seem to be as involved the way Asian parents are." These racist beliefs have material consequences. They are used to justify differential treatment, or what I have described as academic profiling. Asian Americans at SCHS are often given the "benefit of the doubt" and placed into more rigorous courses than their Latina/o schoolmates. Teacher Laura Cooper explains: "No teacher here would say that [they teach to the Asians], and it is not because they don't want to [say it], but I don't think that they really consciously think that way. It's what they internalize."

Just as tracking and the ideologies that maintain it are ingrained in how schools such as SCHS are organized, the criteria used to place students in courses, such as standardized tests and teacher and counselor recommendations, also go unquestioned.[15] However, these are subjective criteria that have historically worked against first-generation, Latina/o, and African American students and in favor of middle-class, English-speaking, white students whose backgrounds, experiences, and cultural references tend to reflect those of test designers and thus affect course placement.[16] As a result, although there are relatively equal percentages of Asian American and Latina/o students at SCHS, middle- and upper-middle-class Chinese and Korean American students predominate in the most prestigious classes, and working-class Latinas/os are largely absent from them. This is a pattern replicated across the nation, where, in general, Latinas/os are underrepresented in honors and advanced courses and overrepresented in non-college preparatory classes.[17]

Such race and class skewing in course placement typically begins before high school and often as early as elementary school. For example, a 2015 report from the second largest school district in the United States—Los Angeles Unified—revealed that relative to their population in the

15. Oakes, *Keeping Track*, 10–13.

16. Ibid., 11–12. Ochoa, *Academic Profiling*.

17. Oakes, *Keeping Track*. Angela Ginorio and Michelle Huston, *Sí, Se Puede! Yes, We Can: Latinas in School* (Washington, DC: American Association of University Women Educational Foundation, 2001).

district Latina/o and African American students are underrepresented by 15 and 30 percent as "gifted and talented" students; in contrast, Asian Americans and Whites are *overrepresented* by 150 and 60 percent based on their enrollment in the district.[18]

The separation of students into distinct academic paths can fuel significant gaps between students—social, cultural, and opportunity gaps.[19] Albert Ortiz, a SCHS sophomore enrolled in college preparatory courses, is aware of these hierarchical social divisions and believes, "They probably won't be talking to me, if they're in honors." With students often forming friendships with those in their classes, tracking hinders opportunities for students to participate in and build their social capital with people outside of their academic programs.[20] Moreover, students' cultural and human capital is also stunted, since tracks are skewed by race/ethnicity and by class.

Not only are these high school classrooms and programs separate, but they are also unequal. Those in the top classes at SCHS describe being assigned novels, creative homework, and papers involving critical thinking. In general, they are granted more liberty at school in their assignments and overall movement. Their opinions are encouraged in classes, and their activities between periods and during lunch are less regulated. Some even report "getting away" with breaking school rules. Through a process of what Annette Lareau (2003) describes as "concerted cultivation," they are taught to "question adults and address them as relative equals."[21] Together, the course curriculum and hidden curriculum are gearing such students toward leadership and decision-making positions in high school and beyond. Access to different types of knowledge and know-how are among the factors leading to unequal forms of the cultural and human capital important for excelling in school.

Inequality in labeling, expectation, and support is also glaring. Students in the school's top-tier program, the International Baccalaureate (IB),

---

18. Arzie Gálvez, *Gifted and Talented Education Update,* Curriculum, Instruction and Assessment Committee (Los Angeles: Advanced Learning Options, April 28, 2015); Annie Gilberston, "LAUSD Schools Most Likely to Label Asian Students as Gifted" (Southern California: Public Radio KPCC, 2015).

19. Gilda L. Ochoa, Laura E. Enríquez, Sandra Hamada, and Jenniffer Rojas, "(De)Constructing Multiple Gaps: Divisions and Disparities between Asian Americans and Latinas/os in a Los Angeles County High School," in *Transnational Crossroads: Remapping the Americas and the Pacific,* Camilla Fojas and Rudy P. Guevarra Jr., eds. (Lincoln: University of Nebraska Press, 2012).

20. See Valenzuela, *Subtractive Schooling.*

21. Annette Lareau. *Unequal Childhood: Class, Race, and Family Life* (Berkeley: University of California Press, 2003), 2.

are labeled "the elite." They have their own counselor who maintains an open-door policy, shares information about colleges, writes letters of recommendation, and provides stress-release sessions. For some in that program, this treatment fuels a sense of entitlement that leads them to expect privileged treatment. Ashley Cordero, a junior previously enrolled in the IB program, observes that "IB students could get kind of big-headed at times because it's only Asian[s] . . . and then I'm Hispanic. It's kind of recognized as the Asian thing because the Asians are supposed to be the smarter ones."

The labels "elite" and "honors" are internalized and can be become self-fulfilling. In this case, they can also perpetuate racist assumptions and racial animosity between Latinas/os and Asian Americans. On the other hand, most students at SCHS are not in the top classes. They are simply "the rest," as referred to above by teacher Mark Durand. Students considered "the rest"—those in college-prep classes—are usually working-class Latinas/os. They typically struggle to name their counselors, are "shooed away" when seeking advice, criticize their structured assignments, and feel watched, disciplined, and treated as suspect. Teacher John Alvarez describes this unequal treatment: "It's almost like the honors are special classes. The AP [advanced placement] classes are special classes. So, they are anointed. They get the blessing, and my other kids basically get whatever is left."

SCHS teacher Michelle Mesa details how race intersects with this inequality: "Some of the Hispanic students come to me and ask where can they find information . . . [I say] 'Well, your teacher should've mentioned it or the counseling department.' But, they only advertise it to the AP and honors classes, and here the majority are Asian students." This racialized and class-based tiered system leads to an accumulation of privileges wherein the students with the most resources receive more support, encouragement, and the valued knowledge, skills, and connections needed to excel in high school and college. They become the "anointed" ones, fulfilling the labels associated with them and their academic paths: "the elite" and "honors." Meanwhile, many of the first-generation Latina/o students are an afterthought, considered "the rest," and given "whatever is left."

WHAT HAPPENS IN HIGH SCHOOL
DOESN'T STAY IN HIGH SCHOOL

Between 2013 and 2015, I visited colleges and universities throughout California, sharing my research from SCHS. During these visits, students continually connected what I was describing in high school with what they were experiencing. Among the most often recurring and haunting comments were those proclaiming, "That sounds just like here—certain students, majors, and colleges get all the resources." As some denounced this inequality, others were still processing a sort of epiphany as they realized that although they had made it to college, often as the first members in their family to do so, they were being shortchanged—denied the same opportunities as others at their university.

The students' comments are accurate. The sorting and selecting of students persists in college. It is apparent in levels of preparation and the types of schools to which students apply and eventually attend, reinforcing a multitiered system that has significant ramifications. As in high school, such sorting and selecting provides unequal access to various forms of capital—human, social, cultural, *and* economic capital. Where there are race and class manifestations, these processes condone a system of racism and class inequality.

Access to rigorous high school curriculum is foundational to college performance. In fact, early quantitative studies reveal that in comparison to test scores and grade point average, high school curriculum is *the* strongest factor determining college graduation. Rigorous high school curriculum is also found to have a greater impact on college graduation for Latina/o and African American students than for white students.[22] These studies define academic rigor as the total number of advanced placement, math, science, laboratory, social science, and English classes a high school student has completed.[23] Within these courses, experiences writing analytical papers, conducting research, and contributing to class discussions better prepare students for college assignments than the rote memorization and note-taking more common in less advanced courses.[24]The college credits provided to high school students who complete AP classes and tests can also reduce the number of required college classes, accelerating their path toward a college degree.

DIFFERENCES FROM SCHOOL TO SCHOOL

Tracking is perhaps nowhere more apparent in higher education than in the differences between and within colleges. Just as there is a hierarchy of academic programs and classes in high school, there is a hierarchy of colleges and universities with unequal enrollments by race and class. From community colleges to research universities, intersecting factors shape college

22. Adelman, *Answers in the Tool Box*; Robert Fry, "Latino Youth Finishing College: The Role of Selective Pathways," (Washington, DC: Pew Hispanic Research Center Report, 2004), 9.

23. Fry, "Latino Youth Finishing College," 9.

24. Oakes, *Keeping Track*; Ochoa and Pineda, "Deconstructing Power, Privilege, and Silence in the Classroom"; Ochoa, *Academic Profiling*.

rankings. These include a school's level of wealth, prestige, and acceptance rate.[25] Despite the fact that higher percentages of Latinas/os are attending college than ever before, over 40 percent of them are enrolled in community colleges.[26] These open-access institutions provide a "primary route to a degree for the great majority of low-income and ethnic minority students."[27] However, only about 20 percent of community college students transfer to four-year colleges. The rates are often lower for Latinas/os and African Americans. Thus, while more Latinas/os are attending college with the hope of earning a four-year degree, their plans are too often cut short.[28]

In general, compared to whites and Asian Americans, Latinas/os are less likely to attend a four-year college, enroll in a selective college, and earn a bachelor's degree.[29] A 2002 study by the Pew Hispanic Center found that even the most academically prepared Latinas/os were less likely than equivalently prepared white students to attend "selective colleges and universities."[30] In fact, many Latinas/os who are considered "most likely to succeed in higher education" are not even applying to selective colleges and universities.[31] As a result, Latinas/os start their post secondary education on "low trajectories."[32]

Access to financial resources influences students' abilities to leave home and attend college full time, but unequal support and enrollment in different high school academic paths cannot be dismissed either. Access to a rigorous high school curriculum influences transfer rates and college selection.[33] Likewise, as teacher Michelle Mesa noted, educators who spend proportionately more time informing students in the top courses about college options and financial aid hinder excluded students' skills, knowledge, and options. If high school students are denied information

25. See Gordon C. Winston, "Subsidies, Hierarchy and Peers: The Awkward Economics of Higher Education," *Journal of Economic Perspectives* (Winter 1999): 13–36.

26. Robert Fry and Paul Taylor, "Hispanic High School Graduates Pass Whites in Rate of College Enrollment," (Washington, DC: Pew Hispanic Research Center Report, 2013), 4–5.

27. Gándara, Alvarado, Driscoll, and Orfield, "Building Pathways to Transfer," 4.

28. Venezia, Kirst, and Antonio, "Betraying the College Dream"; Gándara, Alvarado, Driscoll, and Orfield, "Building Pathways to Transfer."

29. Gándara, Alvarado, Driscoll, and Orfield, "Building Pathways to Transfer"; Fry and Taylor, "Hispanic High School Graduates Pass Whites in Rate of College Enrollment." [My sentence summarizes the overall report.]

30. Fry, "Latino Youth Finishing College," vi.

31. Ibid., 12–13.

32. Ibid., vi.

33. Gándara, Alvarado, Driscoll, and Orfield, "Building Pathways to Transfer."

about different colleges and financial resources, their routes to more selective schools are blocked. A lack of "college-going knowledge" shuts them out of the process.[34]

As with high school classes, the type of college students attend is crucial. There is a positive relationship between college selectivity and graduation rate. The more selective the college, the higher the graduation rate for all students.[35] Research indicates that this is the case, even when comparing Latinas/os who have similar levels of high school academic preparation. That is, Latinas/os who attend more selective colleges are more likely to graduate with a bachelor's degree.[36] More selective schools typically have larger endowments, enabling them to offer additional academic resources for students in counseling, advising, and teaching. Thus, relative to students at less selective colleges, students at selective schools often have access to smaller classes, reduced student-faculty ratios, more extracurricular activities, and multiple forms of support.[37] These resources can enhance retention, academic success, and graduation rates. Lack of access to selective colleges and universities has significant lifetime implications as well. Over their lifetimes, college graduates earn more than 84 percent of what high school graduates earn.[38] This economic reality influences home ownership, wealth accumulation, overall quality of life, and opportunities for future generations. The racial/ethnic and class asymmetry in college selection, access to resources, and completion rate continues societal inequalities.

These inequalities are also apparent within colleges and universities. In many ways, the inequalities that exist *within* schools in the form of honors programs and honors colleges are a continuation of high school tracking. Begun in the 1920s at Swarthmore College, honors programs and honors colleges resurged in the 1950s and have proliferated in public institutions of higher education since the 1980s.[39] Across the United States, more than 1,000 honors programs or colleges exist, a skyrocket increase over the past

---

34. See Roberta Espinoza, *Pivotal Moments: How Educators Can Put All Students on the Path to College* (Cambridge: Harvard Education Press, 2011), 26.

35. Fry, "Latino Youth Finishing College," vi.

36. Ibid., 5.

37. Gordon C. Winston, "Subsidies, Hierarchy and Peers: The Awkward Economics of Higher Education," *Journal of Economic Perspectives* (Winter 1999): 13–36; Fry, "Latino Youth Finishing College."

38. Hsu, Tiffany, "College Graduates Earn 84% More Than High School Grads, Study Says," *Los Angeles Times,* April 5, 2011.

39. Norm Weiner, "Honors is Elitist, and What's Wrong with That?" *Journal of the National Collegiate Honors Council* 10:1 (2009): 19-24; Brenda R. Freeman, "The Development of Honors Colleges in Public Universities" (MS thesis: Texas A&M University, 2015).

30 years.[40] There is vast heterogeneity in type of program and institution, but there are significant trends.

The growth of honors programs and colleges has been linked to demographic and economic shifts.[41] First, the rise has been associated with the post World War II "massification of higher education," a time when the United States experienced the largest expansion of college enrollment in its history.[42] The growth in college honors programs in public institutions also parallels the emergence of curriculum tracking in K-12 education, where, as public schooling became more available, schools, classrooms, and curriculum became more differentiated. This differentiation, in turn, reinforced other hierarchies and additional forms of exclusion. Second, the growth of college honors programs has also been attributed to the shift in the 1980s from need-based to merit-based scholarships, which allow schools to benefit financially and in terms of rankings by recruiting and retaining students with high standardized test scores and grade point averages.[43] As public institutions compete with private schools for select students, there has been a growing trend toward funneling more institutional, state, and federal resources to students defined as the most academically able.[44]

The justifications for honors programs and the criteria used to place students are similar to those used in the K-12 system. Honors programs and colleges have been implemented in an attempt to recruit designated "high-quality" students and faculty, raise the morale of faculty, boost the image of schools, and generate revenue.[45] Underlying these rationales are

---

40. Dena Owens and Jon E. Travis, "College and University Honors Programs in the Southern United States, *Focus on Colleges, Universities, and Schools* 7:1 (2013): 3.

41. For a detailed description of the evolution of honors programs and honors colleges from Swarthmore in 1922 to public universities in the 1950s and 1960s and community colleges in the 1980s, see Elena V. Galinova, "The Construction of Meritocracy within Mass Higher Education: Organizational Dynamics of Honors Programs at American Colleges and Universities" (PhD diss.: Pennsylvania State University, Graduate School College of Education, 2005).

42. Galinova, "The Construction of Meritocracy within Mass Higher Education," 41.

43. Bridget Terry Long, *Attracting the Best: The Use of Honors Programs to Compete for Students,* Chicago: Spencer Foundation [ERIC Reproduction Service No. ED465355] (March 29, 2002), 1–27.

44. Larry D. Singell and Hui-Hsuan Tang, "The Pursuit of Excellence: An Analysis of the Honors College Application and Enrollment Decision for a Large Public University," *Research in Higher Education* 53:7 (2012): 717–737.

45. Judith Pehlke, "The Myth of an Honors Education," *Journal of the National Collegiate Honors Council* 4:2 (2003): 27–33; Peter Sederberg, "Characteristics of the Contemporary Honors College: A Descriptive Analysis of a Survey of NCHC Member Colleges," *Journal of the National Collegiate Honors Council* 6:2 (2005): 121–136; Freeman, "The Development of Honors Colleges in Public Universities."

meritocratic assumptions and beliefs that some students are more worthy of privileged treatment and resources. Galinova (2005) describes this as an "honors ideology," which she explains as "the belief in a differential education [for] students of superior academic ability within the same college or university."[46]

Labels such as "smart," "the best and the brightest," "superior students," and "high quality" fill the literature of college honors programs.[47] In an analysis of three different honors colleges, Galinova (2005) found similar trends in the language used to describe students. As with the use of "the elite" in reference to SCHS students in the school's most prestigious program, these labels can become self-fulfilling and reinforce a sense of entitlement that provides preferential treatment for labeled students and leads them to expect it.

Standardized tests, recommendations, and grades are typically the criteria used for entrance into honors programs.[48] Decades of research demonstrate the racial/ethnic, gender, and class biases in standardized tests.[49] However, as subjective criteria, recommendations can also be biased in favor of middle and upper class White and Asian American students.[50] Thus, as with K-12 track placement, when used in isolation, these instruments can lead to biased measurements that skew access.[51]

Mirroring the privileged support provided to high school students in AP and honors classes, students in honors colleges are also granted valued resources. These resources can include special counseling, additional scholarships, smaller classes, research opportunities, priority registration, and extracurricular activities.[52] Some programs also offer separate honors residence halls, study spaces, and additional technology.[53] Honors-designated courses are often small, seminar-based classes taught by full-time faculty. Courses and other assignments provide opportunities for students to complete research with faculty, write honors theses, and engage in commu-

---

46. Galinova, "The Construction of Meritocracy within Mass Higher Education," 16.

47. For examples, see Owens and Travis, "College and University Honors Programs in the Southern United States."

48. Pehlke, "The Myth of an Honors Education."

49. See González, *Chicano Education in the Era of Segregation.*

50. See Oakes, *Keeping Track*; and Ochoa, *Academic Profiling.*

51. See Pehlke, "The Myth of an Honors Education."

52. Deborah L. Floyd and Alexandria Holloway, "Prioritizing Service to the Academically Talented: The Honors College," *New Directions for Community Colleges* 136 (2006): 43–52.

53. Galinova, "The Construction of Meritocracy within Mass Higher Education"; Freeman, "The Development of Honors Colleges in Public Universities."

nity-based learning classes.[54] Such opportunities enhance students' personal, social, and cultural capital by providing them with skills, networks, and know-how to excel in college—assets that can also increase their post-degree prospects in graduate school and careers.

The very limited scholarship on diversity and enrollment in college honors programs suggests that, like high school academic programs, access to programs and the allocation of resources are tied to race and class. Overall, Latinas/os are "severely unrepresented" in enrollment in honors programs.[55] This was certainly the case in the two Texas universities studied by Freeman (2015), wherein Latina/o, Black, and first generation students were underrepresented in the honors programs and colleges relative to their university enrollment. Some colleges do aim for an honors program that increases opportunities and middle-class access for lower-income, first-generation, and rural students.[56] But when only select students are granted access to honors programs and their accompanying resources, such aspirations are not met. The result is that students entering universities with more economic resources, cultural capital, and other forms of support are likely to receive additional opportunities and privileges—thereby reproducing significant gaps.

In spite of the proliferation of honors programs and honors colleges, there is a dearth of scholarship on them, especially in terms of race, class, and gender. In part, this is due to the absence of a critical analysis of access and retention. It is also due in part to the fact that few studies unpack broad categories such as "diverse" or "non-white" to ascertain how historically underrepresented groups such as Latinas/os in institutions of higher education are faring.[57] With the exception of some notable dissertations, much of the existing literature engages in boosterism. It appears in the *Journal of the National Collegiate Honors Council*, the official journal of the National Collegiate Honors Council and is written by administrative deans and faculty members working within honors programs; this journal provides a platform for proponents of honors programs. A lack of interrogation of such programs suggests that, as with K-12 curriculum tracking,

---

54. Galinova, "The Construction of Meritocracy within Mass Higher Education."

55. Lindsey Malcom-Piqueux, Estela Mara Bensimon, Roberto Suro, Anna Fischer, Alicen Bartle, Jeremy Loudenback, and Jonathan Rivas, *Addressing Latino Outcomes at California's Hispanic-Serving Institutions* (Los Angeles: University of Southern California, Center for Urban Education, 2012), 1–29.

56. See Charlotte Pressler, "The Two-Year College Honors Program and the Forbidden Topics of Class and Cultural Capital," *Journal of the National Collegiate Honors Council* 10:1 (2009): 37–42.

57. For an example, see Singell and Tang, "The Pursuit of Excellence."

college honors programs and the inequalities they reinforce have become so entrenched that they are accepted in the running of today's schools.

Overall, despite the inequities that a system of K-16 tracking perpetuates, it remains largely uncontested. Differential academic paths in the K-12 system have become "the tradition."[58] This pattern is continued in institutions of higher education through a hierarchy of colleges and select programs, and the disparate resources accompanying them. Thus, such institutional practices impact students' opportunities and ensure the reproduction of inequality.

CONCLUSION

Academic and political debates on achievement gaps often focus on the product of schooling rather than the multiple adjunct *processes* that foster opportunity, social, racial/ethnic and economic gaps. As such, this emphasis diverts attention from the ways in which institutional practices reproduce inequality throughout the length of the educational pipeline. Connecting the constructed divides between high school and higher education allows for a more integrated analysis of students' experiences and institutional processes. It can also enhance high school-college transitions.

Just as those in high schools benefit by knowing more about college expectations, opportunities, and dynamics, those of us working within colleges and universities have much to learn by going back to high school. School practices, everyday beliefs, and students' experiences do not exist in isolation. They shape the lives of students long past their four years in high school, and some of the varied K-12 practices that prepare students for disparate paths are often replicated in colleges and universities—and go similarly unquestioned. This is apparent in an analysis of the history, justifications, and ramifications of the longstanding practice of K-12 tracking and the role of higher education in its perpetuation through a hierarchy of colleges and proliferation of honors programs.

Despite being steeped in exclusionary beliefs and manifestations, the unequal practice of sorting and selecting students persists. Its continuation condones, even if unintentionally, racial/ethnic and class inequality. This is largely to the detriment of Latina/o, African American, and first-generation students and communities. As in the past, beliefs that some students are more worthy intellectually and culturally justify an accumulation of privilege: those with the most continue receiving more from our schools.

---

58. Oakes, *Keeping Track*, 15.

REFERENCES

Adelman, Clifford. 1999. *Answers in the Tool Box: Academic Intensity, Attendance Patterns, and Bachelor's Degree Attainment.* Washington, DC: US Department of Education.

Bettie, Julie. *Women without Class: Girls, Race, and Identity.* 2003. Berkeley: University of California Press.

Delgado-Gaitán, Concha. 1992. "School Matters in the Mexican American Home: Socializing Children to Education." *American Educational Research* 29:3, 495–513.

Espinoza, Roberta. 2011. *Pivotal Moments: How Educators Can Put All Students on the Path to College.* Cambridge: Harvard Education Press.

Floyd, Deborah L., and Alexandria Holloway. 2006. "Prioritizing Service to the Academically Talented: The Honors College." *New Directions for Community Colleges* 136, 43–52.

Freeman, Brenda R. 2015. "The Development of Honors Colleges in Public Universities." MS thesis: Texas A&M University.

Fry, Robert. 2004. "Latino Youth Finishing College: The Role of Selective Pathways." Washington, DC: Pew Hispanic Research Center Report, i-viii and 1–32.

Fry, Robert, and Paul Taylor. 2013. *Hispanic High School Graduates Pass Whites in Rate of College Enrollment.* Washington, DC: Pew Hispanic Research Center Report, 1–12.

Galinova, Elena V. 2005. "The Construction of Meritocracy within Mass Higher Education: Organizational Dynamics of Honors Programs at American Colleges and Universities." PhD diss.: Pennsylvania State University, Graduate School College of Education. ProQuest Dissertation Publishing, 3173790.

Gálvez, Arzie. 2015. "Gifted and Talented Education Update." Curriculum, Instruction and Assessment Committee. Los Angeles: Advanced Learning Options.

Gándara, Patricia, Elizabeth Alvarado, Anne Discoll, and Gary Orfield. 2012. *Building Pathways to Transfer: Community Colleges that Break the Chain of Failure for Students of Color.* Los Angeles: University of California: Civil Rights Project/Proyecto Derechos Civiles.

Ginorio, Angela, and Michelle Huston. 2001. *Sí, Se Puede! Yes, We Can: Latinas in School* Washington, DC: American Association of University Women Educational Foundation.

González, Gilbert G. 1990. *Chicano Education in the Era of Segregation.* Philadelphia: Balch Institute Press.

Hamilton, Kendra. 2004. "Courting the Best and the Brightest." *Black Issues in Higher Education* 21:1, 29–31.

Hsu, Tiffany. 2011. "College Graduates Earn 84% More Than High School Grads, Study Says." *Los Angeles Times* (April 5, 2011).

Kao, Grace. 2000. "Group Images and Possible Selves among Adolescents: Linking Stereotypes to Expectations by Race and Ethnicity." *Sociological Forum* 15:3, 407–430.

Killgore, Leslie. 2009. "Merit and Competition in Selective College Admissions." *Review of Higher Education* 32:4, 469–488.

Lareau. Annette. 2003. *Unequal Childhood: Class, Race, and Family Life.* Berkeley: University of California Press.

Lee, Stacey J. 1996. *Unraveling the "Minority Myth" Stereotype: Listening to Asian American Youth.* New York: Teachers College.

Long, Bridget Terry. 2002. *Attracting the Best: The Use of Honors Programs to Compete for Students.* Chicago: Spencer Foundation (ERIC Reproduction Service, No. ED465355), 1–27.

López, Nancy. 2003. *Hopeful Girls, Troubled Boys: Race and Gender Disparity in Urban Education.* New York: Routledge.

Louie, Vivian. 2004. *Compelled to Excel: Immigration, Education, and Opportunity among Chinese Americans.* Stanford: Stanford University Press.

Malcom-Piqueux, Lindsey, Estela Mara Bensimon, Roberto Suro, Anna Fischer, Alicen Bartle, Jeremy Loudenback, and Jonathan Rivas. 2012. *Addressing Latino Outcomes as California's Hispanic-Service Institutions.* Los Angeles: University of Southern California, Center for Urban Education, 1–29.

Oakes, Jennie. 1985. *Keeping Track: How Schools Structure Inequality.* New Haven, CT: Yale University Press.

Ochoa, Gilda L. 2004. *Becoming Neighbors in a Mexican American Community: Power, Conflict, and Solidarity.* Austin: University of Texas Press.

———. 2007. *Learning from Latino Teachers.* San Francisco: Jossey-Bass.

———. 2013. *Academic Profiling: Latinos, Asian Americans and the Achievement Gap.* Minneapolis: University of Minnesota Press.

Ochoa, Gilda L., Laura E. Enríquez, Sandra Hamada, and Jenniffer Rojas. 2012. "(De)Constructing Multiple Gaps: Divisions and Disparities between Asian Americans and Latinas/os in a Los Angeles County High School." In *Transnational Crossroads: Remapping the Americas and the Pacific,* edited by Camilla Fojas and Rudy P. Guevarra Jr., 143–170. Lincoln: University of Nebraska Press.

Ochoa, Gilda L., and Daniela Pineda. 2008. "Deconstructing Power, Privilege, and Silence in the Classroom." *Radical History Review* 102, 54–62.

Outcalt, Charles. 1999. "The Importance of Community College Honors Programs." *New Directions for Community Colleges* 108, 59–68.

Owens, Dena, and Jon E. Travis. 2013. "College and University Honors Programs in the Southern United States. *Focus on Colleges, Universities, and Schools* 7:1, 1–7.

Pehlke, Judith. 2003. "The Myth of an Honors Education." *Journal of the National Collegiate Honors Council* 4:2, 27–33.

Pew Hispanic Foundation/Kaiser Family Foundation. 2004. *National Survey of Latinos: Education.* Washington, DC, 1–22.

Pressler, Charlotte. 2009. "The Two-Year College Honors Program and the Forbidden Topics of Class and Cultural Capital." *Journal of the National Collegiate Honors Council* 10:1, 37–42.

Sederberg, Peter. 2005. "Characteristics of the Contemporary Honors College: A Descriptive Analysis of a Survey of NCHC Member Colleges." *Journal of the National Collegiate Honors Council* 6:2, 121–136.

Singell, Larry D., and Hui-Hsuan Tang. 2012. "The Pursuit of Excellence: An Analysis of the Honors College Application and Enrollment Decision for a Large Public University." *Research in Higher Education* 53:7, 717–737.

Valenzuela, Angela. *Subtractive Schooling: U.S.-Mexican Youth and the Politics of Caring.* 1999. Albany: State University of New York Press.

Venezia, Andrea, Michael W. Kirst, and Anthony L. Antonio. 2003. *Betraying the College Dream: How Disconnected K-12 and Postsecondary Education Systems Undermine Student Aspirations.* Palo Alto: Stanford Institute for Higher Education Research.

Weiner, Norm. 2009. "Honors is Elitist, and What's Wrong with That?" *Journal of the National Collegiate Honors Council* 10:1, 19–24.

Winston, Gordon C. 1999. "Subsidies, Hierarchy and Peers: The Awkward Economics of Higher Education." *Journal of Economic Perspectives* 13:1, 13–36.

Yosso, Tara. 2006. *Critical Race Counterstories along the Chicana/Chicano Educational Pipeline.* New York: Routledge.

The College Choice Process for High-Achieving Latinas

Ebelia Hernández and Antonio G. Estudillo

INTRODUCTION

The current college enrollment rates for Latina/o students in higher education reflect an increase in recent years, yet most of this increase is concentrated in community college enrollments. López and Fry (2013) highlight these demographic shifts, and, whereas Latina/o students are now the largest ethnic-racial minority population in higher education, this same student population still lags far behind its White and African American peers, when it comes to four-year degree attainment. This is particularly troubling when considering that overall population projections for 2020 suggest Latinas/os will represent approximately a quarter of young adults ages 18–29 in the United States (Santiago and Callan 2010). The importance of examining contributing factors influencing initial college enrollment cannot be overstated.

Evidence suggests that all colleges do not offer equal opportunities for success when it comes to attaining a degree, and more competitive schools show higher graduation rates for Latinas/os (Kelly, Schneider, and Carey 2010). But, even Latinas/os who are eligible to attend more selective institutions are not likely to do so. They are more likely to attend regional, less prestigious institutions, and as a result, the probability of their completing a bachelor's degree may be lower, when compared to equally qualified peers attending more selective institutions (Kelly et al. 2010; Reardon, Barker, and Klasik 2012). Simply put, institution choice matters when it comes to closing the achievement gap in higher education.

This article examines the decision-making processes of high-achieving Latinas in the Northeast, who ultimately chose to attend a public, selective, research-intensive institution. College choice is defined here as the process through which students go about implementing their postsecondary educational aspirations. Participants were asked to reflect on their college choice process; in examining their narratives, we can expand the dialogue about college choice, centering on how these Latinas arrive at the decision to enroll in a particular institution. Using critical race theory (CRT) to inform our analysis, we asked which individuals, policies, and institutional factors informed their decision-making processes, what information was used, and whether advantages and constraints influenced the college choice process.

Factors Influencing the College Choice Process for Latinas

Perna's (2006) literature review offers a comprehensive summary of college choice scholarship, citing the ubiquitous use of sociological and economic theories to explain students' decision-making behaviors, as well as the prevalent use of Hossler and Gallagher's (1987) three stage model. The first stage, *predisposition*, refers to the process where students begin to consider plans after high school, which can include postsecondary education or work. The second stage, *search*, involves students exploring and evaluating possibilities in regards to potential colleges and universities for enrollment. In the third stage, *choice*, students select an institution from those that they have considered. A student's academic preparation (Hossler, Schmit, and Vesper 1998), family background (Álvarez 2010), financial aid (Avery and Hoxby 2004; Kim 2004; Perna 2006), ethnic makeup and campus climate of institutions (Cho, Hudley, Lee, and Barry 2008) and social network of family members, counselors, and peers (Pérez and McDonough 2008; Riegle-Crumb 2010) all contribute to the college choice process (Kinzie et al. 2004). Nora (2004) concludes that students use "the heart as well as the head" in deciding which college to attend, by using cognitive and intuitive processes (197). Indeed, students rely more heavily on psychosocial factors (e.g., support from family, sense of welcome and acceptance by particular institutions, family support and encouragement, approval by others) in the final decision of which institution to matriculate.

For Latina students in particular, Álvarez (2010) suggests that "[i]t may be more accurate to think of the Latina college choice process as familial instead of the individual process that Hossler and Gallagher (1987) suggested, and thus reframe the way we . . . think about the Latina college choice process" (58). Considering that many Latina/o parents may not have attended higher education themselves, may be unfamiliar with the American educational system, and/or may have limited English language ability,

Latina/o parents may not have the necessary critical knowledge to guide their daughters through the college choice process, even when they have had older children go through the college application process (Ceja 2006).

High-Achieving Latinas' College Choice Process

Avery and Hoxby (2004) suggest that the characteristics of high-achieving students may contribute to significant differences in the college choice process because this group is "capable of complex analysis are the least risky for creditors, and they tend to be patient people who take future benefits seriously" (240). High-achieving students can be characterized as the group likely to be best informed, given their abilities to problem-solve and seek out information and opportunities, and are most likely to have the resources and opportunities available to them that contribute to the development of competitive academic records. Yet, despite these characteristics, high-achieving Latinas/os are disproportionately enrolling in less selective institutions. Specifically, the number of high-achieving Latinas/os is small, and their enrollment in the most prestigious colleges and universities is severely disproportional compared to other ethnic/racial groups: approximately 8 percent of Latinas/os attend a selective or highly selective institution, compared to 30 percent of Asian Americans, 15 percent of Whites, and 9 percent of African Americans (Swail, Cabrera, and Lee 2004).

Critical Race Theory as a Perspective to Examine Educational Inequities

The theoretical viewpoint taken here, i.e., "the philosophical stance informing the methodology and thus providing context for the process and grounding its logic and its criteria" (Crotty 1998, 3) is CRT, Critical Race Theory. CRT has its roots in critical legal studies, and is grounded on a social justice platform that seeks to expose the often invisible ways that privilege and oppression are perpetuated in American society (Ladson-Billings 1999). This exposure aims to increase awareness, and to foster motivation for change that may yield more equitable policies and practices. CRT has been used by education research scholars to examine the effects of racism and racist educational policies on the experiences of Latinas/os in higher education (Solórzano 1998; Solórzano, Villalpando, and Oseguera 2005).

Ladson-Billings and Tate (2009) propose three central components to guide investigations of educational inequity, which we employed in the present investigation into the college choice process. The first component, which states that race and ethnicity continue to be significant factors in determining inequity in the United States, asserts that "class- and gender-based explanations are not powerful enough to explain all of the differences (or variance) in school experience and performance" (170). The literature review regarding college choice supports this assertion that race is a significant factor and plays a role in the inequities that exist in the representation of Latinas/os in higher education. The second component states that US society is based on property rights. Property, as it relates to the educational system, includes the resources used to develop rich learning environments, and intellectual property such as curriculum. "Thus, intellectual property must be undergirded by 'real' property, that is, science labs, computers, and other state-of-the-art technologies, appropriately certified and prepared teachers" (172). The extent to which these rich learning environments for Latina/o students may promote aspirations for college and information-rich resources (counselors) may help them navigate the college application and selection process has proven to be limited, as many Latinas/os attend underfunded schools. The third proposition states that the intersection of race and property can create an analytic tool to examine social and educational inequities. The use of CRT to examine college choice may provide the focus that not only acknowledges how students of different racial and ethnic groups approach the college choice process differently, but that their processes are also influenced by social norms, levels of resources available to them, and educational practices that may put some populations at an advantage and others (e.g., Latinas/os) at a disadvantage.

RESEARCH DESIGN

We used interviews collected from the first year of a longitudinal research project. Its overarching agenda was to examine the interconnections and interplay between Latinas' college student engagement and their holistic development throughout their undergraduate career. We explain the components of the research design, how the college choice process emerged as an area of study, and the procedures taken to explore college choice.

Epistemology, Theoretical Perspective, and Research Approach

The central aim of this research design is to give voice to a minority population, with the intent of examining how these students make meaning of their lives as Latina women attending college. The research design is grounded in constructionist epistemology and a CRT theoretical perspective—this combination allows for a critical investigation on the impact that context (social forces, institutional environment) plays on the experiences of this specific population (Hernández, 2012). We applied narrative inquiry methodology (Chase, 2008), which "honors people's stories as data that can stand on their own as pure description of experience or be analyzed for connections between psychological, sociological, cultural, political, and dramaturgic dimensions of human experience to reveal larger meanings" (Patton 2002, 478). The narratives were collected by conducting in-depth, semi-structured interviews.

The high-achieving Latina students represent a clear subgroup, as viewed within both the general student population and the general Latina student population. For example, these Latinas attended schools in the northeastern United States, a regional setting often ignored in most educational literature on Latina/os in higher education, despite that roughly over six million Latina/os reside in this region (Brown and López 2013), and that this region reflects distinct and different meanings of Latina/o race/ethnicity. First, the majority of the Latina/o students in this group are not of Mexican descent; thus the historical and immigration legacy is distinct from other regions of the United States. Second, access to educational resources (e.g., public education resources, availability and access of private institutions for Latino families) is distinct from other regions where social norms, diversity mix, and public policy may result in different levels of access to these resources.

Procedures and Participants

The study was based at Eastern University (the pseudonym for a large public institution located in the Northeast). Eastern is Carnegie classified as having a "more selective" undergraduate student profile. After receiving a list of potential students who met the criteria for participation (first-years, women, self-identified as Latina) from the Institutional Research office, the first author randomly selected 100 students. They were emailed an invitation to be part of a longitudinal study about the Latina college experience. Seventeen traditionally aged women participated in the first year of the study and were given a $20 cash incentive. Their cultural backgrounds were a diverse range of Latina ethnic heritages: Dominican, Puerto Rican, Columbian, Peruvian, Ecuadorian, and Honduran; of which four identified as mixed heritage in that they claimed two or more different Latino ethnicities and/or racial groups (White, African American).

Data Collection and Analytic Procedures

Using simultaneous data collection, analysis, and revision of research design to investigate emerging themes (Charmaz 2006) allowed for a focused investigation of the college choice process. The data came from the first-year interviews, built upon questions exploring the students' first year in college, including how they had arrived at the decision to attend Eastern University. Each participant took part in a one-on-one, semi-structured interview with the Principal Investigator, lasting anywhere between 30 to 70 minutes, with an average of 46 minutes. These interviews were digitally recorded and transcribed.

The first phase of data analysis consisted of individual open coding (Strauss and Corbin 1998), and these individual code lists were then combined to form a master code list. In this initial round of analysis, the narratives revealed that the participants' choice to attend Eastern was one of the most significant decisions they had made, and their narratives detailing the college choice process emerged as a topic that merited a more focused examination. In the second phase, the software program Atlas.ti, for qualitative data analysis, was used to recode the first set of transcripts. This recoding allowed for refinement of the codes and identification of emerging themes about college choice. In the final phase, we further developed emerging themes on college choice by coding all transcripts and running Atlas.ti data reports on codes related to the emerging themes for further analysis through axial coding (Strauss and Corbin 1998). We continued the practice of simultaneous data collection and analysis (Charmaz 2006), by sharing with participants our interpretation of emerging themes regarding college choice, allowing their feedback to inform our continued analysis.

Trustworthiness and Positionality

Trustworthiness (Lincoln and Guba 1985) was addressed with peer debriefing, and member checking. Informal member checking was done with participants during the interviews by asking them to assess the research team's developing understanding of college choice. The researchers' identities and experiences played a critical role. Specifically, the cultural background and personal experience as a minority woman in higher education greatly informed the cultural intuition of the principal investigator (first author); cultural intuition contributes to trustworthiness, as it is considered similar to theoretical sensitivity (Delgado Bernal 1998). The principal investigator (first author) identifies as a Mexican American woman. In our study, therefore, we use our own experience of Latino cultural dynamics, whether of a personal or professional nature, to also facilitate information gathering, and acknowledge the salience of supporting Latina college women. In addressing positionality, the first author acknowledges that her Latina identity was an advantage in developing rapport. Trust with the participants may have been developed from shared cultural and gender identities. Positionality "describes the relationship between the researcher and his or her participants and the researcher and his or her topic" (Jones, Torres, and Arminio 2006).

FINDINGS

For this group of women, the college choice process was centered on deciding which school to go to, rather than determining if college was for them. Their narratives revealed the barriers that challenged their access to the most prestigious institutions, the factors they considered in their decision-making process, and the varying levels of influence these factors had. While acknowledging the range of experiences represented in these narratives, a common thread emerged that connected each of their stories to the others: striking a balance between their dreams about having the "full college experience" at a school they and their family would be proud to claim, with the sobering realities of family expectations and finances. Their stories revealed emerging themes of balancing distance (close but far enough away), reputation and cost, and their parents' idealism with the realities of their family finances. Each of these three themes is reviewed in the following section.

"Close, But Far Enough Away"— Balancing Independence and Connection

Balancing distance, or as one participant put it, "close, but far enough away" was a contributing factor in college choice. Julie (all participant names are pseudonyms), who often went home on the weekends to help her family take care of her younger siblings and relatives, represented the thinking of many of the participants, in how she considered balancing her need for connection and independence in the following statement:

> I didn't want to go far from my house but I wanted to be far enough that they couldn't get to me without warning me in advance. That's why I like Eastern.

Choosing a school that was just far enough away to necessitate living on campus was another strategy employed by these participants. As Elisia shared:

> I did not want to stay home. Eastern just seemed it was far enough to move out but not too far that my parents would freak out

although at first my mom was very opposed to me moving out. She wanted me to stay home.

Often, these women had one parent who supported their desire to become independent and explore (most often the mother), and another parent who wanted them to stay home under their protection and commute to school (most often the father). Most of the women shared the struggle to convince a parent to allow them to move away to attend college by choosing an institution that was close enough for them to come home on the weekends and/or for their parents to visit them on a consistent basis. Despite having to deal with parental disapproval of their choice to move away to attend college, some of the women chose Eastern over other attractive offers because its distance from home promised the independence they wanted. Amy chose not to attend an Ivy League school that was close to home because she would have had to continue living at home. Diva also chose not to accept a full ride to a private college close to home because she wanted to experience going away to college and explore a new environment unlike her hometown. Diva remarked, "It wouldn't make sense to live on campus when you live down the street." Both Amy and Diva shared that it was difficult to engage in discussions with their parents about their plans to attend Eastern, and for one of them, it remained a sensitive topic in the family in their first year of college.

"Getting Your Money's Worth"— Balancing Reputation and Cost

For this group of Latinas, the balancing act between dreams and reality played out in their strategy to "get your money's worth" by selecting an institution with the best reputation and academics at the most affordable cost. Cost was often a deciding factor, its influence felt at various stages, affecting both the *search* and *choice* phases of the college choice process.

Julie admitted that despite her struggles with paying tuition, she felt fortunate that she could attend Eastern rather than a community college. Claudia shared that cost was a major consideration, but acknowledged that she did not seriously consider community college, even with the available state tuition assistance, covering high-achieving students' tuition at community colleges for two years, after which grants were offered to support earning a bachelor's degree at a public four-year state institution over another two years. As she stated,

> If I would have gone to a community college, it would have been paid for because I was the valedictorian of my graduating class

> . . . I would have [my tuition] paid for two years and then I could have come to Eastern for half tuition paid or something like that. It would have been a good deal, but no. I feel like if you're here [at Eastern] from the start, it's better for you. I see transfer students and they don't have the same support.

The issue of cost narrowed the field of possibilities for many of the participants, who shared that they did not even look into certain types of institutions if they felt the cost was too far beyond their means. It became apparent that for the few students seriously considering cost during their search phase, Eastern was the top choice; they considered it affordable and having the best academic reputation among in-state public schools. For them, the college choice process was more a matter of being admitted to Eastern.

In the choice phase, the issues of cost and academic reputation played key roles when selecting among the schools offering admission. The process that many described was one of elimination based on letters of offer of financial aid. Indeed, private schools and out-of-state institutions were often the first to be crossed off their lists when many of the women realized the cost of tuition was beyond their means, even with available financial aid in the form of grants and scholarships. As Destiny shared:

> I got accepted to all of [my choice schools]. I actually loved [an out of state institution], but as an out of state student, I didn't have enough money. [A private institution] is a really good school. I was also looking into [another college]. It's private, so it was like $50,000. [A third private institution] is the same thing. . . . Eastern provided the most financial aid so that's why I came here.

Realizing what college costs was a sobering experience for Caroline as well. She also was admitted to her first and second choices, and upon reviewing both offers of financial aid, realized that out-of-state schools and private schools would be out of reach because she did not want to accrue significant student loan debt. Aiming to strike the balance between cost and reputation, and "get your money's worth," was again observed when some of the women shared how they decided between Eastern and other more affordable institutions. In these cases, Eastern's reputation won out over cost.

Balancing Parents' Idealism with Reality

Many of the interviewed students shared that their parents had expressed very high hopes of supporting their daughters' educational dreams, and the students had found themselves in the position of having to temper

their parents' idealism with the family's financial reality. Several participants shared that their parents did not want them to limit their college
aspirations—they believed that their parents held the hope that they could
somehow "make it work," by finding a way to afford college costs despite
limited means and limited financial aid packages. Betsy's recollection of
conversations with her parents illustrated Latina/o parents' aspirations to
support their daughters' college dreams: "They told me it was my decision. Like whatever I did, we would tackle it however we can. Yes, it was
my decision." In Betsy's and similar cases, daughters recognized that this
decision was posed as an individual choice, yet with repercussions affecting the family.

Parents, especially fathers, perceived themselves as providers who felt
a responsibility to support their children's educational aspirations, no matter the sacrifice required. One student shared that she struggled to balance
her father's expectation to support her educational expenses and her own
feelings about overburdening her family's finances. She shared:

> He was like, I told you that I am your provider. So he is like, if
> you need something . . . There were a couple of things that I actu-
> ally needed for school, but he was like if you need something, ask
> me. Like, I am your provider and you weren't supposed to forget
> me. . . . I really don't like asking my parents for money.

Letty's narrative describes the strategy of working around parental
hopes by never challenging her parents' assertion that they could support
her college aspirations directly. Instead, Letty worked in collaboration
with her siblings to make decisions that she felt were more financially
responsible and realistic for the family. In the following, Letty revealed
how balancing her parents' hopes with financial reality informed her college choice process:

> My mom obviously was going to say, 'choose what you want,' but
> I was like, you're crazy . . . And then my sisters were like, 'Let's
> help mom with college costs.' My dad, I told him about [my dif-
> ficulty in choosing a college to attend] too, because we talk, and
> he said 'Eastern is not a bad school. Eastern has a good research
> reputation and a good price.'

Letty acknowledged her mother's unrealistic hopes of somehow being able
to afford any school Letty chose to attend. She also recognized how her
choice of college could impact her siblings' college aspirations. Letty and
her siblings' pact to attend public institutions was a strategy to keep college costs as affordable as possible, and to ensure all siblings had an equal

share of parental financial support. Letty, like other women in the study, admitted that she could not select a school knowing it would require her family to sacrifice more than she was comfortable with, despite parents who assured her that money should not be an issue.

Claudia's discussions about family finances were markedly different from all the other participants. Her narrative allows insight to how the college choice process may be experienced by immigrant families in which daughters handle the family finances, because they are proficient in English and understand American culture. In Claudia's case, she was largely responsible for managing her family's finances—from writing checks to paying bills to calling offices about her parents' accounts. For Claudia, discussing her college choice process with her parents was more about informing them of her choices rather than seeking their advice or support. She stated, "I just told them I'm applying to Eastern, and this and that when I started applying. I feel like they didn't know anything about it."

In summary, the interviewees spoke about acknowledging how their college education would signify financial sacrifices for their families. While many parents had told their daughters to choose the school they wanted, the women, in many cases, first considered the potential effects and impact of a given choice upon their families. The students most often considered whether their parents would have to make sacrifices in order to pay the tuition bill, and particularly whether these sacrifices were acceptable or unacceptable to the student, and how the family's ability to support the college aspirations of their other children would be affected, as well as overall financial stability of the family.

DISCUSSION

Seventeen high-achieving Latina first-year students shared their college choice process to reveal how they selected among multiple offers of admission by considering several important factors: distance from home, reputation of the institution, academic rigor, and most importantly, cost. Their narratives reveal how they tempered their own dreams, as well as those of their parents, with the very real challenges that would be insurmountable in their individual cases. This article seeks to contribute to furthering scholarship in several ways. First, these narratives broaden the representation of Latino college students, to also reflect Caribbean and South American cultures, where many other studies focus primarily on Latinas/os of Mexican descent (e.g., Kiyama 2011; Martínez 2013; Rosas and Hamrick 2002). Second, furthering Hossler and Gallagher's (1987) college choice process review, and adding complexity by providing a more focused examination of the ways that family and culture may influence the choice and selection phases. These findings confirm the conclusion reached by Álvarez (2010) that, for Latina/o students, college choice may best be understood as a familial process rather than an individual decision-making process. Third, the use of CRT reveals how race and ethnicity, the privilege (or lack thereof) of access to resources and information, and financial aid policies affect the college choice process.

A Critical Analysis of College Choice

Examining the college choice process with a CRT lens allows for a more nuanced understanding of the ways in which social factors influence the student's process of selecting a college for matriculation. CRT's three tenets are useful tools of analysis that reveal how Latina college choice is affected by culture, institutional policies, and access.

The influence of race and ethnicity in the college choice process. The first tenet asserts that race and ethnicity are factors that must be considered when attempting to explain educational disparities (Harper 2012; Ladson-Billings and Tate 2009). In this case, participants represented the "cream of the crop" for Latina college students—they were at high levels of academic achievement, were proactive in obtaining information and advice on potential colleges and universities to attend, seeking out the support of counselors, teachers, and family, were highly knowledgeable on college costs, and were confident in their abilities to be academically successful in college. Lack of academic preparation or lack of understanding or initiative regarding appropriate information on college was not something observed in this group, whereas these challenges are often faced by other students, and often result in a thwarted college choice process. This notwithstanding, many of the participants did not ultimately attend their top choice school despite "doing everything right." That is, the participants' academic credentials and self-help behaviors challenge deficiency frameworks and the validity of meritocracy ideologies; such thinking would conclude that Latino students attend less prestigious institutions than those they are eligible for, due to a lack of academic preparation or interest to attend these institutions. CRT challenges such frameworks that place the blame for inequities on individual characteristics or behaviors rather than examining the environmental factors that may privilege certain groups and marginalize others (Solórzano 1998).

The student's focus on her role and sense of commitment to the family was woven throughout each of the themes presented. *Familismo* is a cultural value prevalent in Latino families, where there is an emphasis on family closeness and putting family needs first, even if it may result in personal sacrifice (Vega 1990). The desire to keep family ties strong was often valued by both student and parent, but it frequently created tension with the student's desire for independence. These women shared that they appreciated going to school close to home and their families, but far enough away that they could gain some independence and make living on campus practical.

The participants also showed considerable understanding of and concern for the family finances, by critically evaluating their parents' ability to take on debt to pay for their college costs. This was done despite their parents' assertions that their daughters should not be concerned, and that it was a parents' responsibility to "make it work." This finding challenges the hypothesis by Hossler et al. (1998) that "the amount students expect their parents to pay is correlated with the amount of support and sacrifice parents are willing to make" (93). These daughters depicted parents who were very willing to support and sacrifice for their college education beyond their means, and instead of accepting the sacrifice, they students made the choice to "help out" by choosing a more affordable option.

Property rights and financial aid. The second CRT tenet states that US society is based on property rights. In the case of higher education, property rights can be understood as access to the tools needed for educational success. Within the college choice process we are discussing, property rights are expressed as the access to financial aid. Hossler, Schmitt, and Vesper concluded in 1998 that the purpose of federal and state financial aid is "to promote access to college; it is not intended to promote the decision to attend one school over another" (93). While federal and state aid continue to be solely need-based, institutional aid policies have changed over the decades to increase institutional prestige rather than provide access for low-income students. A report by the New America Foundation (Burd 2013) examined the "net price," or the amount students pay for college minus grants; it revealed that current institutional aid policies at both public and private colleges are making postsecondary education increasingly more expensive for those who can least afford it. In a review of institutional aid practices from the mid 1990s to the 2007–2008 academic year, the policy of directing most institutional aid to need-based seen in the 1990s changed to the current trend, where the percentage of merit-based aid awarded supersedes need-based aid.

During the same period, grants awarded to high-income students increased, while the percentage of low-income students receiving awards fell. Institutional aid at both public and private institutions has become a recruitment tool to attract high-achieving, affluent students with merit aid, rather than a means to increase access for low-income students.

Kim (2004) promotes the role of financial aid as a tool to support equity in higher education and states that "it is crucial to clarify whether financial aid promotes educational opportunity, not just measured in terms of access (getting students into college) but in terms of choice (which college students want to attend the most)" (44). Kim clarified that equity-minded access should include choice, and not be limited to being defined as an either/or proposition of being able to attend college or not. As depicted in these narratives, financial aid played a gatekeeper role by pricing low-income, high-achieving students out of private institutions as well as the most selective, out-of-state public institutions.

The "financial ceiling." The third tenet of CRT states that the intersection of race and property can create an analytic tool to examine social and educational inequities. In the analysis of the intersection of race and financial aid policy, the concept of the "financial ceiling" emerged, which is the barrier of college costs that put elite public, private, and out-of-state institutions out of reach for even the most high-achieving, savvy, and motivated Latina students. This work confounds earlier conclusions that suggested that high-achieving Latinas/os prefer to attend regional public schools despite possessing the credentials that would admit them to institutions of higher prestige, by revealing that many of the Latina students interviewed did dream big, but reached a "financial ceiling" they could not break through.

This financial ceiling showed up at both the search and choice stages in Hossler and Gallagher's (1987) college choice process study. Most of the women shared that they had not initially been aware of the financial ceiling during their search phase, when they were exploring possible colleges and universities, often aspiring to attend an out-of-state school or perhaps a private school. Their aspirations drove them to learn more about those schools, go on campus visits, and apply for admission.

It was surprising that none of the women seriously considered community college, despite its affordability and the opportunity to transfer to a four-year institution. From Avery and Hoxby's (2004) human capital perspective, one potential explanation for why community college was not considered is that students view their college choice process as needing to achieve a balance between costs and benefits, by seeing less resource-rich college options as balanced by larger grants and other benefits. For high-achieving students, community college may not be considered an option because students "will never by tempted by more aid to attend a college that offers such reduced consumption and human capital investment that he is worse off over his lifetime" (244). Indeed, in discussions with participants about the findings emerging from the study, they shared their view of community college as a step backwards in their academic plans. Community colleges were perceived as providing an inferior education, in comparison to a four-year institution, as well as failing to provide any social capital, such as that obtained by attending a prestigious university. These disadvantages were deemed to be too severe to be outweighed by the greater financial affordability of the community institution.

The effects of the financial ceiling on college choice was most fully illustrated in the narratives of several students who had been admitted to their top choices, but were unable to accept due to the prohibitively high costs associated with these out-of-state schools and private institutions. Burd's (2013) analysis of institutional aid practices supports their narratives about the high cost of private schools where "nearly two-thirds of the private institutions analyzed charge students from the lowest-income families, those making $30,000 or less annually, a net price of over $15,000 a year." It led students to opt for the strategy of "getting your money's worth" by choosing the most affordable school with the strongest reputation, even if it meant passing up better offers from less selective institutions, or turning down more prestigious schools that would cause them to accrue large student loan debt to cover costs.

FUTURE STEPS

For educators who wish to support Latinas during the college choice process, we offer several suggestions based on our findings. First, we must recognize the importance that Latinas place on their roles as members of a family unit. Counselors, teachers, and others to whom these students turn for advice, should consider *familismo* as a positive source of support for Latinas to draw from during their college choice process; we would suggest including the student's family members in the conversation, by offering informational sessions which the whole family is encouraged to attend, and ideally conducted in Spanish. Latina daughters may also need support in managing their parents' expectations, as these may conflict with the student's own hopes for independence. Second, we must expand our concept of college accessibility, so that it includes private and elite institutions, as well as high-achieving students, to be fully on par with the complexity of college choice. The narrative of supporting college choice for Latinas/os is often focused only on increasing the number of students in higher education, leaving the experiences of students like those in our study completely out the conversation. Third, we must reconsider the role that financial aid should play in the college choice process. While college choice literature examines the influence that financial aid plays on choice, more analysis is required if we wish to examine the role that financial aid plays in promoting educational equity.

The limitations of the present study provide opportunities for further research. Our sample only included Latinas attending one specific public institution in the Northeast. While the narratives we gathered and present here cannot reflect the college-bound journey of every Latina student, these narratives do offer insight to the ways many individuals balance their dreams and those of their family with the realities of cultural expectations and impenetrable financial ceilings.

REFERENCES

Alvarez, Cynthia Lua. 2010. "Familial Negotiation of the Latina College Choice Process: An Exploration of How Parents and Their Daughters Obtain and Utilize Information to Navigate the Process." *Enrollment Management Journal* 4 (4): 57–78.

Avery, Christopher, and Caroline M. Hoxby. 2004. Do and should financial aid packages affect students' college choices? In *College choice: The economics of where to go, when to go, and how to pay for it*, ed. Caroline Hoxby, 239–301. Chicago: University of Chicago Press.

Brown, Anna, and Mark H. López. 2013. "Mapping the Latino Population, by State, County and City." *Hispanic Trends*. Washington, DC: Pew Research Center.

Burd, Stephen. 2013. *Undermining Pell: How Colleges Compete for Wealthy Students and Leave Low-Income Students Behind*. Washington, DC: New America Foundation.

Ceja, Miguel. 2006. "Understanding the Role of Parents and Siblings as Information Sources in the College Choice Process of Chicana Students." *Journal of College Student Development* 47 (1): 87–104.

Charmaz, Kathy. 2006. *Constructing Grounded Theory: A Practical Guide through Qualitative Analysis*. Thousand Oaks, CA: SAGE Publishing.

Chase, Susan E. 2008. Narrative Inquiry: Multiple Lenses, Approaches, Voices. In *Collecting and Interpreting Qualitative Materials*, ed. Norman K. Denzin and Yvonna S. Lincoln, 57–94. Thousand Oaks, CA: SAGE Publishing.

Cho, Su-Je, Cynthia Hudley, Soyoung Lee, and Leasha Barry. 2008. "Roles of Gender, Race, and Sex in the College Choice Process among First-Generation and Non-First-Generation Students." *Journal of Diversity in Higher Education* 1 (2): 95–107.

Crotty, Michael. 1998. *The Foundations of Social Research: Meaning and Perspective in the Research Process*. Thousand Oaks, CA: SAGE Publishing.

Delgado Bernal, Dolores. 1998. "Using a Chicana Feminist Epistemology in Educational Research." *Harvard Educational Review* 68 (4): 555–583.

Harper, Shaun R. 2012. "Race without Racism: How Higher Education Researchers Minimize Racist Institutional Norms." *The Review of Higher Education* 36 (1): 9–29.

Hernández, Ebelia. 2012. "The Journey Towards Developing Political Consciousness through Activism for Mexican American Women." *Journal of College Student Development,* 53 (5): 680–702.

Hossler, Don, and Karen S. Gallagher. 1987. "Studying College Choice: A Three-Phase Model and the Implications for Policy-Makers." College and University 2: 207–221.

Hossler, Don, Jack Schmidt, and Nick Vesper. 1998. Going to College: How Social, Economic, and Educational Factors Influence the Decisions Students Make. Baltimore, MD: Johns Hopkins University Press.

Jones, Susan R., Vasti Torres, and Jan Arminio. 2006. Negotiating the Complexities of Qualitative Research in Higher Education: Fundamental Elements and Issues. New York, NY: Routledge.

Kelly, Andrew, Mark Schneider, and Kevin Carey. 2010. "Rising to the Challenge: Hispanic College Graduation Rates as a National Priority." Washington, DC: American Enterprise Institute.

Kim, Dongbin. 2004. "The Effect of Financial Aid on Students' College Choice: Differences by Racial Groups." *Research in Higher Education* 45 (1): 43–70.

Kinzie, Jillian, Megan Palmer, John Hayek, Don Hossler, Stacy A. Jacob, and Heather Cummings. 2004. Fifty Years of College Choice: Social, Political and Institutional Influences on the Decisions-Making Process. In *New Agenda Series.* Indianapolis, IN: Lumina Foundation for Education.

Kiyama, Judy Márquez. 2011. "Family Lessons and Funds of Knowledge: College-Going Paths in Mexican American Families." *Journal of Latinos and Education* 10 (1): 23–42.

Ladson-Billings, Gloria. 1999. Just What Is Critical Race Theory, and What's It Doing in a Nice Field Like Education? In *Race Is . . . Race Isn't: Critical Race Theory and Qualitative Studies in Education,* ed. Lawrence Parker, Donna Deyhle, and Sofia Villenas, 7–30. Boulder, CO: Westview Press.

Ladson-Billings, Gloria, and William F. Tate IV. 2009. Toward a Critical Race Theory of Education. In *The Critical Pedagogy Reader,* 2nd edition, ed. Antonia Darder, Marta P. Baltodano, and Rodolfo D. Torres, 167–182. New York, NY: Routledge.

Lincoln, Yvonna S., and Egon G. Guba. 1985. *Naturalistic Inquiry.* Beverly Hills: SAGE Publishing .

López, Mark Hugo, and Richard Fry. 2013. Among Recent High School Grads, Hispanic College Enrollment Rate Surpasses That of Whites. Washington, DC: Pew Research Center, Fact Tank (September 4). http://www.pewresearch.org /fact-tank/2013/09/04/hispanic-college-enrollment-rate-surpasses-whites-for -the-first-time/

Martínez, Melissa A. 2013. "(Re)Considering the Role *Familismo* Plays in Latina/o High School Students' College Choice." *The High School Journal* 97 (1): 21–40.

Nora, Amaury. 2004. "The Role of Habitus and Cultural Capital in Choosing a College, Transitioning from High School to Higher Education, and Persisting in College Among Minority and Nonminority Students. *Journal of Hispanic Higher Education* 3 (2): 180–208. doi: 10.1177/1538192704263189

Patton, Michael Q. 2002. *Qualitative Research & Evaluation Methods*. 3rd ed. Thousand Oaks, CA: SAGE Publishing.

Pérez, Patricia A., and Patricia M. McDonough. 2008. "Understanding Latina and Latino College Choice: A Social Capital and Migration Analysis." *Journal of Hispanic Higher Education* 7 (3): 249–265.

Perna, Laura W. 2006. Studying college access and choice: A proposed conceptual model. In *Higher Education: Handbook of Theory and Research*, ed. John C. Smart, 99–157. New York: Agathon Press.

Reardon, Sean F., Rachel Baker, and Daniel Klasik. 2012. "Race, Income, and Enrollment Patterns in Highly Selective Colleges, 1982–2004." cepa.stanford.edu /publications/working-papers

Riegle-Crumb, Catherine. 2010. "More Girls Go to College: Exploring the Social and Academic Factors Behind the Female Postsecondary Advantage Among Hispanic and White Students." *Research in Higher Education* 51: 573–593.

Rosas, Marisela, and Florence A. Hamrick. 2002. "Postsecondary Enrollment and Academic Decision Making: Family Influences on Women College Students of Mexican Descent." *Equity & Excellence in Education* 35 (1): 59–69.

Santiago, Deborah, and Patrick Callan. 2010. "Ensuring America's Future: Benchmarking Latino College Completion to Meet National Goals: 2010–2020." Washington, DC: Excelencia in Education.

Solórzano, Daniel G. 1998. "Critical Race Theory, Race and Gender Microaggressions, and the Experience of Chicana and Chicano Scholars." *Qualitative Studies in Education* 11 (1): 121–136.

Solórzano, Daniel G., Octavio Villalpando, and Leticia Oseguera. 2005. "Educational Inequities and Latina/o Undergraduate Students in the United States: A Critical Race Theory Analysis of Their Educational Progress." *Journal of Hispanic Higher Education* 4 (3): 272–294.

Strauss, Anselm, and Juliet Corbin. 1998. *Basics of Qualitative Research: Techniques and Procedures for Developing Grounded Theory* (2nd ed.). Thousand Oaks, CA: Sage.

Swail, Watson Scott, Alberto F. Cabrera, and Chul Lee. 2004. "Latino Youth and the Pathway to College." Washington, DC: Pew Hispanic Center.

Torres, Vasti, and Ebelia Hernández. 2007. "The Influence of Ethnic Identity on Self-Authorship: A Longitudinal Study of Latino/a College Students." *Journal of College Student Development* 48 (5): 558–573.

Vega, William A. 1990. "Hispanic Families in the 1980s: A Decade of Research." *Journal of Marriage and the Family* 52: 1015–1024.

Latino Community College Students in California

CHALLENGES AND OPPORTUNITIES FOR LEADERSHIP

Frances Contreras and Gilbert Contreras

T he majority of Latino students who transition to college begin their academic journey in community colleges. Community colleges have open access, are close to home for Latino students, affordable, and have a critical mass of Latinos, particularly in the Southwest. However, the challenges for many students attending community colleges are the time-to-degree and time-to-transfer process that negatively affect the four-year degree completion rate.

This study explores the central challenges for Latino students attending community colleges in California, home to 113 colleges, the largest community college system in the nation. In addition, 98 out of 113 community colleges are Hispanic Serving Institutions (HSIs),[1] making the entire system a "Hispanic Serving" system. Using the CC DataMart, the system that includes data on students, faculty, and staff throughout the California Community College system, we look at developmental education enrollment and success rates, the transfer process, financial aid access, and part-time vs. full-time status. Examining the trends for these select variables for Latino students allows for a more accurate picture of the Latino community college student experience today.

California's community college system serves more than 2.3 million students throughout California. The California community college system is also a very diverse segment of the state, with approximately half of all students coming from historically underrepresented communities. Given the rising tuition costs at the California State University and

---

1. *Excelencia* in Education. Hispanic-Serving Institutions (HSIs): 2015-16 (Washington, DC: *Excelencia* in Education, 2017).

University of California systems over the past decade, community colleges have become an attractive college option for students from low-income, first-generation, backgrounds. Latino students fall into this profile, given that over 39% live in poverty.[2] More than 80% are the children of immigrants.[3] This article provides an overview of Latino students in community colleges in California and the distinct challenges faced by this large population within this postsecondary sector.

Latinos represent over 40% of the community college system-wide enrollment, while African Americans represent 7.1% (California Community College Chancellor's Office 2015). The community college sector is therefore the most popular college choice for Chicano/Latino students in California. First-time Latino freshmen in 2013 were far more likely to enter one of California's community colleges (65%) than to start out in the California State University system (16%) or the University of California (6%), as seen in Figure 1 below.[4]

FIGURE 1. Distribution of Latino/a first-time freshmen in California, 2013

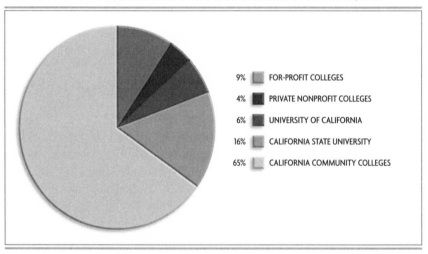

Source: *The State of Higher Education in California: Latino Report.* Produced by The Campaign for College Opportunity, Los Angeles, CA, April 2015.

---

2. Kids Count Data Center, a project of the Annie E. Casey Foundation, 2016, http://datacenter .kidscount.org/data.

3. Patricia Gándara and Frances Contreras, *The Latino Education Crisis* (Cambridge: Harvard University Press, 2009).

4. *The State of Higher Education in California: Latino Report* (Los Angeles, CA: Campaign for College Opportunity, April 2015).

Although the majority of Latino students enter the community college system nationally, few will transfer to a four-year institution, and fewer still will complete a bachelor's degree.[5] This is especially true for Latinos in California, where Latino students have low transfer and completion rates, yet make up the largest proportion of high school graduates in the state, and the single largest ethnic group in K-12 schools. Many have argued that the challenges to college completion are a reflection of students being poorly prepared in the K-12 system.[6] Others note that this uneven achievement begins at the pre-K level. It is well documented that Latino students attend K-12 schools with less resources (e.g., less access to Advanced Placement options, Honors, IB curriculum in schools) and high levels of teacher turnover.[7] Thus, the viable option for many Latinos who may be less prepared—or less aware of college options altogether—has been the community college, and the majority of Latino students who transition to college begin their academic journey there.

In addition to their open-access policies, proximity to the homes of Latino students, and affordability, these institutions often have a critical mass of Latino students, particularly in the Southwest: in California over 86% of them are HSIs. However, there are distinct challenges for many students attending community colleges, including:

- Limited financial resources to attend college
- Limited financial aid packages
- Hours spent working
- Poor academic preparation in high school and the need for developmental education
- A longer time to transfer to the four-year sector and to obtain a degree

These challenges mean that many Latino postsecondary students will drop off at the community college level. Those who do persevere experience

---

5. Gándara and Contreras, 2009; Stella Flores, Catherine Horn, and Gloria Crisp, "Community Colleges, Public Policy, and Latino Student Opportunity," *New Directions for Community Colleges* 133.2 (2006): 71-80; Richard Fry, *Latino Youth Finishing College: The Role of Selective Pathways* (Washington, D.C.: Pew Hispanic Research Center, 2004); Amaury Nora and Gloria Crisp, *Future Research on Hispanic Students: What Have We Yet to Learn? And What New and Diverse Perspectives Are Needed to Examine Latino Success in Higher Education?* White paper prepared for Hispanic Association of Colleges and Universities, 2012.

6. Gándara and Contreras, 2009; Patricia Gándara, Elizabeth Alvarado, Anne Driscoll, and Gary Orfield, *Building Pathways to Transfer: Community Colleges that Break the Chain of Failure for Students of Color*, UCLA Civil Rights Project, 2012; Linda Sera Hagedorn and Rita Cepeda, "Serving Los Angeles: Urban Community Colleges and Educational Success among Latino Students," *Community College Journal of Research and Practice* 28 (2004): 199–211.

7. Gándara and Contreras, 2009.

a longer time-to degree and time-to-transfer process that ultimately lowers their overall four-year degree completion rate. Such low college completion rates are a recipe for economic disaster for current and future generations in California.[8]

An example from 2013: for the 2009 cohort, only 38.4% of Latino students (a total 209,719) transferred or completed a degree within six years. Such low transfer rates can be attributed in part to the limited college preparation rates among Latino high school graduates. In California, for example, only 29% of Chicano/Latino high school graduates complete the A-G college-preparatory curriculum, which serves as the foundation for college readiness.[9] In 2014, some 50,102 Latino students (29.2%) failed to pass a placement exam in math for community colleges and were deemed unprepared for college-level coursework.[10] In addition, over 40% of Latinos were found to be unprepared that same year and placed into developmental education. This high proportion of Latino students in developmental education places an uneven burden on a community college system that is not entirely prepared with respect to having an infrastructure of academic support for students scoring below college level.

As a result, the original short-term solution has turned into a long-term practice. It places large numbers of Latinos, low-income, first-generation, and other underrepresented students into developmental education classes taught by contingent faculty. Failure rates for this pathway are very high and demonstrate high drop-out rates among this population, which starts college with aspirations of transferring. This article also presents a demographic overview of Latino students in community colleges in California and an overview of the central challenges that exist for Latino students as they attempt to navigate the two-year sector. Using the CC DataMart, we examine developmental education enrollment and success rates, the transfer process, and select measures of student success. Assessing the trends for these select variables for Latino students allows for a better understanding of Latino community college students and their experiences in California's community college system today and the opportunities that exist for paving a smoother road to college completion.

---

8. Ibid.

9. Frances Contreras, "The Education Landscape of Latino Students in the Central San Joaquin Valley in California," paper presented at the Latino Education Summit, California State University, Fresno, October 30, 2015.

10. Frances Contreras and Gilbert J. Contreras, "Raising the Bar for Hispanic Serving Institutions: An Analysis of College Completion and Success Rates," *Journal of Hispanics in Higher Education* 14.2 (2015): 151–170.

LITERATURE ON LATINO COLLEGE COMPLETION

Community colleges have long been the primary postsecondary pathway for Latino students, particularly students attending low-performing high schools in California. In addition, it has long been considered the first step toward four-year degree completion among first generation students.[11] As noted, students who enter the community colleges do so often because of a lack of preparation for four-year institutions, affordability, open access, proximity to home, and a social climate that possesses greater diversity than many of the traditional or highly selective four-year institutions.[12] In 2013, for example, only 29% of all Latino students completed an A-G curriculum in California, the courses required for admission to the four-year public sector.

The California Master Plan of 1960 outlines the function of the three tiers of higher education in California. The primary mission of California's community colleges has been to provide open access and carry out multiple missions for students from all backgrounds interested in taking postsecondary classes, seeking specific technical training, or transferring to a four-year institution. Historically, community colleges never had the primary role of transfer and completion and always had multiple missions of serving the broader community, not solely the traditional college-age population (18-24 year olds).[13] However, given the growing demand for postsecondary degrees in the work force and limited economic options for individuals with only a high school education, community colleges have witnessed an expansive increase in students who enter the community colleges with aspirations to transfer. In fact, in 2014, approximately 60% who enrolled in community colleges intended to transfer (NCES 2014).

Given the increasingly important role of community colleges in state and national college completion agendas, it is important to assess both the factors that would ensure two-year completion and transfer outcomes and the barriers that impede them. In an attempt to understand the challenges and opportunities that exist for Latinos navigating community colleges, this article explores the following questions:

- What are the Latino completion rates in the California community colleges and challenges to raising these rates?

---

11. Laura Rendón and Amaury Nora, 1997; Gloria Crisp and Amaury Nora, 2010; Frances Contreras, Adriana Flores-Regade, John Lee, and Keon McGuire. *The Latino College Completion Agenda: Research and Context Brief* (New York: The College Board, 2011).

12. Gándara and Contreras, 2009; F. Contreras and G. Contreras, 2015.

13. Kevin Dougherty and Barbara Towsend, "Community College Missions: A Theoretical and Historical Perspective," *New Directions for Community Colleges 136 (Winter 2006)*.

- How do these rates vary by level of student preparation (developmental vs. prepared students)?

- What gaps exist in the institutional and policy frameworks for measuring student success, progress, and completion?

RESEARCH METHODS

This article uses secondary data to answer research questions related to community college student outcomes in California. The primary data stems from several public data sets, including the California Community College Scorecard (2015), the California Community College Data Mart, California State University system data on transfer pathways, and the Integrated Postsecondary Data System (IPEDS). The secondary data from the California Student Success Card Database includes six-year completion rates for cohorts for the following years:

- 2004-05
- 2005-06
- 2006-07
- 2007-08
- 2008-09

Sample from Community College Data Mart

A total of 2,310,306 students attend California's community colleges. Less than half of them are full-time students (see Table 2). Of this sample, 53% are female, and 46% are male. Data from the California Community College Chancellor's Office (2015) shows that the majority enrolled are between the ages of 20 and 24 (32.3%) and 25 and 39 (26.8%). As noted earlier, the California community college system is among the most diverse in the nation, with 7.1% African American students, 40.2% Latino, 11.3% Asian American, and 29% white (see Table 1). The Community College System in California is essentially a Hispanic-serving system, with over 76% of its entities officially designated as HSIs.

The California Community college system also has a unique composition in that over 40% are first-generation, as Table 2 highlights. Having a high proportion of first-generation students calls for additional counseling services and an infrastructure for academic support. First-generation Latino students are more likely to be low-income and prefer a pay-as-you

TABLE 1. Composition of California community college students, by race/ethnicity, 2015

ETHNICITY/RACE	
African American	7.1%
American Indian/Alaska Native	0.4%
Asian	11.3%
Filipino	2.9%
Latino	40.2%
Pacific Islander	0.5%
White	29.0%
Two or more races	3.5%
Unknown	5.0%

Source: California Community College Chancellor's Office, Data Mart, 2015.

go approach to higher education.[14] First-generation students are also less likely to understand pathways to specific careers, majors that lend themselves to particular industries, and the transfer process.[15]

The system's infrastructure has not kept pace with the volume of students that need support services. The first notable issue is the declining percentage of full-time faculty over the past 25 years. Full-time faculty are central to upholding the mission of an institution, as they have earned job security through tenure and are part of the institutional fabric. The percentage of full-time faculty in 2014 in the community college system was at 56.1% in California. This data point is disconcerting, given the developmental demands of the Latino (and general) student population in community colleges. There is a clear over-reliance on contingent part-time faculty in community colleges, including the faculty who work with developmental education students—the students most in need of experienced instructors. This is a pressing concern for the state system,

14. Alisa Cunningham and Deborah Santiago, *Student Aversion to Borrowing: Who Borrows and Who Doesn't* (Washington, DC: IHEP and Ed. Excelencia, December 2008).

15. Nicole Reyes and Amaury Nora, *A Review of the Literature of Latino First Generation Students,* white paper prepared for the Hispanic Association of Colleges and Universities (HACU), July 2012; Frances Contreras, "*First-Generation* College *Students,*" Encyclopedia of Diversity in Education, J. Banks, ed., 911–916 (Thousand Oaks, CA: Sage Publications Inc., 2012), doi: http://dx.doi.org/10.4135/9781452218533.n290.

TABLE 2. Select characteristics of the California community college system

Full-time equivalent students	1,122,604.7
Credit sections	323,693
Non-credit sections	28,419
Median credit section size	27
Percentage of full-time faculty	56.1%
Percentage of first-generation students	40.1%
Student Counseling Ratio (Fall 2013)	722:1

Source: California Community College Chancellor's Office, Data Mart, 2015. First generation data is derived from the parent education level data as reported by the student.

given the high proportion of students who do not place into college level math or English, and the odds against them for making it out of the developmental tracks.[16]

The second disconcerting feature of the system, given the emphasis on individual student outcomes through the Student Success Act of 2012, is the student-to-counselor ratio, which in 2013 was at 722:1. Because the Student Success Act of 2012 calls on campuses to develop individualized student plans, counselors have become increasingly important to student success and the roadmap process. However, with a student-counselor ratio of more than 700 to 1 detailed attention and oversight to individual education plans present a challenge for the staff and for the infrastructure that exists within California community colleges today.

The third notable challenge to the community college infrastructure in California is assessment. The California community college system has identified a number of distinct measures of student success, including (1) the persistence rate, which is a year-to-year assessment of student progression beyond the first year; (2) the 30-unit rate, which documents the units earned for students; and (3) completion rates (SPAR rates). These rates have long been considered the key "momentum points" predicting progress toward community college success.[17] However, a six-year rate for transfer perhaps is not the most appropriate measure, given the urgency of increasing Latino college completion. It is important to know how many students

---

16. F. Contreras and G. Contreras, 2015.

17. Clifford Adelman, "The Toolbox Revisited: Paths to Degree Completion from High School through College" (Washington, D.C.: U.S. Department of Education, 2006).

actually transfer in a two- and three-year time frame, for example. As far as persistence, is completing 30 units truly a marker of student success? Consider a 30-unit student who drops off in year five, or does not complete a degree at all; the 30-unit measure is not a particularly strong predictor of student success. In earlier work, we have suggested that these models of assessment are outdated and in need of refinement if community colleges are serious about raising Latino college completion and transfer rates.[18]

In addition, two placement exams have dominated the market, the ACCUPLACER (used by 62% of community colleges nationally) and the COMPASS (used by 46% of community colleges). Some colleges use both the ACCUPLACER and COMPASS.[19] What remains unclear is the connection these exams have to course content in California high schools and whether or not these exams have kept pace with the No Child Left Behind Act and, more recently, Common Core alterations to curricular standards. The use of these assessments were to be replaced by CCCAccess, under the Common Assessment Initiative (CAI) which was in part prompted by the Student Success Task Force Recommendations in 2011.[20] However, in October 2017, the Chancellor of the Community College system called for a "reset" on the implementation of this common assessment, calling for colleges to use multiple measures to place students in appropriate courses.[21]

FINDINGS AND ANALYSIS

The California data analyzed suggest considerable challenges for community colleges as they work to raise Latino transfer and completion rates. The data for Latino students who first enroll in community colleges needing developmental education services in math, English, or ESL in 2008-09 is particularly discouraging. Latino students who start community college needing developmental education are not likely to complete a college level course—they do not make it out of the developmental education track. For

18. F. Contreras and G. Contreras, 2015.

19. Katherine Hughes and Judith Scott-Clayton, *Assessing Developmental Assessment In Community Colleges*, CCRC Working Paper No. 19, Assessment of Evidence Series (New York: Columbia University Teachers College, Community College Research Center, 2011).

20. Olga Rodriguez, Marisol Cuellar Mejia, and Hans Johnson. *Determining College Readiness in California's Community Colleges*. Report of the Public Policy Institute of California, San Francisco, 2016.

21. Correspondence by Chancellor Eloy Ortiz Oakley, October 24, 2017, https://www.cccassess.org.

TABLE 3. Students first enrolled in 2008-9 in a developmental course in English, Math, or ESL who completed a college-level course in the same discipline (percentages)

ETHNICITY/RACE	MATH	ENGLISH	ESL
Statewide Average	31%	43.4%	28.4%
	n = 170,416	n = 169,998	n = 32,188
African American	17.4	28.4	26.3
American Indian	25.1	32.1	19.6
Asian American	44.0	59.3	36.5
Filipino	37.9	53.3	31.2
Latino	29.4	40.2	19.5
Pacific Islander	26.7	39.1	24.0
White	35.2	48.3	31.3

Source: *California Statewide Student Success Scorecard*, 2015. Students were tracked for the six years between 2008-9 and 2013-14.

example, in math, only 29.2% of Latinos ended up completing a college-level course in the same discipline (Table 3). And only 40.2% of Latinos complete a college-level English class in six years. The data is even more challenging for ESL students, with 19.5% of Latino ESL students making it through to college-level courses. These data suggest the need for concentrated efforts for students that begin college in developmental education classes, because this track has low "transition-out" rates and ultimately lengthens the time to degree for Latinos and all other students starting college through this pathway.

As noted in previous research on persistence rates, Latinos have relatively high persistence rates, often enrolling for three consecutive terms. For example, Table 4 shows the overall persistence rate for Latinos from 2008-09 through 2013-14 to be 70.4%. The rates for African Americans and Native American students were slightly above 67%. However, persistence for Latinos and their underrepresented peers, as measured by three consecutive terms, does not necessarily guarantee two-year degree completion or transfer, as seen in the low six-year rates in Table 6.[22]

Another measure of student success for California community colleges is the 30-unit rate on the Student Success Scorecard. As with the persistence rate, 63.4% of Latinos earn 30 units or more. The instances of a Persistence attainment and the earning of 30 units appear to be far greater than the

---

22. F. Contreras and G. Contreras, 2015.

TABLE 4. Overall Persistence Rates: Percentage of degree or transfer-seeking students starting in 2008-09, tracked for 6 years through 2013-14, and who were enrolled in the first three consecutive terms

ETHNICITY/RACE	PERSISTENCE
Statewide Average	71.7 (n=209,719)
African American	67.5
American Indian	67.2
Asian American	75.4
Filipino	75.0
Latino	70.4
Pacific Islander	68.6
White	72.9
Unknown	5.0%

Source: *California Statewide Student Success Scorecard,* 2015.

actual completion rates we see after six, eight, or nine years among Latino community college students.[23] That is, even though students may have relatively high Persistence rates or 30-unit rates, they never make it to either degree completion or transfer in a six-year period. Thus, the predictive nature of these momentum points is likely not as accurate as it once was for community college students. These data suggest that these assessment measures may not be the best approach for understanding students' progress or their pathways toward completion.

Since the persistence and 30-unit rates are relatively high among Latinos, the question then becomes this one: are they appropriate and accurate predictors of Latino success and completion, given that completion rates do not represent fruition?[24] Do they truly measure student success? We also examined the overall completion rates of Latinos in six years for cohorts beginning in the years 2004 through 2009. It is important to note that previous research has found that the six-year completion rate overall is an insufficient indicator of progress and far from a reliable measure of student success."[25] The core question is whether or not the measure of college com-

---

23. Sara Goldrick-Rab, "Challenges and Opportunities for Improving Community College Student Success," *Review of Educational Research* 80.3 (2010): 437–469. http://dx.doi.org /10.3102/0034654310370163; Clifford Adelman, 2006.

24. F. Contreras and G. Contreras, 2015.

25. Ibid.; F. Contreras et al., 2011.

TABLE 5. First-time degree, certificate and/or transfer-seeking students achieving at least 30 units between 2008-09 and 2013-14

ETHNICITY/RACE	PERSISTENCE
Statewide Average	66.5 (n=209,719)
African American	55.9
American Indian	56.6
Asian American	74.3
Filipino	70.4
Latino	63.4
Pacific Islander	62.2
White	68.9
Unknown	5.0%

Source: *California Statewide Student Success Scorecard*, 2015.

pletion rate should be linked to a six-year rate. Is it an accurate portrayal of college success today? For community colleges in particular, a six-year rate that accounts for transfer and completion is three times the length described in their long-held mission and their identity as two-year colleges. Over time, the function of the two-year colleges has moved far from the aspiration of transferring or completing a community college degree in the span of two years.

The overall completion rates for Latino students across the five cohorts examined for 2004 to 2009 were less than 40% across all years. The same held true for African American students' completion rates. In fact, the highest six-year completion rates occurred for Asian American students (approximately 65% across all years) and white students (between 51% and 54%).

For those students who enter the community college prepared, as indicated by their passing the entrance level exams in English and math, the six-year completion rates are far higher than that of students needing developmental education. However, it is important to note that this group represents a very small proportion of students. Only 25% of all full-time students across all groups in 2008-09 fell into this Prepared category. And only 5% of all Latino students enrolled full time in 2008-09 fell into that category."

Many scholars have argued that developmental education is one of the greatest challenges facing community college students and institutions

TABLE 6. Overall completion rates of students in 6 years, cohorts 2004-2009

COMPLETION PREPARED	2004-2005		2005-2006		2006-2007		2007-2008		2008-2009	
	COHORT SIZE	COHORT RATE	COHORT SIZE	COHORT RATE	COHORT SIZE	COHORT RATE	COHORT SIZE	COHORT RATE	COHORT SIZE	COHORT RATE
All	161,650	48.1%	169,531	49.0%	179,423	49.2%	194,377	48.2%	209,719	46.8%
Female	88,740	48.7%	91,299	49.9%	95,482	50.1%	102,565	49.3%	109,122	48.1%
Male	71,310	47.4%	76,221	47.7%	82,395	48.1%	90,072	47.0%	97,750	45.3%
< 20 years old	126,026	51.4%	136,452	52.0%	146,757	52.0%	158,628	51.0%	169,494	49.9%
20 to 24 years old	16,100	38.7%	15,474	39.3%	15,415	38.9%	17,160	37.3%	19,058	35.0%
25 to 39 years old	13,068	34.8%	11,617	34.3%	11,551	35.2%	12,271	35.2%	13,634	33.2%
40+ years old	6,350	33.5%	5,889	33.4%	5,657	33.6%	6,282	34.0%	7,489	31.9%
African American	11,834	37.4%	12,543	38.3%	13,075	39.1%	14,628	37.7%	15,523	36.8%
American Indian/Alaska Native	1,362	37.1%	1,449	39.7%	1,579	38.6%	1,674	37.8%	1,803	34.1%
Asian	19,013	65.5%	20,653	66.4%	21,753	66.7%	22,465	65.8%	22,120	64.8%
Filipino	7,100	51.7%	6,961	51.3%	7,318	50.7%	7,557	51.3%	7,947	50.9%
Latino	49,803	37.7%	53,383	38.6%	57,364	39.6%	64,013	39.2%	70,998	38.4%
Pacific Islander	1,423	43.4%	1,570	43.5%	1,710	41.6%	2,038	42.8%	2,118	41.0%
White	57,440	52.7%	58,360	53.7%	61,168	53.5%	64,806	52.6%	67,119	51.1%

Source: *California Statewide Student Success Scorecard*, 2015.

alike.[26] For students who enter community college on this path, the road automatically becomes longer with respect to time-to-degree. This road also is costly, given the opportunity cost these students face for not being able to work full time and the years it takes to transfer and complete a degree. In addition, Latino students still lag behind their white and Asian American peers with respect to academic preparation for college coursework in general. Table 7 shows data for the students classified as Prepared. Less than 65% of Latino students who were classified as Prepared completed or transferred from community college, compared to rates of greater than 80% for Asian Americans and approximately 70% for whites in the same classification. The cohort data convey that even for those Latino students considered "prepared," college completion is uncertain.

It is not surprising then, given the lower overall rates of completion even among those who passed entrance exams, to see extremely low completion rates among students starting at the developmental education level (Table 8). Such students are more likely to drop out of college, given the additional time it takes to persist through developmental course sequences. For example, a study that examined 42 HSIs in southern California found that in select case sites only 4 out of 100 students who started in developmental math went on to college-level math and only 25 of 100 students who began in English made it into college English.[27] These data convey the tremendous drop-off among students who enter community colleges in developmental education. Few will ever make it beyond these courses.

The cohort completion rates for Latino students and for all ethnic groups (except Asians) are less than 50%. For Latino students, the completion rates across all of the years examined is less than 35%. Having slightly over one-third of students complete the two-year degree in a system that is largely Hispanic-serving conveys the need for systemic reform.

These data are devastating for a state that is one of the largest economies in the United States. The community college sector is a critical component of the college completion agenda for the state, given its great student diversity and the opportunity it offers for raising the capital of entire communities through stronger pathways to the four-year degree and beyond for Latino students.

---

26. Gloria Crisp and Chryssa Delgado, "The Impact of Developmental Education on Community College Persistence," *Community College Review* 42.2 (2014): 99–117; Thomas Bailey, "Rethinking the Role and Function of Developmental Education in Community College," *New Directions for Community Colleges* 145 (2009): 11–30; F. Contreras and G. Contreras, 2015.

27. Frances Contreras and Gilbert J. Contreras, presentation at the American Association of Hispanics in Higher Education, Los Angeles, March 8, 2014.

TABLE 7. Completion rates of students prepared for college in 6 years, cohorts 2004-2009

COMPLETION PREPARED	2004-2005		2005-2006		2006-2007		2007-2008		2008-2009	
	COHORT SIZE	COHORT RATE	COHORT SIZE	COHORT RATE	COHORT SIZE	COHORT RATE	COHORT SIZE	COHORT RATE	COHORT SIZE	COHORT RATE
All	42,866	69.4%	44,875	70.8%	47,682	71.3%	49,614	70.4%	52,331	69.7%
Female	21,465	72.3%	22,546	73.5%	23,878	73.9%	24,442	73.4%	25,296	72.8%
Male	20,953	66.4%	21,652	68.0%	23,321	68.6%	24,704	67.4%	26,212	66.7%
< 20 years old	36,487	71.9%	38,950	72.9%	41,940	73.2%	43,538	72.4%	45,898	71.9%
20 to 24 years old	3,338	59.9%	3,245	61.4%	3,152	61.9%	3,362	60.3%	3,511	58.5%
25 to 39 years old	2,085	51.5%	1,810	54.9%	1,796	53.9%	1,848	52.2%	1,865	49.4%
40+ years old	937	47.0%	847	44.6%	777	44.9%	858	44.3%	1,042	45.0%
African American	1,661	63.2%	1,608	66.2%	1,700	65.8%	1,856	65.2%	1,998	63.6%
American Indian/ Alaska Native	289	56.7%	330	60.6%	375	61.1%	334	61.7%	378	57.9%
Asian	6,620	80.2%	7,242	82.1%	7,894	82.0%	8,060	80.9%	7,857	81.5%
Filipino	1,869	72.3%	1,864	72.3%	1,926	71.7%	1,991	71.2%	2,119	72.3%
Latino	7,666	61.5%	8,247	63.3%	9,010	65.0%	9,736	63.7%	10,442	62.7%
Pacific Islander	330	61.8%	361	63.4%	387	58.7%	415	64.3%	432	62.3%
White	20,069	68.8%	20,603	70.2%	21,544	70.5%	22,013	69.9%	22,867	69.1%

Source: *California Statewide Student Success Scorecard*, 2015.

TABLE 8. Completion rates of students starting in developmental education, over 6 years

COMPLETION PREPARED	2004-2005		2005-2006		2006-2007		2007-2008		2008-2009	
	COHORT SIZE	COHORT RATE	COHORT SIZE	COHORT RATE	COHORT SIZE	COHORT RATE	COHORT SIZE	COHORT RATE	COHORT SIZE	COHORT RATE
All	118,784	40.4%	124,656	41.1%	131,741	41.2%	144,763	40.6%	157,388	39.2%
Female	67,275	41.2%	68,753	42.1%	71,604	42.1%	78,123	41.8%	83,826	40.7%
Male	50,357	39.4%	54,569	39.7%	59,074	40.1%	65,368	39.4%	71,538	37.5%
< 20 years old	89,539	43.1%	97,502	43.6%	104,817	43.5%	115,090	42.9%	123,596	41.8%
20 to 24 years old	12,762	33.2%	12,229	33.5%	12,263	33.0%	13,798	31.8%	15,547	29.7%
25 to 39 years old	10,983	31.6%	9,807	30.4%	9,755	31.8%	10,423	32.2%	11,769	30.6%
40+ years old	5,413	31.2%	5,042	31.5%	4,880	31.7%	5,424	32.3%	6,447	29.8%
African American	10,173	33.2%	10,935	34.2%	11,375	35.1%	12,772	33.7%	13,525	32.9%
American Indian/Alaska Native	1,073	31.8%	1,119	33.5%	1,204	31.6%	1,340	31.8%	1,425	27.7%
Asian	12,393	57.6%	13,411	58.0%	13,859	57.9%	14,405	57.3%	14,263	55.6%
Filipino	5,231	44.4%	5,097	43.7%	5,392	43.2%	5,566	44.2%	5,828	43.1%
Latino	42,137	33.3%	45,136	34.1%	48,354	34.9%	54,277	34.8%	60,556	34.2%
Pacific Islander	1,093	37.9%	1,209	37.6%	1,323	36.6%	1,623	37.3%	1,686	35.5%
White	37,371	44.0%	37,757	44.7%	39,624	44.2%	42,793	43.7%	44,252	41.8%

Source: *California Statewide Student Success Scorecard*, 2015.

SUMMARY

The data on Latino college success and completion in California's community colleges convey a story that requires greater attention and targeted investment, if the infrastructure within this sector is to address the academic needs of its student population. The cohort analysis shows high developmental education enrollment rates, and low completion rates, for this population in particular. The data further show that although Persistence and 30-unit rates may be relatively high for Latinos and underrepresented students, this marker of success does not translate into students' eventual college completion or transfer. This suggests that a large proportion of full time students drop out beyond the third year, despite the fact that they have been enrolled on a full-time basis and have met the traditional markers of momentum and academic success.

This analysis calls into question the use of such markers of student success and outcomes in the California community colleges, given the demonstrably low completion rates of the full-time students in this analysis. Additional markers of student success might include grade-point average, transitioning more quickly out of developmental education tracks, and the two, three, and four-year transfer/completion rates. It is important to know how many students are transferring within a shorter time frame and the profiles of these students. This cohort analysis does not consider the part-time student story, but it is important to do so. Given that more than half of California's community college students attend part-time, greater attention to their success and progress is a necessary part of the student experience.

The California Community Colleges represent a large system charged with the mission of educating students from a broad range of academic, financial, ethnic, and personal backgrounds. While it is important to celebrate these strengths, it is equally important to critically engage Latino-serving postsecondary systems, to better meet the needs of their largest base of students. The Hispanic Serving Community College system in California has the opportunity to transform the next generation of Latino students and communities. This analysis shows the opportunity that exists for critical assessment, targeted reform, and investment to better address the needs of Latino and underrepresented community college students, and create an environment where aspirations are realized and come to fruition.

REFERENCES

Adelman, C. 2006. "The Toolbox Revisited: Paths to Degree Completion from High School through College." Washington, D.C.: U.S. Department of Education.

Belfield, Clive, and Peter Crosta. 2012. "Predicting Success in College: The Importance of Placement Tests and High School Transcripts." Working Paper No. 42. New York: Community College Research Center at Teachers College, Columbia University.

Contreras, Frances. 2011. *Achieving Equity for Latino Students*. New York: Teachers College Press.

Contreras, Frances. 2012. "First-Generation College Students." In *Encyclopedia of Diversity in Education*, edited by J. Banks, 911–916. Thousand Oaks, CA: Sage Publications, Inc., doi: http://dx.doi.org/10.4135/9781452218533.n290

Contreras, Frances, and Gilbert Contreras. 2015. "Raising the Bar Among Hispanic Serving Institutions." *Journal of Hispanics in Higher Education* 14:2, 151–170.

Contreras, Frances, Lindsay Malcom, and Estela Mara Bensimon. 2008. "Hispanic-Serving Institutions: Closeted Identity and the Production of Equitable Outcomes for Latino/a Students." In *Understanding Minority Serving Institutions*, edited by M. Gasman, B. Baez, and C. S. V. Turner, 71–90. Albany: SUNY Press.

Crisp, Gloria. 2014. "Understanding the Racial Transfer Gap: Modeling Underrepresented Minority and Nonminority Students' Pathways from Two to Four Year Institutions. *Review of Higher Education* 37:3, 291–320, doi: 10.1353 /Rhe.2014.0017.

Crisp, Gloria, and Amaury Nora. 2010. "Hispanic Student Success: Factors Influencing the Persistence and Transfer Decisions of Latino Community College Students Enrolled in Developmental Education." *Research in Higher Education* 51, 175–194.

Crisp, Gloria, Amaury Nora, and A. Taggart. 2009. "Student Characteristics, Pre-College, College, and Environmental Factors As Predictors of Majoring in and Earning a STEM Degree: An Analysis of Students Attending a Hispanic Serving Institution." *American Educational Research Journal* 46, 924–942.

Dougherty, Kevin and Barbara Towsend. 2006. "Community College Missions: A Theoretical and Historical Perspective." *New Directions for Community Colleges* 126, 136.

Flores, Stella, and Timothy Drake. 2014. "Does English Language Learner Identification Predict College Remediation Designation? A Comparison with Non-ELL Peers by Race and Ethnicity and Time in Program." *Review of Higher Education* 38, 1–36.

Flores, Stella, Catherine Horn, and Gloria Crisp. 2006. "Community Colleges, Public Policy, and Latino Student Opportunity." *New Directions for Community Colleges* 133:2, 71–80.

Gándara, Patricia, and Frances Contreras, *The Latino Education Crisis*. Cambridge: Harvard University Press, 2009.

Hagedorn, Linda Sera, and Rita Cepeda. 2004. "Serving Los Angeles: Urban Community Colleges and Educational Success among Latino Students." *Community College Journal of Research and Practice* 28, 199–211.

Melguizo, Tatiana, Johannes Bos, and George Prather. 2011. "Is Developmental Education Helping Community College Students Persist? A Critical Review of the Literature." *American Behavioral Scientist* 55, 173–184.

Nora, Amaury, and Gloria Crisp. 2012. *Future Research on Hispanic Students: What Have We Yet to Learn? And What New and Diverse Perspectives Are Needed to Examine Latino Success in Higher Education?* White paper prepared for the Hispanic Association of Colleges and Universities (HACU).

Núñez, A-M., P. J. Sparks, and E. A. Hernández. 2011. "Latino Access to Community Colleges and Hispanic-Serving Institutions: A National Study." *Journal of Hispanic Higher Education* 10, 18–40.

Rendón, Laura, and Amaury Nora. 1997. *Student Academic Progress: Key Trends.* Report prepared for the National Center for Urban Partnerships. New York: Ford Foundation.

Reyes, Nicole, and Amaury Nora." 2012. *A Review of the Literature of Latino First-Generation Students.* White paper prepared for HACU.

Rodriguez, O., M. Cuellar Mejia, and H. Johnson. 2016. *Determining College Readiness in California's Community Colleges.* San Francisco, CA: The Public Policy Institute of California.

Latina/o Students Navigating the Labyrinth

PERSISTENCE IN COMMUNITY COLLEGE DEVELOPMENTAL EDUCATION

Nancy Acevedo-Gil

A large percentage of Latina/o students who enroll in postsecondary education begin at the community college. Unfortunately, high enrollments in developmental education courses hinder college completion rates. Given that California serves 25 percent of all community college students in the United States (Bradley 2011), and 42 percent of California community college students identify as Latina/o, the author presents a case study on the condition of Latinas/os in California community college developmental education courses. In particular, the article examines the patterns of Latina/o enrollment and persistence rates in developmental education and the pedagogical practices that they encounter in their coursework. The article begins with an overview of developmental education at the national level, followed by quantitative and qualitative findings. Quantitative data comes from the California Community College Chancellor's Office DataMart and qualitative data from the University of California All Campus Consortium on Research for Diversity (UC/ACCORD) Pathways to Postsecondary Success study (see: Solórzano, Datnow, Park, and Watford 2013). Based on previous literature and the data, the author concludes by offering recommendations for community college policies and practices to foster the academic success of Latina/o students in developmental education.

Nationwide, more than half of first-time Latina/o college students who enter the public higher education sector begin at the community college, also known as a two-year college (American Association of Community Colleges 2015). With 114 colleges, California maintains the largest community college system in the nation (Reed 2008). In 2014-15, Latinas/os represented 42 percent of students enrolled in the California Community College (CCC) system (Chancellor's Office undated-a). Latinas/os represent

179

53 percent of K-12 students (California Department of Education 2013), and of those who pursue a postsecondary education, 80 percent choose a community college (Moore and Shulock 2010). Thus, the representation of Latinas/os in two-year colleges will likely continue to increase. Therefore, California community colleges serve as an essential starting point to examine the experiences of Latinas/os who are pursuing college degrees. This article focuses on developmental education because 70 percent of students entering the CCC system require at least one developmental education course (Chancellor's Office 2014), compared with the national average of 60 percent (NCPPHE and SREB 2010).

Previous studies find that 40 to 70 percent of Latina/o community college students aspire to transfer to a four-year college (Arbona and Nora 2007; Crisp and Núñez 2011; Gándara, Alvarado, Driscoll, and Orfield 2012). Unfortunately, the same studies find that only 5 to 10 percent of Latinas/os will transfer to a four-year college within six years. Thus, transfer is a critical leakage point in the Latina/o baccalaureate educational pipeline (Solórzano, Villalpando, and Oseguera 2005). As indicated in previous research, few Latinas/os complete a college degree, or the requirements to transfer, due in large part to their participation rates in developmental education (Acevedo-Gil, Santos, and Solórzano 2014). Unfortunately, the majority of studies that address student pathways in developmental education do not focus on Latina/o students. This article provides an overview of the challenges and strengths within developmental education, with an emphasis on the experiences of Latinas/os.

DEVELOPMENTAL EDUCATION

Developmental education is also identified as remedial education, basic skills education, compensatory education, and pre-college coursework (Arendale 2007; Grubb and Grabiner 2013). Although developmental education referral and enrollment policies vary by state, a student is generally required to enroll based on assessment of his or her preparation to pass college-level courses. Developmental education courses include English writing and reading, English as a second language, and math, often with reading and writing integrated into one class (Doran 2015).

New applicants to CCC are required to take a standardized multiple-choice math, English, and reading placement exam to measure academic competencies. Those who test below college-level math or English must enroll in developmental courses to increase academic skill sets. Currently, students can place anywhere from college level to four levels below college level (Chancellor's Office undated). If students place below college level, they must complete the required preparation courses before enrolling in college-level and/or transfer-level coursework.

High-Stakes Placement Exams

High-stakes standardized exams are customary to measure college readiness and to determine whether a student should take developmental coursework. However, states take varied positions on whether a student should take the test. On the one hand, Texas requires that all students take the same assessment before enrolling in a public college, as part of the Texas Success Initiative. On the other hand, Florida legislators have made the exam and developmental education optional through the state's Senate Bill 1720. Unfortunately, the majority of students who take placement tests do not prepare for the exam (Fay, Bickerstaff, and Hodara 2013; Venezia, Bracco, and Nodine 2010), and college websites provide only vague information (Flores 2015).

Regardless, studies find that placement exams do not measure college readiness accurately (Belfield and Crosta 2012; Burdman 2012; Grubb and Gabriner 2013). In particular, Conley (2007; 2012) contends that assessment tests do not measure all four college-ready measures of contextual skills and awareness, academic behaviors, key content, and key cognitive strategies. Furthermore, researchers argue that the exams do not measure important psychosocial and non-cognitive factors that can identify and measure the behaviors that shape students' abilities to learn, academic persistence, and motivation (Farrington et al. 2012). While exams are not diagnostic and do not determine academic needs, they do allow for college administration systems to work more efficiently (ACT 2006; James 2007; K. L. Hughes and Scott-Clayton 2011). For prospective students, the tests often serve as deterrents to college enrollment and persistence. For example, almost two thirds of students assessed for and assigned to developmental education do not enroll in developmental coursework (Bailey et al. 2010). In addition, placement in developmental education can decrease students' academic confidence (Bickerstaff, Barragán, and Rucks-Ahidiana 2012).

Despite the downfalls of relying on assessments to place students into developmental education courses, California's community colleges relied heavily on that approach: in 2010, the system spent 1.8 billion dollars on placement tests (Chancellor's Office 2011). Although the verdict for *Romero-Frias et al. v. Mertes et al.* (1988) resulted in students being able to use multiple measures to assess math and English skill sets, studies find that placement test scores are used most often across the CCC system (Bracco, et al. 2014; Willett & Karandjeff 2014). Furthermore, multiple measures allocate the largest weight on placement test scores, which reduces the influence of high school courses (Bracco, et al. 2014). Nevertheless, research supports the argument that high school coursework and non-cognitive variables can increase the accuracy of placement decisions (Willett and Karandjeff 2014). To address concerns, California has taken steps to improve placement practices by developing the California Common Assessment Initiative, where students enrolling in CCC would take the same placement test, and the Multiple Measures Assessment Project (MMAP), which would facilitate the process of using measures other than placement test scores.

Pedagogical and Curricular Approaches in Developmental Education

In the various studies of developmental education, there is no single consensus about how to increase student success rates. What is clear, however, is the need to revamp pedagogical practices and curriculum. Pedagogical and curricular practices are important, given that classroom learning environments and instructor pedagogies influence student understandings of the learning process (Bickerstaff et al. 2012; Cox 2009). Furthermore, if an instructor recognizes learning capabilities and fosters a student's academic self-confidence, there is a positive influence on academic effort and achievement (Dweck 2006).

A primary concern with teaching in developmental education is the use of remedial pedagogy, defined as an ineffective approach that emphasizes the correct answer through a drill-and-practice approach (Grubb and Gabriner 2013). Remedial pedagogy is decontextualized, does not emphasize student interactions, and leads to student disengagement (Grubb and Gabriner 2013). Moreover, developmental education instructors in community colleges often do not have the institutional resources, time, and/or professional development to implement varied and engaging teaching approaches (Gerstein 2009; Grubb 1999). Contreras and Contreras (2015) find that community college leaders and instructors often perceive developmental education courses and students as inferior. In addition, college instructors and leaders often maintain low expectations of students in developmental education courses (Contreras and Contreras 2015).

Nevertheless, various classroom interventions exist to improve outcomes in developmental education courses. Such strategies include accelerating coursework by decreasing the time spent in classes, specializing content, contextualizing course content with interdisciplinary or vocational elements, and providing additional academic support (Fong and Visher 2013). Reducing the number of required courses in a sequence helps to decrease the number of possible exit points and can increase the opportunities for completion (Adams, Miller, and Roberts 2009; Edgecombe 2011; Hern 2012; Jenkins, Speroni, Belfield, Jaggars, and Edgecombe 2010; Levin, Garcia, and Morgan 2012; Fong and Visher 2013). In addition, studies find that pedagogical interventions that both contextualize course content and center on collaborative learning improve outcomes, increase credits earned, and support course progress (Zachry Rutschow and Schneider 2011). Finally, learning communities can contextualize course material and strengthen relationships between students and faculty (Weissman, et al. 2011). In particular, students participating in learning communities tend to attempt and pass math developmental education courses at higher rates than those not in learning communities (Weissman, et al. 2011). Thus, despite the widespread implementation of remedial pedagogy, various strategies exist to improve student outcomes within developmental education.

EXPERIENCES OF LATINAS/OS IN DEVELOPMENTAL EDUCATION CLASSROOMS

Previous research finds that Latina/o students in community college learning environments can experience both invalidation and validation (Rendón-Linares and Muñoz 2011). When instructors maintain deficit perspectives and low expectations, students do not develop a collegiate identity and perform poorly academically (Acevedo-Gil, Santos, Alonso, and Solórzano 2015; Howard 2003; Steele and Aronson 1995). In addition, invalidating and sterile classrooms do not support the academic success of Latinas/os, low-income, and first-generation students (Belenky, Clinchy, Goldberger, and Tarule 1986; Rendón 1994; Terenzini et al. 1994). When individuals are uncertain about belonging in college, student engagement and academic performance in developmental math courses suffer (Yeager, Muhich, and Gray 2011).

Students are more likely to learn in classroom environments that are validating, which can include connecting the curriculum to student experiences and culture and viewing students from a strength-based approach (Acevedo-Gil, Santos, Alonso, and Solórzano 2015; Cazden 2002; Gonzalez and Moll 2002; Grubb, Lara, and Valdez 2002; Pradl 2002). Using interview data, researchers find that instructors and institutional agents can provide academic validation by emphasizing high expectations, focusing on social identities, and improving academic skills (Acevedo-Gil, Santos, Alonso, and Solórzano 2015). In short, academic validation can support the completion of both math and English developmental education courses. Doran (2015) finds that when instructors are mandated by state policies to revise developmental English education courses, the effort can lead to incorporating culturally relevant pedagogies if faculty understand student needs. As opposed to remedial pedagogy, the culturally relevant approach fosters student success through students reading Latina/o authors and writing about issues pertinent to their communities (Doran 2015). Although limited, the available research establishes a need to move away from a deficit remedial pedagogy with low expectations and toward a culturally relevant caring pedagogy.

TRAJECTORIES OF LATINAS/OS IN DEVELOPMENTAL EDUCATION

If developmental education courses functioned as intended, students would progress through them and move on to college-level and transfer-level coursework. Unfortunately, the majority of Latina/o students do not progress through the developmental education course sequence in a timely manner (Acevedo-Gil et al. 2014), which is also in line with all other students who enroll in low levels of developmental education (Bailey 2009; Hern 2012). Because students typically do not receive credits for developmental courses, the process increases time-to-degree and can affect financial aid awards (Burdman 2012).

Figure 1 reveals that of the 40,216 Latinas/os enrolled in developmental English courses in Fall 2009, approximately 36 percent passed transfer-level English within a four-year period (Acevedo-Gil et al. 2014). The majority of Latinas/os (51 percent) enrolled at one level below transfer-level English (Intermediate Reading and Composition), and about half passed transfer-level English. Some 32 percent placed two levels below transfer-level English (Foundations in Reading and Composition), and about one-third of that group completed the course sequence. Evident in Figure 1 is that the lower the level at which a student initially enrolls, the less likely it is that the student will complete a transfer-level English course.

However, students struggle more with math, in which initial placement also influences likelihood of success. As indicated by Figure 2, approximately 17 percent of the 54,384 Latina/o students who enrolled in developmental math during Fall 2009 completed a transfer-level math

FIGURE 1. Completion of a transfer-level course for Latina/o students initially enrolling in developmental English (Fall 2009 to Spring 2013)

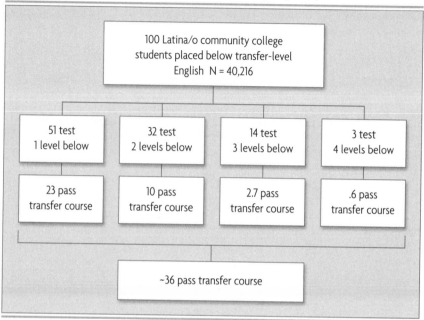

Source: Adapted from Acevedo-Gil, Santos, and Solórzano 2014.

course within four years. The majority of students began two levels below transfer-level math (Elementary Algebra); the next largest group enrolled at three levels below transfer-level math (Pre-Algebra). In the next sections, this article continues by examining the persistence and navigation experiences of Latinas/os as they make multiple attempts to pass each level.

METHODS AND DATA

Given the low completion rates in the transfer-math course sequence, this study aimed to challenge deficit perspectives. Using quantitative and qualitative data, the article examines the persistence rates of Latina/o students in community college developmental education and their experiences as they persisted. I defined persistence as the multiple attempts made by students to pass a course. To examine the pathways of Latinas/os in developmental math, I collected data from the Basic Skills Progress Cohort Tracking Tool (Progress Tracker) provided by the California Community College Chancellor's Office Data Mart, and I calculated developmental

FIGURE 2. Completion of a transfer-level course for Latina/o students initially enrolling in developmental Math (Fall 2009 to Spring 2013)

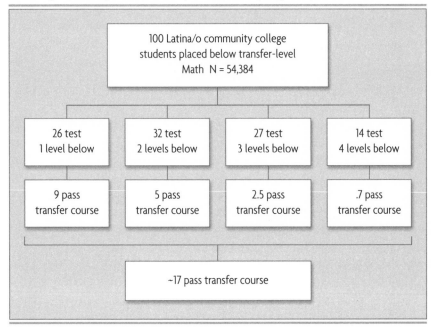

Source: Adapted from Acevedo-Gil, Santos, and Solórzano 2014.

education pipelines. The Progress Tracker follows cohorts of students in the California Community College system in four general areas: English reading, English writing, ESL, and math. The data entailed a cohort of students who first enrolled in math basic skills courses in fall 2009. I disaggregated the data by race and institution and captured student enrollment, course attempts, and course success numbers. A limitation of the data was that it did not allow for student-level analysis in order to calculate a more accurate number of multiple attempts.

According to Skinner (2012), about 85 percent of California Community College students are assessed into developmental math, with the largest group placing at two levels below transfer-level math (Elementary Algebra). Latinas/os in 2010-11 accounted for 45 percent of students enrolled in for-credit basic skills and 52 percent of students in noncredit basic skills (Skinner 2012). In this article, I focused on the progress of Latina/o students in developmental math course sequences over the four-year period from fall 2009 to spring 2013. For each level, I focused specifically on the number of Latina/o students who enrolled in a course. Then I compared the number of attempts to pass the courses with the original enrollment numbers, and the number of students who passed each level. Finally, I compared the number of students who enrolled in a course with the number who passed the previous level to examine the number of students who stopped-out.

To provide context for the quantitative descriptions, this article also used qualitative data from the UC/ACCORD Pathways to Postsecondary Success study (see: Solórzano, Datnow, Park, and Watford 2013), a five year, multi-method study funded by the Bill and Melinda Gates Foundation. I utilized qualitative data from the Los Angeles case study. Between December 2010 and September 2012, the Pathways research team conducted three waves of semi-structured interviews with 110 low-income students at three community colleges in southern California. For this article, I selected data from the 73 participants who identified as Latinas/os. I selected data identified with pre-established codes of "basic skills," "repeated course," and "failed course." I then analyzed transcripts from the first- and second-round interviews, using open, axial, and selective coding (Strauss and Corbin 1990) to understand the experiences of participants when navigating developmental education math courses after not passing a class.

FINDINGS

In this section, first I detail the developmental education quantitative pipelines, and then I provide qualitative findings that contextualize the pipelines. Regardless of the initial level of enrollment, the data revealed that students attempted to pass courses multiple times. In particular, once students reached the transfer-level math course, the number of attempts increased greatly. Each pentagon in the figures below represents one course level. I selected the figure of a pentagon to emphasize visually that the number of attempts to pass a course was much greater than the number of students who enrolled in the course, and the number of students who passed the course was smaller compared to both the number enrolled and the number of attempts. In other words, students made multiple attempts to pass each course. The dashed arrow between each figure represented the transition from one level to the next. Figure 3, Figure 4, and Figure 5 represent educational pipelines for the cohort of students who began their developmental education during fall 2009. As in previous pipeline studies (Solórzano, Villalpando, and Oseguera 2005), I reduced the number of students to 100 and calculated the numbers by adjusting the actual number of students to the 100-student figure.

Findings from Quantitative Data

Findings from quantitative data highlight the persistence of Latina/o students in developmental education. Persistence, in this case, was framed as the multiple attempts made by students to pass a course. As indicated earlier, in fall 2009, approximately 26 percent of Latina/o students (14,344) in developmental education began one level below transfer-level math; Figure 3 reflects the pathways of these students. Findings in Figure 3 depict that 100 students who began one-level below transfer-level math made 148 attempts to pass the course and 68 students passed the course. Nevertheless, in alignment with the literature noted earlier, the transition from one level to the next served as an exit point, and, of the 68 who passed the initial course, 46 students enrolled in the transfer-level course. Among the 46 students, there were 98 attempts to pass the course, and 34 students passed the transfer-level course within four years.

Moreover, 32 percent of Latina/o students in developmental math began two levels below transfer-level math. Figure 4 represents the trajectories of 17,603 Latinas/os who initially enrolled in developmental education courses that were two levels below transfer math. As indicated by Figure 4, the trend of students enrolling in courses multiple times in order to pass continued, as did the stopping-out of students when transitioning between course levels. Of the 100 students who enrolled two levels below transfer math, there were 140 attempts to pass the course and 63 students passed.

FIGURE 3. Educational pipeline for Latina/o students initially enrolling one course below transfer-level Math (Fall 2009 to Spring 2013). *n = 14,344 students*

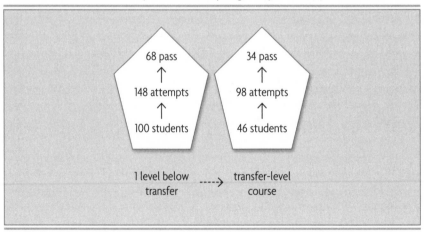

Data Source: Progress Tracker, California Community College Chancellor's Office DataMart

FIGURE 4. Educational pipeline for Latina/o students initially enrolling two courses below transfer-level Math (Fall 2009 to Spring 2013). *n = 17,603 students*

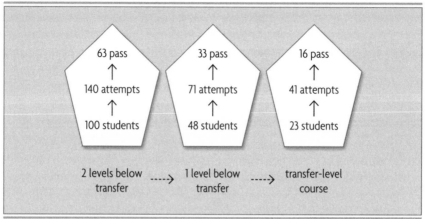

Data Source: Progress Tracker, California Community College Chancellor's Office DataMart

Of those 63 students, 48 enrolled in the next level and made 71 attempts to pass, but only 33 passed the course. Of the 33 students, 23 enrolled in transfer-level math and made 41 attempts to pass the course. After four years of enrollment, only 16 of the 100 Latina/o students completed a transfer-level math class if they placed two levels below the transfer math course. Findings in Figure 4 depict a notable increase in attempts to pass the transfer-level course in comparison to the two lower levels.

Furthermore, 27 percent of Latinas/os, or 14,658 students, began developmental math by enrolling three levels below transfer. The data revealed a reduction in passing rates for students who enrolled initially at three levels below transfer level, with only 9 percent passing the transfer course after four years. Findings in Figure 5 highlighted the multiple attempts made by students at every level. However, in this sequence students were attempting to pass a total of four courses within a four-year period, and there was a reduction in the percentage of attempts. Regardless, the number of attempts in this sequence continued to be greater in the transfer-level course, which was similar to the findings depicted in Figures 3 and 4. Although there were fewer attempts in the lowest level of math when compared to Figures 3 and 4, there were also fewer students who stopped-out between each level. In other words, upon passing a course, a larger percentage of students who began three levels below transfer math continued within the course sequence, compared with students who began one or two levels below transfer math.

FIGURE 5. Educational pipeline for Latina/o students initially enrolling three courses below transfer-level Math (Fall 2009 to Spring 2013). *n = 14,658 students*

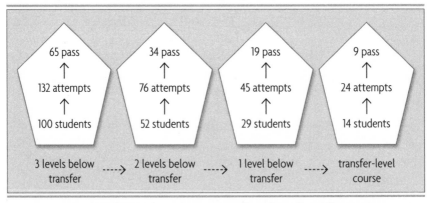

Data Source: Progress Tracker, California Community College Chancellor's Office DataMart

Finally, 14 percent of students, or 7,779, who participated in the developmental math sequence began four levels below transfer math. If these students hoped to transfer from the community college to a four-year institution, they had to take at least five math courses before being eligible to transfer. If a student were planning to transfer into a science or math major, the five courses would be only the beginning of the math courses required for the majors. Unfortunately, for students who began developmental math four levels below transfer, less than five percent passed the transfer-level course within four years. However, Figure 6 can be misleading in that students could be persisting at higher rates by attempting to pass courses but the data only included a four-year period. Data in Figure 6 revealed that larger percentages of students stopped-out when transitioning from four levels below to three levels below. Nevertheless, Figure 6 also revealed the lowest stop-out rate between the other levels, which highlights the often unacknowledged strengths of this student population. As noted in previous literature, while community college leaders and instructors may view students in developmental education as deficient, the multiple attempts evident in these pipelines demonstrated the determination and persistence present in Latina/o students who navigated developmental education. The following section presents qualitative findings to contextualize student decisions.

Findings from Qualitative Data

Qualitative data was analyzed to contextualize the quantitative persistence pipelines. Interview data complemented the quantitative findings by high-

FIGURE 6. Educational pipeline for Latina/o students initially enrolling four courses below transfer-level Math (Fall 2009 to Spring 2013). *n = 7,779 students*

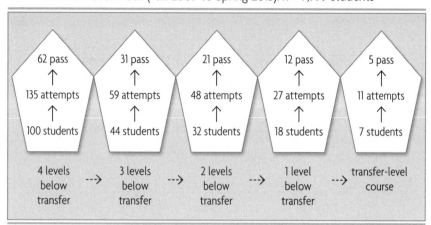

Data Source: Progress Tracker, California Community College Chancellor's Office DataMart

lighting that students enrolled in developmental courses multiple times in order to meet transfer requirements. Students revealed the intricacies involved in deciding to repeat a course after not receiving a passing grade, often due to an instructor's pedagogy. Strategies included taking the course in a different format, withdrawing from a course, and focusing solely on developmental education for one term.

For example, Natalia, a student who was majoring in radiology and aimed to transfer to California State University, Northridge, explained her ongoing struggle with passing the developmental education math course: "I'm thinking this time I'm going to get a math class that . . . I tried the big classroom twice a week, four hours: didn't work. I tried a small classroom twice a week, four hours: didn't work. So, now I'm going to get a small classroom every day for an hour." Natalia attempted to complete the same math course twice, each time choosing a different course format in hopes of fostering academic success. Her experiences highlighted the strategies of participants who made multiple attempts to pass a course because they aimed to transfer.

Similarly, Alicia explained that she had taken two levels of math courses twice; within two years, she had advanced two levels on the developmental math pipeline. Alicia stated:

> I've only taken Math 115 and Math 125 . . . I retook those classes
> . . . I knew the material. I guess for me, it's like I have to take the
> class at least twice in order to understand it. So, it's like if
> I don't get it the first time, I'll get it the second time.

Alicia explained that final exam scores lowered her grade and she would repeat the math courses in order to earn a passing grade. Student participants discussed having to repeat developmental math courses, which increased their time-to-degree completion.

However, based on college policies, students had three opportunities to pass a developmental education course. A student who did not pass the class after three attempts would have to enroll in the course at another community college. For example, Sandra aspired to earn her associate's degree and transfer to a public four-year college. She explained her struggle and her persistence in attempting to pass a developmental math course:

> I tried math. I can't find the professor that I can—I don't know—that I can ask for help. They always expect us to know and learn, and I'm very hardheaded when it comes to math. I hate math, but I'm hoping that I can pass this summer because it would be my second time taking it, and I can't take it any more than three [times] anyway. So, there's no "ifs" or "buts"—I have to pass.

Sandra's experiences exemplified that limiting the number of attempts to pass a course added pressure. Under such circumstances, students entered the class knowing that it would be the final opportunity to pass the course. Having already failed the course twice was an added stigma that supported low academic self-perceptions through stereotype threat (Steele 1995) and invalidation (Rendón 2002).

Other participants explained that they would plan to repeat a course, even if they had not yet received a failing grade. For instance, Javonne explained her decision to withdraw from and repeat a course. She recalled:

> (The instructor) would take off, I think, two points if we didn't write down the fact that we did something . . . I think (I got) a C on the first exam just for little things that he was nitpicking about, and in class . . . it didn't really click, so I thought it'd be better to get a W than to fall behind in the class . . . which is fine. I'm planning to retake that one in the summer, it would just be my only class and I can focus on it.

Javonne's experience reinforced the importance of instructor pedagogy and curricular decisions. Similar to Sandra, Javonne encountered an instructor who she was not able to ask for support. Javonne's experiences highlighted various strategies utilized by students. First, students chose to drop courses after the college deadline and accepted the "Withdraw" notation on their transcript. Second, students chose to retake developmental education courses with different instructors in hopes of finding one that had strong pedagogy. Finally, students chose to isolate the course that they struggled with and enrolled only in the developmental education course during a term, the goal being to focus all learning efforts on the course.

While Javonne's strategies exemplified the experiences of other participants, if students did not drop the course, they risked receiving a failing grade. For instance, Sonia noted:

> I'm going to retake it, just because I don't like the fact that I got a D . . . I didn't learn anything in her class . . . I think she should have done more exercises. Instead of writing everything down, do exercises so we could know what to do . . . It's kind of hard to teach that math, because it's mainly like theorems and postulates that you have to learn.

Sonia's experiences reinforced the importance of an instructor's pedagogy and its influence on the learning process, which was a theme present in the experiences of all participants who were developmental education students. Regardless of whether a student chose to withdraw from the course or receive a failing grade, repeating a course increased the time-to-degree. Nevertheless, findings from both the quantitative and qualitative data highlighted the continued attempts to pass developmental education courses and exemplified the persistence efforts of Latina/o students.

SUMMARY OF FINDINGS AND RECOMMENDED ACTIONS

The findings reveal that Latina/o students persist in developmental education by attempting multiple times to pass courses and that instructor pedagogies are important for student success. Although community college leaders often perceive developmental education students from a deficit perspective (Contreras and Contreras 2015), the findings in this article reinforce the notion that instructors and administrators should emphasize the strengths of Latina/o students. Thus, while numerous students do not pass developmental education courses successfully in the first attempt, educators can focus on the persistence and commitment to complete the courses.

Moreover, pedagogy and curriculum matter in developmental education. As indicated in previous work, a critical race-validating pedagogy, or CRVP (Acevedo-Gil, et al. 2015), supports the completion of developmental education courses. CRVP aims for Latinas/os to reflect on social identities within the context of developmental education and cultivate academic skills. CRVP within developmental education entails fostering a learning environment wherein students: (a) reflect on previous moments of academic invalidation, (b) believe in their academic abilities to complete transfer-level courses, (c) view social identities as sources of strength that can support the completion of transfer-level math and English, and (d) experience culturally relevant curriculum and socially just courses. By implementing a contextualized CRVP, community college leaders can increase Latina/o student completion rates in developmental education course sequences.

Given the findings of this article and considering previous literature, I propose five key recommendations to increase the retention and persistence rates of Latina/o students in developmental education courses.

1. As indicated earlier, reducing the length and number of courses can improve the time-to-degree completion rates. Findings revealed that students repeated the same course numerous times and/or stopped-out of the developmental education sequence. Therefore, the first recommendation is for college leaders to decrease the number of developmental courses.

2. Given that student participants persisted by attempting to pass a course multiple times, I recommend that institutional leaders and counselors provide additional support systems for students who fail a developmental education course. For instance, college leaders should avoid policies that limit the number of times a student can attempt to pass and instead support student success by tracking students who fail a developmental math or English course. College leaders can foster success by reaching out and providing institutionalized supports to students who do not pass a class, such as a learning community tailored to students who did not passed the course in the previous term. College leaders and instructors must reframe deficit perspectives, which suggest that a student who fails a developmental education course does not deserve to re-enroll, and instead tap into the student's commitment to persist and complete developmental education.

3. As indicated in this article, developmental math is a particular leakage point in the educational pipeline. Given the various approaches to teaching the same mathematical concept, seeking support outside of the classroom often resulted in more questions from the student. Therefore, I recommend that community college leaders allocate funds to provide in-class tutors in developmental education math courses. Having a tutor in the class could facilitate easier access to problem-solving information and allow students to ask someone other than the instructor, if the instructor is not approachable.

4. A concern revealed by the qualitative data was the need to improve classroom pedagogy. College leaders must facilitate engagement in culturally relevant pedagogical practices. Various studies document effective

culturally relevant practices in minority-serving institutions (Conrad and Gasman 2015) and for Latina/o students in particular (Acevedo-Gil, Santos, Alonso, and Solórzano 2015; Doran 2015). Community college leaders and instructors must learn from culturally relevant practices, such as the Puente program, and adapt such strategies to each specific learning context. To do so, English and math department chairs and faculty must be open to moving away from traditional and deficit-oriented pedagogical practices. Implementing anti-deficit and culturally relevant pedagogies can foster academic success of students.

5. Finally, I recommend that institutional leaders consider implementing a critical race-validating pedagogy (Acevedo-Gil, et al. 2015) throughout the campus. By implementing a CRVP, community college leaders will foster an institutional culture wherein all institutional agents expect and foster student success in developmental education courses, whether or not the agents themselves teach a developmental course.

CONCLUSION

The majority of Latina/o students begin postsecondary education by enrolling in developmental math and/or English courses, which points to a disjuncture between the academic preparation received in K-12 and college readiness. Until the public educational system provides equitable learning opportunities in the K-12 context, community college leaders must collaborate with K-12 leaders to bridge the academic preparation. Despite encountering ineffective and invalidating pedagogical practices, Latina/o students navigate and persist in developmental education courses. Education stakeholders must continue to address the institutional obstacles present in developmental education to eliminate a major exit point in the higher education pipeline. Given the persistence strategies revealed in this article, college leaders and instructors can focus on the strengths of Latina/o students to foster academic success within and beyond developmental education courses.

REFERENCES

Acevedo-Gil, Nancy, Ryan E. Santos, Lluliana Alonso, and Daniel G. Solórzano. 2015. "Latinas/os in Community College Developmental Education: Increasing Moments of Academic and Interpersonal Validation." *Journal of Hispanic Higher Education* 14:2, 101–127.

Acevedo-Gil, Nancy, Ryan E. Santos, and Daniel G. Solórzano. 2014. "Examining a Rupture in the Latina/o College Pipeline: Developmental Education in California

Community Colleges." *Perspectivas: Issues in Higher Education Practice and Policy* 3, 1–20. http://www.aahhe.org/_resources/pdf/perspectivas-vol3.pdf.

Adams, Peter, Sarah Gearhart, Robert Miller, and Anne Roberts. 2009. "The Accelerated Learning Program: Throwing Open the Gates." *Journal of Basic Writing* 28:2, 50–69.

Arbona, Consuelo, and Amaury Nora. 2007. "The Influence of Academic and Environmental Factors on Hispanic College Degree Attainment." *Review of Higher Education* 30:3, 247–269.

Bailey, Thomas R. 2009. "Challenge and Opportunity: Rethinking the Role and Function of Developmental Education in Community College." *New Directions for Community Colleges* 145, 11–30.

Bailey, Thomas R., and Sung-Woo Cho. 2010. "Developmental Education in Community Colleges." Columbia University Academic Commons, Community College Research Center Brief, September, 1–8. https://ccrc.tc.columbia.edu/publications/developmental-education-in-community-colleges.html.

Bailey, Thomas R., Dong Wook Jeong, and Sung-Woo Cho. 2009. "Student Progression Through Developmental Sequences in Community Colleges." Columbia University Academic Commons, Community College Research Center Brief No. 45, 1–6.

Belfield, Clive, and Peter Michael Crosta. 2012. "Predicting Success in College: The Importance of Placement Tests and High School Transcripts." Columbia University Academic Commons, Community College Research Center Working Papers, No. 42, 1–45.

Bickerstaff, Susan E., Melissa Barragán, and Zawadi Rucks-Ahidiana. 2012. " 'I Came in Unsure of Everything': Community College Students' Shifts in Confidence." Columbia University Academic Commons, Community College Research Center Working Papers, No. 48, 1–29.

Bracco, Kathy R., Mina Dadgar, Kim Austin, Becca Klarin, Marie Broek, Neal Finkelstein, Susan Mundry, and Dan Bugler. 2014. "Exploring the Use of Multiple Measures for Placement into College-Level Courses: Seeking Alternatives or Improvements to the Use of a Single Standardized Test." San Francisco, CA: WestEd. https://www.wested.org/wp-content/files_mf/1397164696product55812B.pdf

Burdman, Pamela. 2012. "Where to Begin? The Evolving Role of Placement Exams for Students Starting College." Achieving the Dream. Washington, DC: Jobs for the Future.

Bureau of Economic Analysis. 2012. *Widespread Economic Growth across States in 2011.* US Department of Commerce. http://www.bea.gov/newsreleases/regional/gdp_state/2012/pdf/gsp0612.pdf

California Community Colleges, Chancellor's Office. 2011. *CCCASSESS: Centralizing Student Assessment in the California Community Colleges.* Sacramento: California Community College Chancellor's Office.

California Community Colleges, Chancellor's Office. 2014. *Annual/Term Student Count Report.* Management Information Systems DataMart. http://datamart.cccco.edu/students/student_term_annual_count.aspx.

California Department of Education. 2013. *Statewide Enrollment by Ethnicity, 2012-13.* Sacramento: California Department of Education. http://dq.cde.ca.gov/dataquest /enrollethstate.asp?level=stateandtheyear=2013-14andcchoice=enrolleth1andp=2

Cazden, Courtney B. 2002. "A Descriptive Study of Six High School Puente Classrooms." *Educational Policy* 16:4, 496–521.

College Board. 2003. *Accuplacer Online: Technical Manual.* New York, NY: College Board.

Community College Fast Facts. 2012. Washington, DC: Association of Community Colleges. http://www.aacc.nche.edu/aboutcc/documents/factsheet2012.pdf.

Conley, David T. 2012. "A Complete Definition of College and Career Readiness." Eugene, OR: Educational Policy Improvement Center. http://www.avid.org/dl /eve_natcon/nc12_four_keys_handout2.pdf

———. 2007. *Redefining College Readiness.* Eugene, OR: Educational Policy Improvement Center.

Contreras, Frances, and Gilbert J. Contreras. 2015. "Raising the Bar for Hispanic Serving Institutions: An Analysis of College Completion and Success Rates." *Journal of Hispanic Higher Education* 14:2, 151–170.

Corbin, Juliet, and Anselm Strauss. 2014. *Basics of Qualitative Research: Techniques and Procedures for Developing Grounded Theory.* Thousand Oaks, CA: Sage Publications.

Cox, Rebecca D. 2009. *The College Fear Factor: How Students and Professors Misunderstand One Another.* Cambridge, MA: Harvard University Press.

Dweck, Carol. 2006. *Mindset: The New Psychology of Success.* New York, NY: Penguin Random House.

Doran, Erin. 2015. "What's Expected of Us As We Integrate Reading and Writing? Constructing Developmental Education at a Hispanic-Serving Community College." PhD diss., University of Texas at San Antonio.

Edgecombe, Nicole Diane. 2011. "Accelerating the Academic Achievement of Students Referred to Developmental Education." Columbia University Academic Commons, Community College Research Center Working Papers, No. 30, 1–42. http://hdl.handle.net/10022/ac:p:13142

Engstrom, Cathy, and Vincent Tinto. 2008. "Access without Support Is Not Opportunity." *Change: The Magazine of Higher Learning* 40:1, 46–50.

Farrington, Camille A., Melissa Roderick, Elaine Allensworth, Jenny Nagaoka, Tasha Seneca Keyes, David W. Johnson, and Nicole O. Beechum. 2012. *Teaching Adolescents to Become Learners: The Role of Noncognitive Factors in Shaping School Performance—A Critical Literature Review.* Chicago: Consortium on Chicago School Research.

Fay, Margaret P., Susan E. Bickerstaff, and Michelle Hodara. 2013. "Why Students Do Not Prepare for Math Placement Exams: Student Perspectives." http://academic commons.columbia.edu/catalog/ac:170472

Fong, Kelly, and Mary G. Visher. 2013. "Fast Forward: A Case Study of Two Community College Programs Designed to Accelerate Students through Developmental Math. Achieving the Dream." New York: MDRC. http://files .eric.ed.gov/fulltext/ed544248.pdf.

Gándara, Patricia, Elizabeth Alvarado, Anne Driscoll, and Gary Orfield. 2012. "Building Pathways to Transfer: Community Colleges That Break the Chain of Failure for Students of Color." Civil Rights Project. Los Angeles: University of California.

Gerstein, Amy. 2009. "Community College Faculty and Developmental Education: An Opportunity for Growth and Investment." Stanford, CA: Carnegie Foundation for the Advancement of Teaching, Problem Solution Exploration Papers, 1–34. http://archive.carnegiefoundation.org/pdfs/elibrary/community_college _faculty.pdf.

González, Norma, and Luis C. Moll. 2002. "Cruzando el puente: Building Bridges to Funds of Knowledge." Educational Policy 16:4, 623–641.

Grubb, Norton. 1999. Honored But Invisible: An Inside Look at Teaching in Community Colleges. New York, NY: Routledge.

Grubb, Norton, and Robert Gabriner. 2013. Developmental Education: Basic Skills Education in Community Colleges Inside and Outside of Classrooms. New York, NY: Routledge.

Grubb, W. Norton, Claudia M. Lara, and Susan Valdez. 2002. "Counselor, Coordinator, Monitor, Mom: The Roles of Counselors in the Puente Program." Educational Policy 16:4, 547–571.

Hern, Katie. 2012. "Increasing Community College Students' Completion: Toward an Action Agenda for Legislators, Policy Makers, and System Leaders." Presentation at the National Association of Latino Elected Officials, San Jose, California.

Hughes, Katherine L., and Judith Scott-Clayton. 2010. "Assessing Developmental Assessment in Community Colleges: A Review of the Literature." Community College Research Center, Columbia University, Working Paper No. 19.

James, Cindy L. 2007. "Accuplacer™ Online: Accurate Placement Tool for Developmental Programs?" Journal of Developmental Education 30:2, 2.

Jenkins, Davis, Cecilia Speroni, Clive Belfield, Shanna Smith Jaggars, and Nikki Edgecombe. 2010. "A Model for Accelerating Academic Success of Community College Remedial English Students: Is the Accelerated Learning Program (ALP) Effective and Affordable?" Columbia University Academic Commons, Community College Research Center, Working Paper No. 21. http://files.eric.ed.gov /fulltext/ed512398.pdf

Levin, Henry, and Emma Garcia. 2012. Cost-Effectiveness of Accelerated Study in Associate Programs (ASAP) of the City University of New York (CUNY). Center for Benefit-Cost Studies of Education. New York, NY: Columbia University Teachers College. www.cuny.edu/academics/programs/notable/asap/levin_report_web.pdf.

Moore, Colleen, and Nancy Shulock. 2010. "Divided We Fail: Improving Completion and Closing Racial Gaps in California's Community Colleges." Sacramento, CA: Institute for Higher Education Leadership and Policy.

Núñez, Anna-Marie, and Diane Elizondo. 2013. "Closing the Latino/a Transfer Gap: Creating Pathways to the Baccalaureate." *Perspectivas; Issues in Higher Education Practice and Policy* 2, 1–15.

Pradl, Gordon M. 2002. "Linking Instructional Intervention and Professional Development: Using the Ideas Behind Puente High School English to Inform Educational Policy." *Educational Policy* 16:4, 522–546.

Reed, Deborah. 2008. "California's Future Workforce: Will There Be Enough College Graduates?" San Francisco, CA: Public Policy Institute of California.

Rendón, Laura I. 1994. "Validating Culturally Diverse Students: Toward a New Model of Learning and Student Development." *Innovative Higher Education* 19:1, 33–51.

Rendón, Laura I., and Susana M. Muñoz. 2011. "Revisiting Validation Theory: Theoretical Foundations, Applications, and Extensions." *Enrollment Management Journal* 2:1, 12–33.

Rutschow, Zachry, Elizabeth Schneider, and Emily Schneider. 2011. "Unlocking the Gate: What We Know about Improving Developmental Education." New York: MDRC.

Skinner, Erik. 2012. *Basic Skills Accountability: Supplement to the ARCC Report.* Sacramento: California Community Colleges Chancellor's Office, 1–46. http://californiacommunitycolleges.cccco.edu/Portals/0/reportsTB/REPORT_BASICSKILLS_FINAL_110112.pdf

Solórzano, Daniel, Amanda Datnow, Vicki Park, and Tara Watford. 2013. "Pathways to Postsecondary Success: Maximizing Opportunities for Youth in Poverty." UC/Accord Pathways to Postsecondary Success Project, http://pathways.gseis.ucla.edu/publications/pathwaysreport.pdf.

Solórzano, Daniel, Octavio Villalpando, and Leticia Oseguera. 2005. "Educational Inequities and Latina/o Undergraduate Students in the United States: A Critical Race Analysis of Their Educational Progress." *Journal of Hispanic Higher Education* 4:3, 272–294.

Steele, Claude M., and Joshua Aronson. 1995. "Stereotype Threat and the Intellectual Test Performance of African Americans." *Journal of Personality and Social Psychology* 69:5, 797.

Terenzini, Patrick T., Laura I. Rendón, M. Lee Upcraft, Susan B. Millar, Kevin W. Allison, Patricia L. Gregg, and Romero Jalomo. 1994. "The Transition to College: Diverse Students, Diverse Stories." *Research in Higher Education* 35:1, 57–73.

Tinto, Vincent, Anne Goodsell-Love, and Pat Russo. 1994. "Building Learning Communities for New College Students: A Summary of Research Findings of the Collaborative Learning Project." Syracuse, NY: Syracuse University, National Center on Postsecondary Teaching, Learning, and Assessment.

Venezia, Andrea, Kathy Reeves Bracco, and Thad Nodine. 2010. "One Shot Deal? Students' Perceptions of Assessment and Course Placement in California's Community Colleges." San Francisco, CA: WestEd.

Visher, Mary. G., Heather Wathington, Lashawn Richburg-Hayes, and Emily Schneider. 2008. "The Learning Communities Demonstration Rationale, Sites, and Research Design." National Center for Postsecondary Research, Working Paper, 1–49.

Weissman, Evan, Kristin Butcher, Emily Schneider, Jedidiah Teres, Herbert Collado, and David Greenberg. 2011. "Learning Communities for Students in Developmental Math: Impact Studies at Queensborough and Houston Community Colleges." National Center for Postsecondary Research Brief, 1–4.

Willett, Terrence, Craig Hayward, and Eden Dahlstrom. 2008. *An Early Alert System for the Remediation Needs of Entering Community College Students: Leveraging the California Standards Test.* Report 2007036. Encinitas, CA: California Partnership for Achieving Student Success.

Yeager, D., J. Muhich, and N. Gray. 2012. "What We're Learning about Productive Persistence: Early Evidence from the Statway." Community College Research Center, Working Paper No. 48.

Un cuento de nunca acabar

EXPLORING THE TRANSFER CONDITIONS FOR LATINX TEJANX COMMUNITY COLLEGE STUDENTS IN TEXAS

José Del Real Viramontes and Luis Urrieta Jr.

As of 2012, according to the National Center for Education Statistics (NCES 2013), Latinxs[1] constituted approximately 17% of the total US population. Within the K-12 system, Latinx students represent the largest minority population in the western and southern regions of the United States, 41% and 21% respectively. In a Latinx policy and issues brief published by UCLA's Chicano Studies Research Center, Pérez Huber, Malagón, Ramírez, Camargo González, Jiménez, and Vélez (2015) revealed that out of 100 Latinx students who begin at the elementary school level, only 63 Latinas and 60 Latinos graduate from high school. The policy brief indicates that the apparent increase in overall Latinx educational attainment in the last decade may be due to a general nationwide Latinx population increase of 18 million, or 5%, inferring that the gains may be attributed to the demographic change and not necessarily to more equitable education (Pérez Huber et al. 2015).

Latinxs who do graduate from high school are less likely to start off at a four-year university, and more likely to enter higher education through the community college system (Kurlaender 2006). NCES (2013) data indicate that 46% of all Latinx students in US higher education are enrolled at a community college. NCES (2013) reports indicate that Latinxs were the second largest group enrolled in community colleges accounting for 20% of the student population. Although Latinxs were more likely to enroll in

---

1. We use Latinx and Tejanx to break down the existing gender binaries and acknowledge all intersecting identities within the Latino community. Further, we also seek to acknowledge and be inclusive of people who may identify as trans, queer, agender, non-binary, gender non-conforming, or gender fluid.

community colleges, however, Latinx transfer rates to four-year universities were disproportionately low among all transfer students (National Center for Public Policy in Higher Education 2011).

In Texas, an overall 53% of students chose community college as their entry point into higher education, according to the Texas Higher Education Coordinating Board (THECB 2013); of those, 25% eventually transferred to a four-year institution within six years (THECB 2014). A 2008 report showed that only 14.1% of all community and technical college students who were first-time entering undergraduates (FTEC) during the fall of 2008 graduated within six years (THECB 2008b). Among the Latinx student population in Texas, 63% choose community college as an entry point into higher education, a percentage higher than the national average. Unfortunately, the majority of FTEC Latinx community college students withdraw without obtaining a degree (THECB 2008a).

This article contextualizes some of the issues that affect Latinx community college students' limitations, affordances, and experiences in accessing higher education, specifically those related to transferring to four-year colleges and universities in Texas. The article is organized in three sections that specifically address the conditions supporting transferability, promising transfer models, and institution-specific efforts being made to support transfer students at six major Texas universities. The first section draws attention to Latinx students' schooling conditions at the community college level with an emphasis on Latinx student characteristics and the academic and non-academic barriers they face. The second section explores transfer models that offer the potential to improve the transferability of Latinx community college students in light of existing "transfer culture" frameworks (Handel 2012; Herrera and Jain 2013; Jain, Herrera, Bernal, and Solórzano 2011; and Pérez and Ceja 2010). The third section focuses on current transfer policy and practice efforts at six top public universities in Texas. The final section shows how the four-year universities profiled are implementing elements of the transfer culture frameworks presented in the previous section. The overall goal of this article is to draw attention to these universities' efforts to increase the access, retention, and graduation rates for Latinx community college students in Texas.

LATINX AND TEJANX COMMUNITY COLLEGE STUDENTS IN TEXAS

Discussing the school context in Texas is important as a starting point to address community college transferability for Latinx students, especially since it is founded on a socio-historical and political context of discriminatory practices that have negatively affected the Latinx Tejanx community (Valenzuela 1999). Key factors such as school and residential segregation, racially segmented labor incorporation, denial of political access, and surveillance and containment by policing forces have an enduring legacy that influences the current context of Latinx Tejanx lives in Texas. These conditions of inequality continue to deny equal educational opportunities to Latinx Tejanx students, often leading them into the community college system, rather than four-year universities. Valencia (2000) describes, for example, the widespread school failure of African American and Mexican American students in Texas public schools by citing long-standing systemic public school inequities. He goes on to show that Latinx student failure is often the result of historic school segregation and the consequent limitations in the learning opportunities afforded to African American and Mexican American students in Texas public schools.

Using data from the Austin Independent School District (AISD), Valencia (2000) shows the detrimental impact segregated schooling has on African American and Mexican American student academic achievement. He demonstrates that segregated schools produce inferior schooling and diminish academic performance, evidenced by lower scores on high-stakes standardized tests; an increase in the percentage of minority student enrollment in AISD schools correlated with an increase in the percentage of students who failed the Texas Assessment of Academic Skills (TAAS). In the same study, Valencia also found that students who attended high minority schools were more likely to be taught by noncertified teachers, who in turn were often more likely to teach in schools with lower test scores, indicating that there is a direct correlation between teacher certification and students' test performance.

Fassold (2000) also showed that exit-level testing ultimately harms African American and Latinx students, especially because they attended schools with the lowest accreditation scores. Latinx and African American students are also disproportionally tracked into lower-level math courses, which has a long lasting impact on educational access. Advanced math courses are often gatekeeping subjects (Fassold 2000, 477). Poor school quality and culturally irrelevant school curricula have a negative impact on learning opportunities and correlate to poor test performance, which is strongly associated with disparity in educational opportunity in Texas public schools (Fassold 2000). Additionally, since the implementation of the high school exit exam in 1991, 35 to 40% of African American and Latinx students do not persist through high school graduation (Haney

2000, 92). Given the sociopolitical context of education in Texas, Latinx Tejanx students, especially those of low socioeconomic backgrounds, generally have limited opportunities for positive learning, making it difficult for them to be academically prepared for enrollment at four-year colleges or universities. Coupled with dwindling funding opportunities, Latinx Tejanx students are often funneled to community college systems as their only option for entry into higher education.

Community colleges are the largest postsecondary education segment in the United States, enrolling 47% percent of the undergraduate student population (Handel and Williams 2012). Malcom (2013) describes the diversity of the student population in US community colleges; students are more likely than their university peers to be first-generation college students, low-income, and adult learners. More than 60% of Latinx students in postsecondary education begin their college careers in the community college, but fewer than 1% transfer to four-year colleges or universities (Yosso and Solórzano 2006). There are multiple factors leading to Latinx students enrolling in community colleges versus four-year universities. Nora and Rendón (1990) measured student transfer behaviors and attitudes across five categories: student background, initial commitments, social integration, academic integration, and predisposition to transfer. Their results revealed significant implications for community colleges: they emphasized that over 50% of the Latinx community college students in their study attended community college because it was affordable, close to home, offered self-improvement or enrichment courses, and allowed them to work while going to school in their hometown.

Notably, Latinx students enrolled in community colleges maintained high educational aspirations. A 2007 study by Rivas, Pérez, Álvarez, and Solórzano showed that 40% of entering Latinx community college students indicated an aspiration to transfer to a senior institution and earn a bachelor's degree. In comparing them to white (70%) and African American (68%) transfer students, Bailey, Jenkins, and Lainbach (2007) similarly noted that 79% of Latinxs aspired to transfer, earn a bachelor's degree, and pursue a graduate degree.

Latinx community college students face many barriers that interrupt, delay, or prevent them from transferring to a four-year college or university. Using 1992 data from the first-time-in-college (FTIC) cohort comprised of 51,903 students attending community colleges in Texas, Burley, Butner, and Cejda (2001) found that about two-thirds of the students who participated in the study were enrolled in developmental education courses. Results from this study showed that the drop-out/stop-out patterns experienced by FTIC students were highly associated with GPA. The best-performing students were those who did not stop out, but instead enrolled for five consecutive semesters. Of students who enrolled for five consecutive semesters, 75% had a GPA of at least 2.0, as opposed to students who enrolled for only one semester; only 25% of the latter group earned a 2.0 GPA or higher.

Suárez's (2003) exploratory study reveals an additional academic barrier within the Latinx community by analyzing the difficulties impeding the forward transfer of Latinx community college students. Suárez discovered that one major barrier for Latinx community college students is their over-representation in remedial English courses, which limits their opportunity to participate in transferable English courses and decreases the likelihood of their transferring to a four-year university. Alexander, García, González, Grimes, and O'Brien (2007) similarly used participant observation and case studies to examine transfer barriers for US Latinx and Latinx immigrant students in the Dallas County Community College District (DCCCD). Alexander et al. (2007) demonstrated the importance of Latinx student enrollment in college preparatory courses throughout high school as a way to prevent future enrollment in remedial courses at the community college, which ultimately delay and/or prevent Latinx community college students from transferring to four-year colleges and universities.

Non-academic barriers also affect the transferability of Latinx community college students. Using the Lanaan-Transfer Students Questionnaire (L-TSQ) with 66 students who transferred from one of the seven Dallas County Community College District Colleges (DCCCD) to an in-state public research university in Texas, Lanaan and Starobin's (2004) study revealed key student attitudes and behaviors regarding the transfer process. They found that students generally believed their future success at the university depended on their community college improving their transfer articulation agreements because this would ensure that their prerequisite classes to transfer were completed.

Students also identified the need to have supportive advisors to assist with the transfer process and, especially, the need to be introduced to the admissions office at the four-year college (Lanaan and Starobin 2004). Alexander et al. (2007) found two additional non-academic barriers for Latinxs: limited financial aid resources, which either delayed or prevented a transfer, and the cultural and social disconnection that Latinx students experience upon transferring to four-year institutions. Latinx community college students tend to experience alienation and isolation, especially since many selective colleges and universities are predominately white institutions (PWIs), whereas community colleges tend be more diverse (Alexander, et al. 2007).

Addressing the Latinx transfer gap, Núñez and Elizondo (2013) echo some of Lanaan and Starobin's (2004) findings regarding students' attitudes and behaviors around the transfer process. They make the following suggestions regarding areas where community college personnel can work to improve the experience for Latinx students during their time at the community college by (a) building relationships with community college faculty and staff, (b) providing access to critical information about how to navigate the community college/four-year university systems, and (c) ensuring that the community college is an affirming and welcoming environment for Latinx students with similar backgrounds.

Despite the academic and non-academic barriers and challenges, Latinx students do transfer, albeit in small numbers, to four-year colleges and universities. Klement (2012), for example, analyzed how effectively selected institutional characteristics explain the variance in Latinx community college students' transfer rates to four -year institutions. Her findings suggest that the presence of Latinx faculty on community college campuses is the highest indicator of positive influence on the transfer rates for Latinx Tejanx students. Her study also supports college readiness as a factor in their transfer rates, as indicated in the positive relationship between successful Texas Success Initiative (TSI) scores and their effect on community college transfer rates. In the same study, Klement also found that there was no significant correlation between locale (location) and transfer rates for Texas community college students.

Identifying these successful Latinx community college student transfer characteristics is important for addressing policy and practice. The following section describes potentially promising models that higher education practitioners at four-year universities can implement to ensure that more Latinx community college students transfer to their institutions.

AFFIRMING TRANSFER CULTURE MODELS
FOR LATINX TEJANX STUDENTS

Researchers and practitioners have developed affirming transfer culture models in an effort to diminish the institutional barriers and strengthen the transfer function from community college to four-year universities for Latinx Tejanx students (Handel 2012; Herrera and Jain 2013; Jain, Herrera, Bernal, and Solórzano 2011; and Pérez and Ceja 2010). Such models address the structural, social, and academic barriers Latinx community college students often face during the transfer process. To highlight some of the most promising practices supporting the transfer of Latinx community college students, two transfer culture models and their components are discussed below.

Emerging Transfer Culture Model

Handel (2012) formulated the Emerging Transfer Culture Model, as a way to systematically identify and provide the necessary resources for students to transfer and earn a baccalaureate degree from two-and four-year institutions. According to Handel (2012), the transfer-affirming culture has five elements (416):

1. Envisions transfer as a shared responsibility between community colleges and four-year institutions.

2. Views transfer and attainment of the bachelor's degree as expected and attainable.

3. Offers curricula and academic support services that make transfer and degree completion possible.

4. Leverages the social capital that students bring to college in service to their educational goals.

5. Includes transfer as an essential element of an institution's mission and strategic vision.

The transfer-affirming culture model mandates that four-year institutions recognize their role in the transfer function. It asks both the community college and the four-year university to make transfer commitments an institutional priority: by actively engaging students during the pre-transfer activities of the transfer process, by having high expectations, and by supporting students throughout the completion of their bachelor's degree.

A Latinx Transfer Culture Model

Latinx scholars have also made recommendations for developing a Latinx transfer culture model. For example, Pérez and Ceja (2010) used previous scholarship and existing data related to transfer objectives and Latinx transfer rates to outline a Latinx transfer culture model. Pérez and Ceja's (2010) model includes seven components that can make an immediate impact on the schooling and educational experiences of Latinx students:

1. High school, community college, and university faculty and staff should reflect the Latino student population. Latino role models and mentors who mirror the students provide invaluable resources to show that college attendance, transfer, and graduation are possible.

2. Educational partnerships should connect middle schools with high schools and high schools with higher education institutions to begin

preparing Latino students early for college. This includes focusing on improving academic skills, strengthening basic skills (writing, reading, and arithmetic), and providing the necessary college and financial aid information, preferably in small learning communities. This strategy would also give students the tools necessary to enroll into some form of higher education directly, as they come out of high school.

3. College and universities must streamline their articulation agreements. These agreements are not limited to community colleges or to state system transfer requisites but should also include the transfer requirements for moving from community college to a university and into a specific discipline.

4. College outreach programs should be culturally responsive and reflect the needs of the Latina/o student population they serve. Such programs would promote college attendance and transfer while instilling in participants a sense of pride in their heritage.

5. Higher education institutions should prioritize and fund outreach programs, practices, and partnerships that facilitate transfer. Part of this funding should be set aside for program evaluation and assessment, with the aim of constant improvement. A related recommendation includes establishing funding for a higher education administrator whose sole responsibility is to coordinate appropriate constituencies and support student transfer.

6. Incentives should be provided to higher education institutions that support transfer through evidence-based practices such as an increase in the rate of students transferring, and the maintenance of continuous enrollment. Evidence might be a decrease in the rate at which students drop classes, or an increase in the percentage of students who complete an orientation program/course.

7. Scholarships based on financial need should be available for Latina/o students at the community college and the four-year institution. Such scholarships would increase the possibility that students could maintain continuous enrollment, attend full-time, and perhaps reduce work hours (16–17).

The model developed by Pérez and Ceja highlights the need to increase the number of Latinx faculty and staff in higher education, especially because they often reflect the cultural values of Latinx students and can become sources of support and mentorship (Urrieta and Méndez Benavidez 2007). Strengthening and streamlining academic programs throughout the K-16 pipeline is also important, as are increasing commitments for financial support and culturally responsive outreach and support efforts that show evidence-based results. Effectively, these are essential elements to eliminate structural, social, and academic barriers Latinx community college students often face and increase their transferability from community college to four-year universities.

We highlight the transfer culture frameworks developed by Handel and by Pérez and Ceja as a basis for the development of models to increase transferability for all minority and low-income students, but for Latinxs in particular, given current and projected demographic growth. The shared commitment to increase and facilitate Latinx transferability based on these frameworks can result in purposeful and meaningful initiatives in policy and practice that can have positive impacts. In the following section we provide an overview of current policies and practices in place at six prominent universities in Texas. We focus on these institutions' promising efforts to increase transferability and promote increased transfer rates, retention, and graduation of Latinx students in Texas community colleges.

PROMISING EFFORTS TO INCREASE TRANSFERABILITY IN SIX TEXAS UNIVERSITIES

The following sections highlight promising efforts geared to assisting potential transfer students at six Texas universities. These universities are the University of Houston, University of North Texas, University of Texas at Austin, Texas A&M University, Texas State University, and Texas Tech University. Although these efforts to support successful transfers are not explicitly geared toward Latinxs, these institutions are highlighted here to show the variety of ways in which they reflect their commitments to transfer students.

University of Houston

The University of Houston (UH) has a transfer admissions web page that provides potential transfer students with general information about applying for admissions. The page includes a link guiding potential transfer students to Transfer FAQs, where potential questions regarding the application process, transferring credits, Texas residency, and student life are answered. UH also has a Transfer Advising Program (TAP), which provides potential students with steps on transferring to UH and other useful links; it includes a TAP advising syllabus with important terms and information. Links to contact information and instructions for making an appointment with a TAP advisor, including the location of their transfer centers within Houston and the surrounding areas, are also provided. At these centers, potential students can meet with a transfer advisor. UH also provides potential transfer students with a link to its transfer and equivalency guides by major, with up-to-date information on major requirements. Once admitted, all new transfer students are invited to attend a one-day advising and registration program (ART). Transfer students are also eligible for two scholarships: the Transfer Excellence and the Terry Foundation transfer scholarships. The UH joint admissions program offers guaranteed admissions for students who begin their postsecondary education at any of their partner schools and then enroll at UH upon fulfilling the predetermined requirements.[2]

WEBSITES FOR UNIVERSITY OF HOUSTON TRANSFER STUDENTS

http://www.uh.edu/admissions/apply/apply-transfer/

http://www.uh.edu/admissions/apply/apply-transfer/faq/

http://eto.uh.edu/tap/

http://www.uh.edu/admissions/apply/apply-transfer/by-major/

http://www.uh.edu/admissions/admitted/conferences/transfer/index.php

http://uh.edu/financial/undergraduate/types-aid/scholarships/index
     #transfers

http://eto.uh.edu/jointadmissions/

University of North Texas

The University of North Texas (UNT) offers potential transfer students the opportunity to meet with a transfer counselor prior to applying to UNT. Transfer counselors can take potential students through the entire transfer process and answer any questions students may have. Students are encouraged to attend a Transfer Debut, an event in which they tour the campus, meet with current transfer students, and learn how their course credits will transfer. Students also have access to four-year plans that provide with a roadmap of what courses to take at their community colleges and then at UNT, as well as other tools to ensure they stay on track during the transfer process. Transfer students are also guaranteed admission through the Eagle-Bound Program, UNT's partnership with local community colleges.

Once admitted, transfer students have several resources to support their transition. For example, students are encouraged to attend a transfer

---

2. Note: Joint Admissions applicants must also apply to UH using the Apply Texas Application and meet all applicable admissions requirements and deadlines. Visit www.uh.edu for more information.

student orientation. Students may also participate in the Transfer Student REAL community, a community designed with transfer students in mind, through UNT housing. Through Transfer Student REAL, which began during the 2015-16 academic year, transfer students can live together as a community in a designated residence hall. Transfer Student REAL offers students a built-in support group to smooth the difficult transitional period often face by transfer students. UNT also has a transfer center that offers student resources, services, and programs specifically designed for them.

Transfer students are eligible for UNT transfer scholarships. They also have access to an off-campus program of student resources, geared for nontraditional students. The UNT definition of "nontraditional" includes students with some or all of the following characteristics: older than the perceived "traditional" college age, returning to higher education after time away from initial enrollment, enrolling in higher education after time away from secondary education, having dependents other than a spouse (usually children, family members, or others), being a single parent (either unmarried, or married but separated, with dependents), working at least 35 hours per week, commuting to campus, or being enrolled only in online or off-campus courses. Nontraditional students are provided with resources and opportunities to join a listserv for nontraditional students and the Union of Non-Trad Students, a student organization that advocates and supports nontraditional students at UNT.

WEBSITES FOR UNIVERSITY OF NORTH TEXAS TRANSFER STUDENT PROGRAMS

https://transfernow.unt.edu/contact-us

http://admissions.unt.edu/transfer-open-house

http://registrar.unt.edu/resource-plans

http://admissions.unt.edu/eagle-boundand

http://studentaffairs.unt.edu/orientation#transfer

http://housing.unt.edu/real_communities/transfer_student_community

http://studentaffairs.unt.edu/transfer-center

http://financialaid.unt.edu/scholarships/unt-transfer-scholarship

http://studentaffairs.unt.edu/off-campus-student-services#non-trad

University of Texas at Austin

The University of Texas at Austin (UT Austin) offers potential transfer students information through a transfer admissions webpage, where they can find information about the components of a transfer application and the documents required. UT Austin offers guaranteed transfer admission under Texas Senate Bill 175 (SB 175) for qualified transfer applicants in the top 10 percent of their graduating high school class who begin their studies at a Texas community college following high school graduation. Potential students have two additional paths to admission to UT Austin: the Coordinated Admissions Program (CAP), and Path to Admissions through Co-Enrollment (PACE). CAP is a program that makes it possible for first-year applicants to UT Austin to begin their studies at another university in the UT system; CAP students are guaranteed admission to UT Austin's College of Liberal Arts upon completing the program requirements and do not have to reapply for admission. CAP transfer students are also able to compete for admission to majors other than those in liberal arts, the same as any other prospective transfer student.

The PACE program offers a pathway into UT Austin to select students who spend their first year taking one class per semester at the UT Austin campus while completing the majority of their coursework at the Rio Grande campus, which is part of the Austin Community College system. At the end of the year, those who successfully complete the PACE requirements continue their undergraduate studies at UT Austin as full-time students and are on track for on-time graduation. PACE students can be automatically admitted to a number of majors in the College of Liberal Arts and are also eligible to compete for admission into majors in other colleges and schools.

Once admitted, transfer students are invited to participate in a Transfer Orientation and can access important information regarding their specific session by college and program and registration dates online. UT Austin recently launched a Transfer-Year Experience Program through the School of Undergraduate Studies, offering transfer students programs that support their successful transition into the university. The Transfer-Year Experience offers courses, called Transfer Student Signature Courses, designed to help connect students with their transfer peers and acclimate to the academic rigor of UT Austin. Another program offered within the Transfer-Year Experience is the Transfer-Year Interests Groups (TRIGS). Students who join a TRIG can reserve a seat in high-demand courses, plug into a built-in network of fellow transfer students, and obtain a peer mentor with the experience and training to help them navigate their transition to UT Austin.

The university's Division of Diversity and Community Engagement (DDCE) offers UTransition, a program that provides a variety of resources for transfer students enrolled at UT Austin and introduces them to services such as academic support; social, cultural, and recreational activities; free tutoring; graduate school preparation support; Achieving College Excellence workshops, and membership to Tau Sigma National Honor Society, a national honor society exclusively for transfer students. Finally, UT Austin also offers transfer students scholarship opportunities through the UT Austin Continuing & Transfer Scholarship Application program.

WEBSITES FOR UNIVERSITY OF TEXAS AT AUSTIN TRANSFER STUDENTS

http://admissions.utexas.edu/apply/transfer-admission

http://catalog.utexas.edu/general-information/admission/undergraduate -admission/transfer-admission/

http://admissions.utexas.edu/enroll/cap

http://admissions.utexas.edu/enroll/pace

http://deanofstudents.utexas.edu/nss/transfer-orientation/index.php

http://www.utexas.edu/ugs/tye

http://ddce.utexas.edu/academiccenter/utransition/

http://www.texasscholarships.org/apply/continuing/CSA.html

Texas A&M University

Texas A&M University (TAMU) has two transfer initiatives to facilitate admission. Texas Senate Bill 175 guarantees admission to the top 10 percent of Texas high school graduates within a four-year period prior to the semester for which the student applies for admission.[3] Students can also gain admission through the Program for Transfer Admission (PTA).[4] PTA is designed for students attending Texas community colleges and offers potential students more than 65 degree plan options. Upon completing the coursework outlined in the degree plan, and additional requirements of the PTA program, students become eligible for automatic admission to TAMU.

Additional resources provided to potential transfer students include Transfer Course Sheets, worksheets on which students can track their transferable coursework, and a transfer course equivalency website that contains a searchable database of course equivalencies for US colleges and universities. Potential transfer students also have the opportunity to attend transfer information sessions that are held throughout the academic school year, including Aggie Day at an Austin Community College or at the Tarant County College campus, two of Texas A&M University's community college partners. Admitted students are required to attend a conference for incom-

---

3. Additional requirements and restrictions apply. For details see, http://admissions.tamu.edu /transfer/admitted.

4. Additional requirements apply. For details, see http://admissions.tamu.edu/PTA.

ing transfer students; this is an informational event that provides them with essential knowledge for joining the Aggie Family. Transfer students are also eligible for transfer student scholarships, including but not limited to the Aggie Transfer Scholarship and the Terry Transfer Scholarship.

TAMU also offers incoming transfer students the opportunity to attend Aggie Transition Camp (ATC), which supports incoming students' transition into the Aggie family. Incoming transfer students can also participate in the Transfer Student Program (TSP), which is designed to help them learn more about the resources at TAMU; make connections with other transfer students, faculty, and staff; and encourage engagement at all levels of the university. Other programs offered through TSP include the Transfer Service Project, which offers volunteer opportunities to transfer students; the Real Transfers Share Challenges, a blog where transfer students can share challenges they face during their first semester at TAMU; and the Transfer Student Peer Mentors, a group made up of former transfer students hired to offer academic and social support to incoming transfer students.

WEBSITES FOR TEXAS A&M UNIVERSITY TRANSFER STUDENTS

http://admissions.tamu.edu/transfer/admitted

http://admissions.tamu.edu/transfer/majors

https://compass-ssb.tamu.edu/pls/PROD/bwxkwtes.P_TransEquivMain

http://admissions.tamu.edu/transfer/programs

http://newaggie.tamu.edu/transfer/

https://scholarships.tamu.edu/TRANSFER/Available-Scholarships

http://atc.tamu.edu/%3Cfront%3E

http://successcenter.tamu.edu/Programs/Transfer-Student-Program

Texas State University

Texas State University (TSU) identifies two types of transfer students: students with between one and 29 hours of course credit and transfer students with 30 or more hours. Dedicated websites provide students with information about their individual applications and the application process. Potential transfer students also have access to a transfer course equivalency system that allows them to keep track of which of their course credits will transfer to TSU. They are provided with a link to the General Education Core Curriculum, a guide that provides a list of courses and alternate courses that fulfill the General Education Core Curriculum for TSU, including equivalent course numbers.

TSU also provides potential transfer students with transfer planning guides that function as agreements between TSU and Texas community colleges. Upon admission, transfer students can attend one of three transfer orientations, depending on the number of transfer credit hours they have completed. The three orientation groups are: Gold (0–15 hours), Transfer Orientation, On-Campus (16–29 hours), and Transfer Orientation, Online (30 + hours). Once admitted, transfer students have access to services and programs that support a healthy and positive transition into TSU. Transfer students can also attend transfer student events, including a transfer student welcome, throughout the academic school year. They are also eligible for scholarships, including but not limited to the Terry Foundation Transfer Scholarship and Martha St. Clair (Phi Theta Kappa) Scholarship.

WEBSITES FOR TEXAS STATE UNIVERSITY TRANSFER STUDENTS

http://www.admissions.txstate.edu/future/transfer/how-to-apply-1-29.html

http://www.admissions.txstate.edu/future/transfer/how-to-apply-30plus.html

http://www.admissions.txstate.edu/future/transfer/equivalency-guides.html

http://www.admissions.txstate.edu/future/transfer/curriculum

http://www.admissions.txstate.edu/future/transfer/tpg

http://www.admissions.txstate.edu/admitted/orientation

http://www.studentsuccess.txstate.edu/resources/transfer-student-resources.html

http://www.studentsuccess.txstate.edu/programs/transfer-events.html

http://www.finaid.txstate.edu/scholarships/transfer/schol.html

Texas Tech University

Texas Tech University (TTU) has a Community College & Transfer Relations (CCTR) office that supports the needs of potential community college transfer students who want to learn about the transfer process, high school students who want to learn about dual enrollment, and current transfer students. CCTR offers specific application guides for students applying to transfer from a community college and those transferring from a four-year university. The university also hosts Transfer Friday, a campus visit experience that allows potential transfer students to meet current transfer students and connects them with a variety of services to support a successful transition into TTU. Potential transfer students also have access to an Optimal Transfer Plans service that provides them not only with course selection and sequencing information but also information about academic departments, undergraduate research opportunities, study abroad, graduate studies, work options, and common careers. In addition, TTU has partnership agreements with Texas community colleges to make the transfer process to TTU less complicated. Once admitted, students are encouraged to attend a Red Raider orientation (RRO), designed for either students transferring with 23 or fewer credits or students transferring with 24 or more credits. Transfer students are eligible for three scholarships at TTU, including the Proven Achievers Scholarship, the President's Transfer Scholarship, and the IMPACT President's Transfer Scholarships. They can also take advantage of the Transfer Connection, which provides students with programs and services to ensure a successful transition to TTU, including Transfer Welcome Day, when students can meet and connect with current transfer students. The Transfer Connection also offers students the Transfer Ambassadors program, which supports transfer students during their transition and engages them throughout their first semester on campus. Transfer Techsans is also a peer mentor network, designed to help students create connections once they transfer to TTU by providing social events, community service projects, and other activities. Finally, there is the Transfer Leadership Connection, a three-day student-led retreat for new undergraduate transfer students, filled with activities to help transfer students build connections to TTU, develop their abilities as student leaders, and prepare to have a positive impact on the student transfer climate for at TTU.

WEBSITES FOR TEXAS TECH UNIVERSITY TRANSFER STUDENTS

http://www.depts.ttu.edu/uesa/cctr/index.php

http://www.depts.ttu.edu/uesa/cctr/TimeframeAndResources/Incoming
    Students/TransferStudent/Steps2-yearTransfer.pdf

http://www.depts.ttu.edu/uesa/cctr/TimeframeAndResources/Incoming
    Students/TransferStudent/Steps4-yearTransfer.pdf

https://apply.texastech.edu/Undergraduate/Pages/EventDetailsaspx?id=
    4b7367d1-7c31-e511-b2d6-0050569b36a6

http://www.depts.ttu.edu/uesa/cctr/plans.php

http://www.depts.ttu.edu/uesa/cctr/partnership_agreement.php

https://www.depts.ttu.edu/redraiderorientation/index.php

http://www.depts.ttu.edu/scholarships/transferStudentsScholarships.php

http://www.depts.ttu.edu/studentengagement/transferconnection/

http://www.depts.ttu.edu/studentengagement/transferconnection
    /transfertechsans.php

http://www.depts.ttu.edu/studentengagement/transferconnection
    /leadershipconnection/retreat.php

INCREASING LATINX TEJANX ACCESS, RETENTION, AND GRADUATION RATES IN TEXAS

Having looked at the policies and practices in place at six universities, we now focus on analyzing these institutions' efforts to increase Latinx Tejanx access, retention, and graduation rates in Texas community colleges, using the transfer culture models presented earlier in this article. In general, each institution profiled meets, to an extent, Handel's (2012) transfer-affirming framework of shared responsibility, high expectations, support services, and essential university mission. All six of the four-year institutions envision the transfer function as a shared commitment between themselves and their local and state community college partners. This is evident in both the articulation agreements and the joint admissions programs set in place at some of these universities. The underlying assumption is that both successful transfer and a bachelor's degree are expected and attainable. Additionally, these universities provide students with general transfer student programming, including academic and social support through outreach and retention programs, increasing the likelihood that community college students will be able to transfer and complete their bachelor's degree. Again, these programs reflect the expectation that students who do transfer will be academically successful. Generally, there is an expressed commitment to diversity, usually in a university mission statement that supports explicitly, or strongly implies, the idea that community college transfer students form part of the diversity the university strives for and values (Urrieta and Villenas 2013).

Using Pérez and Ceja's (2010) Latinx transfer culture model, however, it becomes evident that the current transfer policy and practice efforts at these six public four-year institutions are not sufficient to increase the access, retention, and graduation rates for Latinx Tejanx community college students. This evidence is especially telling in two areas. First, none of the outreach programming instituted by these universities has a culturally responsive component focusing on the specific needs of Latinx Tejanx community college students, or racial or ethnic minority transfer students in general. These policies and programs assume that what they have instituted will meet the needs of any transfer student, generally assumed to be a white student. By this we mean that there are no deliberate institutionalized efforts, programs, or policies to address Latinx students and the socioeconomic, cultural, linguistic, and socio-emotional needs of those students and their families in the transfer process, including (minimally) providing information in Spanish to reach out to Spanish-speaking families. The university efforts we have highlighted are in line with neoliberal, equal-opportunity, colorblind educational policies that ignore issues of race and culture in addressing educational inequities as they normalize solutions to a white-student-majority norm (Urrieta 2006).

Second, although all of the universities offered some type of financial aid and scholarships for transfer students, the awards are not specific to racial-minority transfer students, which includes Latinx community college transfer students. This is important, especially because financial difficulty is often an impediment for accessing higher education for Latinx Tejanx students. Financial hardship especially affects undocumented students, even in states like Texas that offer undocumented students the opportunity to apply for financial aid. Finally, Latinx transfer students' retention, and eventual graduation, is significantly tied to university efforts to recruit, support, and retain minority faculty (including the granting of tenure). This deficiency is especially marked in the case of Latinx faculty, who often express and manage significant Latinx community commitments in addition to their teaching responsibilities, despite the ways in which the tenure and promotion processes discourage and undervalue these efforts (Urrieta, Méndez, and Rodríguez 2015).

CONCLUSIONS AND IMPLICATIONS

Our goal was to draw attention to current transfer policies and practices at six top public universities in Texas and to evaluate their efforts to increase the access, retention, and graduation rates for Latinx community college students in the context of Texas higher education. Given the apparently disproportionate enrollment rates of Latinx students in community colleges and the small percentage of those who eventually transfer to, and graduate from, four-year universities, we argue that creating transfer policies and transfer student programming that focuses on Latinx Tejanx community college student transfer culture in Texas is of critical importance. Failure to address these issues will result in the continuation of a disproportionately low rate of Latinx Tejanx community college students transferring to four-year institutions and more generally to the lack of Latinx achievement and attainment in higher education.

We conclude that public four-year universities, including the six Texas universities we profiled in this article, should develop transfer policies and practices specific to the needs of Latinx community college students. These might include: (1) the development of culturally relevant outreach programs focusing on the specific needs—including the financial needs—of Latinx community college students; (2) the development of guaranteed admission pathways into four-year universities for Latinx community college students; and (3), the development of programming specific to increasing the retention and graduation of Latinx community college transfer students. This should include financial aid awards and scholarships specifically for Latinx community college transfer students. The demographic imperative surrounding this issue highlights the urgency with which these access, retention, and graduation efforts must be advanced, especially in Texas.

REFERENCES

Alexander, B. C., V. Garcia, L. Gonzalez, G. Grimes, and D. O'Brien. 2007. "Barriers in the Transfer Process for Hispanic and Hispanic Immigrant Students." *Journal of Hispanic Higher Education* 6:2, 174–184.

Bailey, Thomas, Davis Jenkins, and D. Timothy Leinbach. 2007. *The Effect of Student Goals on Community College Performance Measures.* Community College Research Center, Brief No. 33. Columbia University.

Burley, Bonita Butner, and Brent Cejda. 2001. "Dropout and Stopout Patterns among Developmental Education Students in Texas Community Colleges." *Community College Journal of Research and Practice* 25:10, 767–782.

Conrady Klement, Emily. 2012. "Transfer Rates of Texas Hispanic Community College Students to 4-Year Institutions: Selected Institutional Factors." PhD diss.: University of North Texas.

Fassold, M. 2000. "Disparate Impact Analyses of TAAS Scores and School Quality." *Hispanic Journal of Behavioral Sciences* 22, 460–480.

Handel, S. J. 2012. *Increasing Higher Education Access and Success Using New Pathways to the Baccalaureate: The Emergence of a Transfer-Affirming Culture.*

Handel, S. J., and R. A. Williams. 2012. "The Promise of the Transfer Pathway: Opportunity and Challenge for Community College Students Seeking the Baccalaureate Degree." New York, NY: Advocacy and Policy Center, The College Board.

Haney, W. M. 2002. "The Myth of the Texas Miracle in Education." *Education Policy Analysis Archives,* online serial, http://epaa.asu.edu.

Herrera, A., and D. Jain. 2013. "Building a Transfer Receptive Culture At Four-Year Institutions. *New Directions for Higher Education* 162, 51–59.

Jain, D., A. Herrera, S. Bernal, and D. Solórzano. 2011. "Critical Race Theory and the Transfer Function: Introducing a Transfer-Receptive Culture." *Community College Journal of Research and Practice* 35:3, 252–266.

Kindler, A. L. 2002. *Survey of the States' Limited English Proficient Students and Available Educational Programs and Services.* Washington, DC: Office of English Language Acquisition, Language Enhancement and Academic Achievement for Limited English Proficient Students.

Kurlaender, M. 2006. "Choosing Community College: Factors Affecting Latina/o College Choice." *New Directions for Community Colleges* 133, 7–16.

Malcolm, L. E. 2013. "Student Diversity in Community Colleges: Examining Trends and Understanding the Challenges." In *Understanding Community Colleges*, edited by J. S. Levin and S. T. Kater. New York: Routledge.

National Center of Education Statistics. 2013. *Digest of Education Statistics 2013*, Table 101.20, https://nces.ed.gov/programs/digest/d13/tables/dt13_101.20.asp.

National Center for Public Policy in Higher Education. 2011. *Affordability and Transfer: Critical to Increasing Baccalaureate Completion Degree Completion*, http://www.highereducation.org/reports/pa_at/

Nora, A., and L. I. Rendón. 1990. "Determinants of Predisposition to Transfer among Community College Students: A Structural Model." *Research in Higher Education* 31:3, 235–255.

Núñez, A., and Elizondo, D. 2013. *Closing the Latino/a Transfer Gap: Creating Pathways to the Baccalaureate*, https://www.academia.edu/4105129/closing_the_latino _a_transfer_gap_creating_pathways_to_the_baccalaureate

Pérez, P. A., and M. Ceja. 2010. "Building a Latina/o Student Transfer Culture: Best Practices and Outcomes in Transfer to Universities." *Journal of Hispanic Higher Education* 9:1, 6–21.

Pérez Huber, Lindsay, Maria C. Malagón, Brianna R. Ramírez, Lorena Camargo González, Alberto Jiménez, and Verónica N. Vélez. 2015. *Still Falling Through the Cracks Revisiting the Latina/o Education Pipeline*. CSRC Research Report No. 19. UCLA Chicano Studies Research Center.

Rivas, M. A., J. Pérez, C. R. Álvarez, and D. G. Solórzano. 2007. *Latina/o Transfer Students: Understanding the Critical Role of the Transfer Process in California's Postsecondary Institutions*. CSRC Research Report No. 9. UCLA Chicano Studies Research Center.

Solórzano, D. G., O. Villalpando, and L. Oseguera. 2005. "Educational Inequities and Latina/o Undergraduate Students in the United States: A Critical Race Analysis of Their Educational Progress." *Journal of Hispanic Higher Education* 4:3, 272–294.

Suárez, A. L. 2003. "Forward Transfer: Strengthening the Educational Pipeline for Latino Community College Students." *Community College Journal of Research and Practice* 27, 95–117.

Texas Higher Education Coordinating Board. 2014. *Texas Public Higher Education Almanac, 2014*, http://www.thecb.state.tx.us/index.cfm?objectid=ce293eed -dd31-bcde-51eb322ff8b856a8andflushcache=1andshowdraft=1

Texas Higher Education Coordinating Board. 2013. *Higher Education Enrollment, Fall2013*, http://www.tacc.org/uploads/tinymce/data%20and%20info/enrollment /fall13_highereduc.pdf.

Texas Higher Education Coordinating Board. 2008a. *Community and Technical Colleges 6-Year Graduation Rates of First-Time Entering Undergraduates, Fall 1999,*

Enrolled for 12 or More Student Credit Hours, http://www.thecb.state.tx.us /reports/pdf/1274.pdf

Texas Higher Education Coordinating Board. 2008b. *Community and Technical Colleges 6-Year Graduation Rates of First-Time Entering Undergraduates (Full-Time and Part-Time), Fall 2008*, http://www.thecb.state.tx.us/reports/docfetch .cfm?docid=6406

Urrieta, L. Jr. 2006."Community Identity Discourse and the Heritage Academy: Colorblind Educational Policy and White Supremacy." *International Journal of Qualitative Studies in Education* 19:4, 455–476

Urrieta, L. Jr., and L. Méndez Benavidez. 2007. "Community Commitment and Activist Scholarship: Chicana/o Professors and the Practice of Consciousness." *Journal of Hispanic Higher Education* 6:3, 222–236.

Urrieta, L. Jr., and S. Villenas. 2013/ "The Legacy of Derrick Bell and Latina/o Education: A Critical Race Testimonio." *Race, Ethnicity and Education* 16:4, 514–535.

Urrieta, L. Jr., L. Méndez, and E. A. Rodríguez. 2015. "A Moving Target: A Critical Race Analysis of Latina/o Faculty Experiences, Perspectives, and Reflections on the Tenure and Promotion Process." *International Journal of Qualitative Studies in Education* 28:10, 1149–1168.

Valencia, R. R. 2000. "Inequalities and the Schooling of Minority Students in Texas: Historical and Contemporary Conditions." *Hispanic Journal of Behavioral Sciences* 22:4, 445–459.

Yosso, T. J., and D. G. Solórzano. 2006. *Leaks in the Chicana and Chicano Educational Pipeline*. Latino Policy and Issues Brief, No. 13. UCLA Chicano Studies Research Center.

Shattering the Deficit Grand Narrative

TOWARD A CULTURALLY VALIDATING LATINO STUDENT SUCCESS FRAMEWORK

Laura I. Rendón, Vijay Kanagala, and Ripsimé K. Bledsoe

As the growth of the nation's Latino population continues in dynamic mode—with projections indicating they will be one-third of the nation by 2050—many more colleges and universities will be transformed into Hispanic-Serving Institutions (HSIs) whose student body is at least 25 percent Latino. Yet, despite a diverse array of academic and student support services targeting students of color, disparities in educational attainment persist at both the high school and college level. Further, educational attainment data from 2010 show that Mexican Americans were the least educated cohort among Hispanics, with 57 percent graduating from high school (or equivalent), compared to 75 percent for Puerto Ricans and 81 percent for Cubans. In higher education there was a similar scenario: Mexican Americans had lower college completion rates with 11 percent earning a bachelor's degree compared to 18 percent for Puerto Ricans and 26 percent for Cubans (US Bureau of the Census Bureau 2012).

How can these achievement gaps be addressed? This essay contends that deficit-based thinking has become the default perspective in considering low-income students of color. Whereas it would be unthinkable for elite, wealthy colleges and universities to assume deficit-based perspectives regarding their students, views that cast low-income students as deficient, unprepared, and inept not only go widely unchallenged but have become entrenched and normalized. Further, many educators are unfamiliar with Latino social and political histories and how these forces have shaped their students' educational experiences and communities. Nor do educators fully understand or acknowledge the cultural wealth Latinos employ to overcome and survive adversity. The authors of this article believe that

223

the future of Latino student achievement must be based on an asset-based framework that incorporates a Latino-centric lens. The purposes of this essay are a) to shatter the pervasive deficit-based model that has worked against Latino and other underserved students and 2) to provide two- and four-year college and university educators with a contemporary, culturally validating model of Latino student success.

EMPLOYING ASSET-BASED THEORETICAL FRAMEWORKS

Over the past decade, a number of critiques about deficit-based frameworks have expressed the role of racial and class biases in creating entrenched views about low-income students of color, views that pathologize, stereotype, and marginalize these students (Conchas 2006; Valenzuela 1999; Volpp 2000; Valencia 2010, 1997; Moll et al. 2001; Yosso 2005; Rendón, Nora, and Kanagala 2014; Zambrana and Hurtado 2015; Stanton-Salazar 1997). Deficit-based thinking is centered on the grand narrative that parents and Latino communities do not value education, the belief that low-income communities are inferior, and the pervasive view that most, if not all low-income students are "at risk," "marginal learners" and "culturally deprived." Absent from this deficit-based discourse is a focus on Latino cultural wealth and the experiential ways of knowing that students employ to transcend their socioeconomic circumstances, build on their instinct to survive, and excel in education. Below are some asset-based theoretical perspectives intended to dismantle the deficit model of education.

Community Cultural Wealth

Tara Yosso's (2005) community cultural wealth model represents "an array of knowledge, skills, abilities, and contacts possessed and utilized by Communities of Color to survive and resist macro- and micro-forms of oppression" (77). Employing a Critical Race Theory lens, Yosso posits that cultural capital comes in the following forms:

- Aspirational: "holding on to hope in the face of structured inequality and often without the means to make such dreams a reality" (77)

- Linguistic: "intellectual and social skills attained through communication experiences in more than one language and/or style" (78)

- Familial: "cultural ways of knowing in the immediate and extended family that maintain a healthy connection to community and its resources" (78)

- Social: "networks of significant others and community resources who provide instrumental and emotional support to navigate through institutions" (78)

- Navigational: "ability to maneuver social institutions which were not created particularly for Communities of Color" (79)

- Resistant: "oppositional behaviors brought forth when Communities of Color recognize and challenge social inequities" (79).

Rendón, Nora, and Kanagala (2014) validated Yosso's model and added four more *ventajas*/assets and *conocimientos*/ways of knowing that Latino students employ to survive, overcome obstacles, and push themselves to complete college. Table 1 presents the combined model.

Scholarly works focusing on Latino students have to a significant extent validated the existence of the cultural strengths listed in Table I (Zambrana and Hurtado 2015; Lozano 2015; Foxen 2015). Additional strengths include the following:

- *Leadership*. Distinctive qualities include a holistic attitude that is oriented toward community and action-oriented, with aims of social activism and coalition building sustained through faith and hope. Latinos seek to push, inspire, motivate and empower others through their actions (Lozano 2015; Beatty 2014; Bordas 2013; Guardia 2015).

- *Resilience*. Many Latino students overcome significant challenges (Kann and Rodríguez 2015; Foxen 2015), such as dealing with racism and deficit views, financial difficulties, learning and navigating a new institutional culture, and dealing with personal challenges.

- *Responsibilidad/Responsibility*. Latino students often take on an obligation to contribute to the family's financial situation and well-being (Suarez 2015). Gender roles include women taking care of their brothers and sisters and young men becoming the "man of the house." Students may also send money home to help with family finances.

Funds of Knowledge

Luis Moll, Cathy Amanti, Deborah Neff, and Norma González (2001) worked with the concept of "funds-of-knowledge," which refers to "the historically accumulated and culturally developed bodies of knowledge and skills essential for household or individual functioning and well-being" (133). Funds of knowledge is an asset-based theory whereby teachers can become learners and come to know their students and the families of their students in new ways. The theory of funds of knowledge

TABLE 1. Latino student *Ventajas y Conocimientos*

VENTAJAS/ASSETS	CONOCIMIENTOS/FUNDS OF KNOWLEDGE
Aspirational	Ability to set high aspirations
	Ability to recognize value of education
	Ability to remain hopeful about the future
Linguistic	Ability to use two or more languages to communicate and to form relationships with others
	Employment of diverse forms of communication skills in multiple contexts
Familial	Modeling the strength and determination of the family
	Ability to use knowledge gained through the value of family *consejos, respeto, testimonios y educación*
	Validation and encouragement from siblings, parents, relatives
Social	Ability to create social networks
	Ability to make new friends and to form new relationships
Resistant	Ability to resist stereotypes and combat micro-aggressions
	Ability to overcome hardships, such as poverty and lack of resources
Ganas/ Perseverance	Ability to develop inner strength, become self reliant and determined to succeed
	Ability to recognize and embrace the sacrifices that must be made to attend college
Ethnic Consciousness	Having cultural pride
	Exhibiting pride in attending an HSI
	Having a deep commitment to Latino community ("giving back")
	Being focused on the betterment of the collective whole
Spirituality/Faith	Turning to faith in God/ higher power
	Having a sense of meaning and purpose
	Understanding the importance of gratitude, goodness, and compassion
Pluriversal	Ability to operate in multiple worlds (college, peers, work, family, native country) and diverse educational and geographical contexts
	Ability to hold multiple and competing systems of meaning in tension in diverse social and educational contexts

Sources: Rendón, Nora, and Kangala 2014, *Ventajas y Conocimientos;* Anzaldúa 2005, Conocimientos; Moll, Amanti, Neff, and González 2001, Funds of Knowledge.

debunks the pervasive, deficit-based notion that linguistically and culturally diverse working-class minority households lack worthwhile knowledge
and experiences. When faculty and staff take time to get to know students—to acknowledge and validate their backgrounds, culture, family
sacrifices, and the challenges they have overcome, for example—they can
view students with more respect and understanding. In the process of
working more closely with students, faculty can potentially draw out hidden talents and abilities.

Mestiza Consciousness

In the Latino culture, *mestiza* or *mestizo* means a person of mixed race and
cultural heritage, neither fully Spanish nor fully indigenous. In her book,
Borderlands/La Frontera: The New Mestiza, Latina feminist scholar Gloria
Anzaldúa (1999) argues that the mixture provides an advantage: when
two or more genetic streams "are constantly 'crossing over,'" this mixture
of races, rather than resulting in an inferior being, provides hybrid prog-
eny, a mutable, more malleable species with a rich gene pool. From this
racial, ideological, cultural and biological cross-pollination, an 'alien' consciousness is presently in the making—a new *mestiza* consciousness, *una
conciencia de mujer*. It is a consciousness of the Borderlands (99)."

Anzaldúa recognizes the "psychic restlessness" that can occur as a
result of occupying liminal spaces, of being neither here nor there, of being
in a state of seemingly perpetual transition, and of living between two
cultures. This state she calls *nepantla*. The shadow side of nepantla is that it
is messy, confusing and chaotic: individuals are removed from familiar
contexts to those that are unknown. Yet, nepantla can also be the threshold
space where transformation can occur, where new knowledge emerges,
worldviews are shattered, personal growth is realized, and new identities
emerge. Many Latino students are of mixed ancestry, have lived in their
homeland and in the United States, speak more than one language, have
experienced dislocation and relocation and cultural collision, and often
find themselves straddling more than one culture in their families, work,
colleges, peers, and relationship to their native country. A consequence
of these varied experiences is that the *mestiza* develops such strengths as
tolerance for ambiguities and contradictions, adaptability in more than one
culture, and the capacity to operate in a pluralistic mode. Students who
share this *mestiza* consciousness mode are pluriversal and exercise a significant strength that goes beyond dualistic thinking (this/that; us/them)
to embrace a collective consciousness that heals the wounds of separation
and seeks connections and points of agreement.

Pedagogies of the Home

Drawing on the work of Gloria Anzaldúa (1987), Dolores Delgado Bernal (2001) expands the concept of "*mestiza* consciousness" to "include how a student balances, negotiates, and draws from her bilingualism, biculturalism, commitment to communities, and spiritualties. With this lens, what are often perceived as deficits for Chicana students—limited English proficiency, inferior cultural/religious practices, or too many non-university responsibilities—can be understood as cultural assets or resources that Chicano students bring to higher education" (628). Pedagogies of the home comprise the communication, practices and learning that can occur within the home and community. This constitutes the cultural knowledge base and strategies of resistance that students employ to survive in educational systems that are alien to them and that often cast students within deficit-minded frameworks.

Validation

Validation theory (Rendón 1994; Linares-Rendón and Muñoz 2011) provides an asset-based approach to working with students in a way that recognizes and affirms students as knowledgeable and capable of college-level work, and builds supportive relationships between validating agents and students. Validation theory stresses the importance of authentic affirmation, support and encouragement from family members, and in- and out-of-class validating agents (faculty, student affairs staff, coaches, advisers), and considers the whole as critical to student success. Validation is an enabling, confirming, and supportive process initiated by in- and out-of-class agents that fosters academic and personal development (Rendón 1994), and it exists in two forms:

- *Academic.* In- and out-of-class validating agents assist students in learning to trust their innate capacity to learn and in acquiring the confidence to be a college student.
- *Interpersonal.* In- and out-of-class validating agents take action to foster students' personal development and social adjustment.

Validation, when administered early in students' transition to college, and consistently throughout their college experience, may be the key to helping students get involved and believing they can learn and achieve their goals (Rendón 1994).

Liberatory Pedagogy

Scholars such as Freire (1970), Rendón (2009), hooks (1994), Shahjahan (2005), and Lather (1991) have proposed epistemological arguments that education should incorporate an inclusive curriculum, be relationship-centered, honor diverse ways of knowing, and take action against colonization and other forms of oppression. This education should also focus on social justice, interdependence, diversity, sustainability, and human rights, endorse students' ability to think critically about their educational situations, and welcome student voices in the classroom. A liberatory pedagogy rejects what Freire (1970) calls the banking model of education, wherein students, who are presumed to be deprived of knowledge, wait to have experts "deposit" knowledge in their vacuous minds. For example, Rendón's (2009) *Sentipensante* [Sensing/Thinking] *Pedagogy* offers a pedagogic model that views individuals as whole human beings, connects inner and outer learning, deeply engages the learner through the use of contemplative practices, promotes the acquisition of both knowledge and wisdom, and emphasizes activism, liberation, healing and social change. Students are assisted to find their self-worth, identity, sense of purpose and voice—key assets needed to succeed in college.

TOWARD A CONTEMPORARY FRAMEWORK OF LATINO STUDENT SUCCESS

Newly developed, culturally validating student success initiatives must be grounded in the experiences, strengths, and culture of Latino students and not on models that were framed with middle- and upper-class majority students in mind. Latino students are succeeding in their own way, employing their own ways of knowing, tools for academic survival, and resistance strategies to take them to the finish line of college completion. Table 2 outlines key differences between dominant models and the proposed Culturally Validating Latino Student Success Framework. Examples of institutional policies and practices that align with the proposed framework are also provided. Institutional agents are encouraged to engage as reflective practitioners to generate innovative strategies that will leverage Latino student success.

Theory

In the 1970s and 1980s, research on student retention began to catch the attention of higher education faculty and student affairs administrators.

TABLE 2. Comparison: Dominant success framework and culturally validating Latino student success framework

	DOMINANT MODEL	CULTURALLY VALIDATING FRAMEWORK	INSTITUTIONAL POLICIES & PRACTICES
Theory	Deficit-based understanding of students; deficit grand narrative unchallenged Definition of success based on emulating experiences of white middle- and upper-class students Academic and social integration/involvement required for success Primary focus of change is student	Establishes asset-based understanding of students Focuses on aligning institutional policies and practices with student ways of knowing Recognizes cultural wealth, allowing students to succeed in their own way Fosters success through validating agents who work with ethic of care, support, and affirmation Places primary focus on critical role of institution's faculty and staff to foster success	Develops asset-based framework for student success Employs asset-based theories to serve as foundation for academic and student affairs programs Provides professional development for faculty and staff to serve as validating agents and to develop an asset-based understanding of students
Historical/ Political	Apolitical Little or no discussion of history and oppressive structures Equity not an explicit concern	Recognizes Latino history in state and local community Recognizes significant inequities that impact Latinos (poverty, segregated schooling, school finance inequalities, etc.) Places equity and ethnic/racial justice at the forefront of concern	Assesses history of local and state community Gives consideration to quality of schooling; history of inequality; extent that the institution is focused on equity as well as ethnic/racial justice
Transition to College	Linear transition Cultural aspects of transition not considered	Accepts nonlinear, messy, multidirectional, transitional process Considers cultural aspects of liminality, separation anxiety, dislocation and relocation, as well as dealing with microaggressions	Develops programming that assists students to make the transition to college, for example, Center for the Transition to College Develop programming that assists students to navigate and decode the world of college
Institutional Culture	Race-neutral Overlooks difference and race/ethnic inequalities	Is culturally validating Accounts for difference Builds community, tolerance, acceptance and sense of belonging	Establishes principles of community Implements programs that foster sense of belonging Trains professional staff to deal with issues of equity, difference and social justice

	DOMINANT MODEL	CULTURALLY VALIDATING FRAMEWORK	INSTITUTIONAL POLICIES & PRACTICES
Student Support Services	Inconsiderate of the needs of changing student demographics Unwelcoming campus traditions and practices that perpetuate covert and/or overt racist ideologies	Develops culturally relevant student affairs practices that cater to the co-curricular, social, cultural and emotional needs of students Creates residential identity based learning communities Develops strategic academic affairs partnerships to ensure Latino student success	Develops Latino student-centric programs that value and validate diversity of cultures Demonstrates commitment to Latino student success by hiring Latino staff and institutional leaders who can support students
Pedagogy	Expert model Faculty distance themselves from students Monocultural curriculum; excludes equity and social justice themes Focus on individual student achievement Student voice not considered Singularly focused on intellectual development and academic knowledge	Implements relational model: co-creation and multidirectional flow of knowledge Uses faculty as in- and out-of-class validating agents Includes multicultural and inclusive curriculum Emphasizes community of learners Welcomes student voice and experience Considers Latino ways of knowing/conocimientos Strives for holistic student development (intellectual, social, emotional, spiritual)	Provides professional development to faculty and staff to: Focus on Latino HIPs (High-impact practices)— applied learning, learning communities, contemplative pedagogy, Latino studies, study groups, service learning, research with faculty member, etc. Design curricula that is inclusive and multicultural Design relationship-centered classrooms
Assessment	Data presented in aggregate Excludes equity concerns	Student achievement data are disaggregated by race, ethnicity, and gender Equity-minded	Conducts assessment of student assets Involves faculty and staff in collecting, assessing, and learning from data

Source: *California Statewide Student Success Scorecard*, 2015.

Much of this early research (Tinto 1975; 1987; Astin 1984) posed the notion that persistence toward graduation was a linear process that assumed the most successful students were those able to become academically and socially integrated and involved with the institution. More recently, "student engagement" (Kuh 2001; Kuh et al. 2008) has become the buzzword for student success. These early theoretical views of student persistence are widely accepted, enjoy paradigmatic status, and continue to play a dominant role in higher education. Nonetheless, scholars have critiqued student success theories for failing to challenge the deficit-based grand narrative, which excludes the experience of students of color in the framing of early theoretical perspectives, overlooks structural inequalities that have worked against low-income students and families, and fails to interrogate the assumptions regarding assimilation that underlie these perspectives. These scholarly critiques also take issue with research that overly emphasizes the role of the student—as opposed to the responsibility of the institution—to account for success. Critiques also question the misguided assumption that all students, regardless of social background and economic resources, must find ways to get involved/integrated/engaged and that in fact this is the only way to achieve educational success.

Absent from this entrenched discourse is the fact that many low-income students have to work to help the family survive and that they have multiple demands on their lives that preclude full engagement (Rendón, Jalomo, and Nora 2000; Rendón, Nora, and Kanagala 2014; Hurtado, 2006; Cantú 2006; Zambrana and Hurtado, 2015). The fact that many of these students do succeed pushes educators to take into account the other assets and alternatives those students must have employed and the various other ways and measures for attaining success, which are not acknowledged or well understood.

The proposed Culturally Validating Latino Student Success Framework dismantles the deficit-based grand narrative and poses the consideration that students have cultural wealth they employ to succeed in their own way. The key to Latino success is not so much that the student takes the initiative to get academically and socially involved. Instead, it must be considered that students can succeed in engaging their own ways of knowing and coming into contact with those colleges and universities that marshal their faculty, staff and institutional resources to assist them to become achievers.

Specifically, students can succeed by attending to the following suggestions:

1. Employing their reservoir of cultural assets. Accordingly, institutional agents are called to understand, validate, and leverage the array of Latino student strengths (see Table 1).

2. Working toward supportive, affirming interactions with in- and out-of-class validating agents. College faculty and staff must be validating champions for students both in and out of class and throughout their college experience. With an ethic of authentic care, validating agents (faculty, counselors, advisers, coaches, tutors, mentors) can assist students' transition to college. Among the elements of support are these:

help them to access resources, navigate and negotiate the academic and sociocultural aspects of the institution, overcome micro-aggressions, develop a sense of belonging, bring their voice and experience to the classroom environment, and acquire confidence in their ability to be successful college students (Center for Community College Engagement, 2014; Rendón-Linares and Muñoz 2011). Indeed, "institutional agents" (Stanton-Salazar 1997) can serve to empower students as agents share knowledge, resources and opportunities needed to decode institutional bureaucracy, language, values, conventions and traditions that are unfamiliar to first-generation, low-income students.

3. Participating in building engaged colleges and universities that marshal diverse, interconnected programs in their academic, social and cultural ecosystem and gear them toward student success. Institutions should ensure that policies, practices and behaviors are aligned with Latino ways of knowing.

Historical and Political Frameworks

Early student retention models and theories were largely, if not exclusively, apolitical. They excluded historical and political forces that have created social and racial injustices and inequitable conditions for students of color. Understanding this helps to contextualize the Latino education experience. More recent views are cognizant that the Latino cultural experience includes a history of successes in overcoming poverty, poor schooling, racial subordination, discrimination, and violence. These societal forms of oppression are very difficult to deal with and to overcome, yet many examples exist of Latino men and women who did just that (Zambrana and Hurtado 2015; Valenzuela 1999; Hurtado 2006).

Transition to College

Key characteristics of early student retention models were based on assumptions of linearity. Simply put, the transition to college was thought to be marked by the student initially separating from personal cultural realities to incorporate into the academic and social fabric of the institution. The result of this integration was deemed to be student success. More recent views argue that the transition to college is not linear. In fact, the educational trajectory of students of color is often messy, with students moving back and forth from college to their personal worlds of home, work, community, native country, and peers (Rendón, Nora, and Kanagala 2014; Hurtado 2006; Jalomo 1995).

In a study of Latino student college completion Rendón, Nora, and Kanagala (2014) found that Latino students operated "*entre mundos*" (in multiple worlds), including their personal worlds and the new world of college. In doing so, students dealt with the following complex dynamics:

Liminality. A liminal space is an "in-between" space, where students can find themselves caught and pulled toward more than one way of being and doing. It can also be the experience of feeling that one is neither here nor there, *ni aquí, ni allá*. During the early transition to college, students are trying to adapt to a new world while staying connected to their old one. They can experience both the "highs" of excitement about being in college and learning new things and the "lows" of loneliness and doubt about whether college is really worth it and really for them.

Choque/Cultural collision. As students move from their familiar cultural realities to the foreign context of college, they can experience what Anzaldúa (1999) calls *un choque,* or a cultural collision. This is substantiated by scholars (Boyte 2014; Putman 2015; Stephens et al. 2012; Rendón, Jalomo, and Nora 2000) who have noted that there are cultural mismatches between low-income and upper-class cultural norms that can create a social performance gap and reproduce social inequalities. For instance, norms such as "doing your own thing," and "realizing your own potential" can run counter to the values of first-generation students, who typically focus on "giving back" and "collective success." Further, the world of college includes academic values and conventions such as merit and independence, along with specific formal and informal forms of language expression, codes of behavior, and belief systems that are often foreign to first-generation, low-income students.

Separation anxiety. Loneliness, depression, and guilt can occur when students feel that they can no longer stay closely connected to family and friends who choose not to leave their home communities.

Dislocation and relocation. Students can experience multiple forms of geographical or educational dislocation and relocation as they transition to college: breaking away from high school, transferring from a community college, moving from one state to another, or moving from their native country to the United States.

Micro-aggressions. For students of color, navigating a new college world often involves experiences with racial and gender micro-aggressions (Minikel-

Lacocque 2012; Sue 2010). Micro-aggressions can include being made to feel embarrassed for playing Spanish music or speaking Spanish, being treated as a cultural outsider, being laughed at for cooking ethnic foods in a residence hall, being made fun of because of an accent, or being made to feel as though as a Latino, one is not as smart as white students.

Institutional Culture

The race-neutral view of an institution that does not account for difference can serve to discounting, masking, and overlooking diverse student cultures, communities, and experiences (Dowd and Bensimon 2015; Harper and Hurtado 2007). The Latino community is quite diverse and includes biracial and multiracial students. Other forms of diversity include sexuality, gender, military status, religion, age, political affiliation and ability. The essentialist framing of the term "Latino" can mask these complexities and nuances. What is needed is a validation-rich institutional culture that accounts for difference while building community. The culture should also foster a sense of belonging, critically engage questions of inequalities and race and social injustices, validate minoritized students, and build on student assets (Malcom-Piqueux and Bensimon 2015).

Student Support Services

As the demographic diversity at institutions of higher educations increases across the nation, departments of student affairs, which have a long history of advocacy for underserved and underrepresented student populations, need to adapt and transform their functions and practices. This is particularly true in communities that have witnessed significant demographic growth in the Latino population. Community colleges, which have traditionally served students of color, are witnessing an increased enrollment of Latino students, and in the process, attaining Hispanic-Serving Institution (HSI) designation (Núñez, Crisp, and Elizondo 2016). In concert with faculty-driven pedagogies that ensure academic success, student affairs professionals should consider embracing culturally relevant practices that attend to the co-curricular, social, cultural, and emotional needs of Latino students. These may include developing learning communities that create a collaborative environment and a sense of belonging through validating experiences (Jehangir, Williams, and Jeske 2012); transforming academic advising practices to meet the unique needs of first-generation, low-income Latino students; expanding outreach to engage Latino families and communities in the recruitment of Latino youth to attend college; supportive cultural centers that cater to the social and cultural needs of Latino students; and communicating with families using bilingual resources (Pérez and Ortiz 2014). Institutions should also consider diversifying their student services staff by hiring more Latinos, who could serve as mentors and role models to students.

Pedagogy

Dominant pedagogic views adhere to the expert model, in which faculty tend to distance themselves from students and maintain a monocultural curriculum. The focus is on individual student achievement, to the exclusion of student voice, and is accompanied by a singular focus on intellectual development. In contrast, culturally validating pedagogic perspectives are relationship-centered, inclusive, and multicultural. A community of learners is created and faculty engage as validating agents who provide support, encouragement, and affirmation. The curriculum includes a focus on racial and social justice, and there is an effort to incorporate student voice and cultural experience. Faculty adhere to holistic student development, attending to intellectual, social, emotional, and spiritual aspects of academic and developmental student growth (Center for Community College Engagement 2014; Freire 1970; Rendón 2009).

Assessment

The entrenched model of student and institutional assessment focuses on collecting data to assess student learning and institutional performance. In fact, performance-based standards of excellence have recently taken center stage. Colleges and universities are rewarded, for example, on the extent to which they can document gains in student course completion, credit attainment, and degree completion. However, a singular focus on performance can have the effect of masking equity issues behind data. Malcom-Piqueux and Bensimon (2015) propose that examining educational outcomes for Latino students is central to institutional assessment practices. They propose that institutional leaders (presidents, vice presidents, deans, department chairs, and directors of divisions and programs) should be attentive to the following assessment practices: disaggregation of educational outcome data by race/ethnicity and gender; the adoption of metrics of equity and their application to disaggregated student outcomes; engagement in performance benchmarking to set equity goals in specific educational outcomes; and the implementation of model practices of equity-minded data interpretation. Accordingly, new equity-minded data collection practices should be guided by both performance and equity considerations and include equity metrics for Latinos as well as for other student cohorts (Malcom-Piqueux and Bensimon 2015).

WORKING WITH LATINO STUDENTS' *CONOCIMIENTOS*/WAYS OF KNOWING

The "Culturally Validating Latino Student Success Framework" described in this essay may be employed as a model to assist two- and four-year institutions to transform academic and student support programs and align them toward Latino students' ways of knowing. Steps toward this outcome include the following:

Provide Extensive Faculty and Staff Development

This training and development should focus on understanding Latino cultural wealth and leveraging Latino student assets, becoming in- and out-of-class validating agents, designing a holistic, culturally relevant pedagogy, considering cultural issues and challenges inherent in the transition to college, facilitating the navigational aspects of learning a new academic culture, and becoming adept in conducting equity-minded assessment practices.

Design Innovative Latino-Centered Practices of High Impact

High-impact practices include experiential and deep learning, applied learning, internships, validation, learning communities, service learning, capstone courses, and research with a faculty member (Kuh 2008; Rendón-Linares and Muñoz 2011; Center for Community College Student Engagement, 2014). These practices can have a significant impact on all students regardless of ethnic/racial background. In addition there are Latino-centered programs and strategies that can have high impact on student learning, socialization, and leadership development, as well as academic and personal growth. These include Culturally Validating Contemplative Experiences that involve deep teaching and learning experiences wherein students can connect their culture to course material; find self worth, purpose, and voice; and acquire the knowledge and wisdom needed to ensure holistic student development. The idea is to go beyond academic understandings and to allow students to develop their emotional, social, and inner-life skills as they seek to build on their ethnic consciousness and become transformative social justice agents. This kind of learning experience can take place in learning communities such as service-learning and arts-based projects that incorporate music, poetry, and the visual arts (Rendón, 2009). For instance, Pulido (2002) and Kanagala and Rendón (2013) have employed what they call the "*cajitas* project," in which students construct boxes that are cultural representations of their history, family, and life experiences. Rooted in liberatory pedagogy and practice, this project allows for deep reflection, self-examination, and mindful learning. The future of teaching and learning calls for much needed culturally validating innovations that foster student academic learning and personal development.

Create Ethnic-Themed Learning Communities

The Puente Project has a long-standing history as an exemplary learning community in two-year colleges and high schools in California and Texas. The Puente model combines accelerated instruction in reading and writing, counseling and a course in student success techniques, and one-on-one mentoring by community role models (http://catchthenext.org/our-program/).

Latino Student Support Programming

Examples include culturally relevant spaces of support: multicultural centers, Latino fraternities and sororities, Latino cultural centers, Latino leadership retreats, intergroup dialogues, and ethnic studies courses. These kinds of programs can facilitate student academic and personal growth as well as leadership development. Programs can assist students who struggle with how to navigate the world of college as they work through issues of identity development, deal with campus micro- and macro-aggressions, and foster *hermandad*/brotherhood and sisterhood (Lozano 2015; Guardia 2015).

CONCLUSION

The next generation of student success programming must work with Latino students by employing an asset-based foundation that is aligned with their ways of knowing and with contemporary research that speaks to the experience of Latino students in society and in higher education. The fact that after at least 30 years of research and practice Latinos are still trailing white students in terms of college access and completion speaks to the notion that some aspects of the dominant models employed to foster success are simply not working. Further, they may be inappropriate or even harmful for Latino students. What is needed is a validating, Latino-centric student success framework that locates two- and four-year institutions at the center of shaping innovative solutions and making transformative changes in academic and student support services. As we experience the browning of American higher education and a growing populace destined to shape the nation's economic and political future, the challenge of ensuring Latinos' success in college must be addressed in ways that lead to breakthroughs and novel advances in study and practice.

REFERENCES

Anzaldúa, Gloria. 1999. *Borderlands/La Frontera. The New Mestiza.* 2nd. ed. San Francisco: Aunt Lute Books.

———. 2005. "To Live in the Borderlands Means You." *American Identities: An Introductory Textbook.* Malden, MA: Blackwell Publishing, 316.

Astin, Alexander W. 1984. "Student Involvement: A Developmental Theory for Higher Education." *Journal of College Student Personnel* 12: 297–308.

Beatty, Cameron Carl, 2014. "Exploring the Leadership Identity Development of Students of Color at a Selective Liberal Arts College." PhD diss.: Iowa State University. *Graduate Theses and Dissertations.* Paper 14050, http://lib.dr.iastate.edu/etd/14050.

Bernal, Dolores Delgado. 2001. "Learning and Living Pedagogies of the Home: The Mestiza Consciousness of Chicana Students." *International Journal of Qualitative Studies in Education* 14:5, 623–639. doi: 10.1080/095183390110059838.

Bordas, Juana. 2013. *The Power of Latino Leadership: Culture, Inclusion, and Contribution.* San Francisco: Berrett-Koehler Publishers.

Boyte, Harry C., ed. 2014. *Democracy's Education: Public Work, Citizenship, and the Future of Colleges and Universities.* Nashville: Vanderbilt University Press.

Catch the Next. 2009. http://catchthenext.org/our-program/.

Center for Community College Student Engagement. 2014. *A Matter of Degrees: Practices to Pathways (High-Impact Practices for Community College Student Success.* Austin: University of Texas at Austin, Program in Higher Education Leadership.

Conchas, Gilberto Q. 2006. *The Color of Success: Race and High-Achieving Urban Youth.* Teachers College Press.

Dowd, Alicia C., and Estela Mara Bensimon. 2015. *Engaging the "Race Question": Accountability and Equity in US Higher Education.* Teachers College Press.

Foxen, Patricia. 2015. *Resilient Latino Youth: In Their Own Words.* Washington, DC: National Council of La Raza.

Freire, Paolo. 1970. *Pedagogy of the Oppressed.* New York: Herder and Herder.

Guardia, Juan R. 2015. "Leadership and Identity Development through a Latino/a Fraternity and Sorority Lens." In *Latina/o College Student Leadership: Emerging Theory, Promising Practice,* edited by Adele Lozano, 65–82. Lanham, MD: Lanham Books.

hooks, bell. 1994. *Outlaw Culture: Resisting Representations.* Routledge.

Harper, Shaun R., and Sylvia Hurtado. 2007. "Nine Themes in Campus Racial Climates and Implications for Institutional Transformation." *New Directions for Student Services* 120: 7–24. doi: 10.1002/ss.254

Hurtado, A. 2006. "Un cuadro–A framing." In N. E. Cantú (ed.), *Flor y Ciencia: Chicanas in Science, Mathematics, and Engineering* (pp.1-10). San Antonio, TX: The Adelante Project.

Hurtado, Sylvia, and Deborah Faye Carter. 1997. "Effects of College Transition and Perceptions of the Campus Racial Climate on Latino College Students' Sense of Belonging." *Sociology of Education* 70:4: 324–345. doi: 10.2307/2673270.

Jalomo, Romero Espinoza. 1995. *Latino Students in Transition: An Analysis of the First-Year Experience in Community College.* Unpublished doctoral dissertation, College of Education, Arizona State University, Tempe.

Jehangir, Rashné, Rhiannon Williams, and Judith Jeske. 2012. "The Influence of Multicultural Learning Communities on the Intrapersonal Development of First-Generation Multicultural Students." *Journal of College Student Development* 53:2, 267–284. doi: 10.1353/csd.2012.0035

Kanagala, Vijay, and Laura I. Rendón. 2013. "Birthing Internal Images: Employing the *Cajita* Project as a Contemplative Activity in a College Classroom." *New Directions for Teaching and Learning* 134 (summer). 41-51. doi: 10.1002/tl.20053

Kann, Veronica, and Alicia Rodríguez. 2015. "Voices on the Margin: The Latina/o Resilience Network and Retention Strategies." In *Latina/o College Student Leadership: Emerging Theory, Promising Practice,* edited by Adele Lozano, 85–100. Lanham, MD: Lanham Books.

Kuh, George D. 2001. "Assessing What Really Matters to Student Learning: Inside the National Survey of Student Engagement." *Change: The Magazine of Higher Learning* 33:3, 10–17. doi: 10.1080/00091380109601795.

Kuh, George D. 2008. *High-Impact Practices: What They Are, Who Has Access to Them and Why They Matter.* American Association of Colleges and Universities, http://secure.aacu.org/store/detail.aspx?id=E-HIGHIMP.

Kuh, George D., Ty M. Cruce, Rick Shoup, Jillian Kinzie, and Robert M. Gonyea. 2008. "Unmasking the Effects of Student Engagement on First-Year College Grades and Persistence." *Journal of Higher Education* 79:5, 540–563.

Lather, Patricia. 1991. *Getting Smart: Feminist Research and Pedagogy with/in the Postmodern.* New York: Routledge.

Lozano, Adele, ed. 2015. *Latina/o College Student Leadership: Emerging Theory, Promising Practice.* Lanham, MD: Lanham Books.

Minikel-Lacocque, Julie. 2012. "Racism, College, and the Power of Words: Racial Microaggressions Reconsidered." *American Educational Research Journal*. 50:3, 432-465. doi: 10.3102/0002831212468048.

Malcom-Piquex, L., and Estela Bensimon. 2015. *Design Principles for Equity and Excellence at Hispanic-Serving Institutions. Perspectivas.* Policy brief sponsored by the American Association of Hispanics in Higher Education and Educational Testing Service. No. 4, Spring 2015. http://education.utsa.edu/crpe.

Moll, Luis C., Cathy Amanti, Deborah Neff, and Norma González. 2001. "Funds of Knowledge for Teaching: Using a Qualitative Approach to Connect Homes and Classrooms." *Theory into Practice* 31:2, 132–141. doi: 10.1080 /00405849209543534.

Núñez, Anne-Marie, Gloria Crisp, and Diane Elizondo. 2016. "Mapping Hispanic-Serving Institutions: A Typology of Institutional Diversity." *Journal of Higher Education* 87:1, 55-83. doi: 10.1353/jhe.2016.0001

Perez, Eyra A., and Noé C. Ortiz. 2014. "The Impact of Financial Aid on Student College Access and Success: The San Antonio Experience." Washington, DC: *Excelencia* in Education.

Pulido, Alberto I. 2002. "The Living Color of Students' Lives: Bringing Cajitas Into the Classroom." *Religion & Education* 29:2, 69–77.

Putnam, Robert. 2015. *Our Kids. The American Dream in Crisis.* New York: Simon & Schuster.

Rendón, Laura I. 2009. *Sentipensante (sensing/thinking) Pedagogy: Educating for Wholeness, Social Justice and Liberation.* Sterling, VA: Stylus Publishing.

Rendón, Laura I. 1994. "Validating Culturally Diverse Students: Toward a New Model of Learning and Student Development." *Innovative Higher Education* 19:1, 33–51.

Rendón-Linares, Laura I., and Susana M. Muñoz. 2011. "Revisiting Validation Theory: Theoretical Foundations, Applications, and Extensions." *Enrollment Management Journal* 5:2, 12–33.

Rendón, Laura I., Romero E. Jalomo, and Amaury Nora. 2000. "Theoretical Considerations in the Study of Minority Student Retention in Higher Education." *Reworking the Student Departure Puzzle* 1, 127–156.

Rendón, Laura I., Amaury Nora, and Vijay Kanagala. 2014. *Ventajas/Assets y Conocimientos/Knowledge: Leveraging Latin@ Strengths to Foster Student Success.* San Antonio: University of Texas at San Antonio, Center for Research and Policy in Education.

Shahjahan, Riyad Ahmed. 2005. "Spirituality in the Academy: Reclaiming From the Margins and Evoking a Transformative Way of Knowing the World." *International Journal of Qualitative Studies in Education* 18:6, 685–711. doi:10.1080/09518390500298188.

Stanton-Salazar, Ricardo. 1997. "A Social Capital Framework for Understanding the Socialization of Racial Minority Children and Youths." *Harvard Educational Review* 67:1: 1–41.

Stephens, Nicole M., Stephanie A. Fryberg, Hazel Rose Markus, Camille S. Johnson, and Rebecca Covarrubias. 2012. "Unseen Disadvantage: How American Universities' Focus on Independence Undermines the Academic Performance of First-Generation College Students." *Journal of Personality and Social Psychology* 102:6, 1178. doi: 10.1037/a0027143

Suárez, Cecilia. 2015. "Never Created with Nosotros in Mind: Combating Colorblind Leadership Education with Cultural Competency and Intersectionality of Identities." In *Latina/o College Student Leadership: Emerging Theory, Promising Practice*, edited by Adele Lozano, 29–44. Lanham, MD: Lanham Books.

Sue, Derald Wing. 2010. *Microaggressions in Everyday Life: Race, Gender, and Sexual Orientation*. Hoboken, NJ: John Wiley & Sons.

Tinto, Vincent. 1975. "Dropout From Higher Education: A Theoretical Synthesis of Recent Research." *Review of Educational Research* 45:1, 89–125.

———. 1987. *Leaving College: Rethinking the Causes and Cures of Student Attrition*. Chicago: University of Chicago Press.

US Bureau of the Census. 2012. *Educational Attainment by Race and Hispanic Origin: 1970 to 2010*. 229, http://www.census.gov/compendia/statab/2012/tables/12s0229.pdf

Valencia, Richard R. 2010. *Dismantling Contemporary Deficit Thinking: Educational Thought and Practice*. New York: Taylor and Francis.

———. 1997. *The Evolution of Deficit Thinking: Educational Thought and Practice*. Washington, DC: Falmer Press.

Valenzuela, Angela. 1999. *Subtractive Schooling: US-Mexican Youth and the Politics of Caring*. Albany: State University of New York Press.

Volpp, Leti. 2000. "Blaming Culture for Bad Behavior." *Yale Journal of Law and the Humanities* 12:1, 89–116.

Yosso, Tara J. 2005. "Whose Culture Has Capital? A Critical Race Theory Discussion of Community Cultural Wealth." *Race Ethnicity and Education* 8:1, 69–91. doi: 10.1080/1361332052000341006

Zambrana, Ruth Enid, and Sylvia Hurtado, eds. 2015. *The Magic Key: The Educational Journey of Mexican Americans from K-12 to College and Beyond*. Louann Atkins Temple Women & Culture series, Book 38. Austin: University of Texas Press.

Nuestra Excelencia

BUILDING AN INSTITUTIONAL CULTURE OF EXCELLENCE THROUGH A LATINA/O EXCELLENCE PEDAGOGY AT THE POST-SECONDARY LEVEL

Louie F. Rodríguez

ABSTRACT

It is fair to say that the trending patterns among Latina/o college students in the United States, when it comes to their challenges, struggles, and achievements, continue to garner attention in the empirical, policy-making, and scholarly realms. While the challenges facing Latina/o college students have been widely recognized, there is a clear dearth of research into how institutional culture shapes Latina/o student success. Using an additive conceptual lens, our goal here is to identify an excellence-based pedagogical framework, aiming to promote a college/university culture that facilitates Latina/o student success. Implications for A Latina/o Excellence Pedagogy are also explored.

SETTING THE CONTEXT

Over the last several years, there has been an upsurge of attention on the enrollment of Latina/o students in post-secondary institutions across the United States (Núñez 2015). Known as Hispanic-Serving Institutions (HSIs), colleges and universities qualify for HSI status when the overall Latina/o enrollment reaches 25 percent. In effect, the growing number of Latinas/os in colleges and universities over the last twenty years has generated significant attention among researchers, policy-makers, and practitioners in the field of education (Santiago 2010). While the enrollment of Latina/o students in colleges and universities has grown considerably over the last decade, there has also been criticism of certain institutions when seen as or referred to as Hispanic "Enrolling" Institutions, suggesting that merely enrolling Latina/o students does not necessarily equate to serving this population, particularly through equity and outcome lenses (Núñez and Elizondo 2012). In fact, some Predominately White Institutions (PWI) that have recently found themselves inching toward the 25 percent Latina/o enrollment threshold have publicly celebrated this milestone. Yet scholars have often questioned whether this designation is a call to action, in actual response to the needs of Latina/o students, or whether this designation just qualifies the institutions for federal funds to "serve" this population (Contreras, Malcolm, & Bensimón 2008). While evidence will continue to emerge, this article is concerned with the ways in which Institutions of Higher Education have responded to the needs of Latina/o students, particularly in the ways they can use specific pedagogical practices to help transform institutional culture.

RECENT DEVELOPMENTS

Historically, there have been important efforts to engage Latina/o students. For instance, in California, the Puente (Bridge) program has been around for several decades with the aim to help historically marginalized students transfer to four year institutions. More recent examples include programs that have revolved around students with STEM-related majors, and programs aimed at first-generation students. At the university level, there have historically been EOP and TRIO-related programs focused on the engagement of success of Latinas/os and other students of color at the university level (Rodríguez, Mosqueda, Conchas, and Nava 2013). The increasing need for remediation at the college and university levels has helped bring attention to college preparedness and a "college readiness" discourse. Such efforts are theoretically supposed to reduce the number of remediation courses needed by unprepared freshman and at the same time provide them with support systems that facilitate their transition and success in college.

Some institutions have also taken a closer look at residential programs that require college freshman to live on campus, especially since the research suggests that when students live on campus, their engagement and persistence rates increase. However, when such programs and policies are contextualized, there are nuances of considerable importance, such as the responsibilities and stress factors faced by first-generation, low-income, and immigrant students, who are often Latinas/os attending a Hispanic-Serving Institution or not. Additionally, we see greater attention—both at national and state levels—around the so-called High Impact

Practices (HIPs). For instance, the California State University system has created a division specifically focused on orienting and engaging campus-level stakeholders in ways that they can implement HIPs at the campus level.

While the actual number and definition of specific High Impact Practices varies, practices include a focus on internship experiences for students, research experiences, and service learning, among many others. The idea is to ensure that all university students have one, two or more of these experiences which have been associated with greater college student persistence and success. What is largely overlooked, presumably, is the power and impact of student-faculty connections and the relationships that are either constructed or not at the college or university level. In fact, research across the educational pipeline suggests that student-teacher or student-faculty relationships are central to the success of students, particularly low-income students of color, and Latina/o students specifically (Rodríguez & Oseguera 2015). Yet, when all these responses, practices, and policies are considered, scant attention is given to the effects that student-teacher/faculty dynamics have, for better or for worse, on students' persistence and overall success. This is more troubling given that solid empirical evidence already exists to show that said dynamics are vital to the success of Latina/o students.

The exclusion of this critically vital component is likely the result of an education culture that avoids conversation about the social and cultural dynamics within institutions, while continuing to focus heavily on technical approaches (such as the implementation of specific programs, polices, and practices). Student-faculty dynamics at the post-secondary level are likely to be overlooked for the same reasons they are at the K-12 level: emphasizing the role of teacher/faculty implies their responsibility and accountability for ensuring that students are successful. It is not solely a matter of faculty responsibility and accountability, but we often fail to acknowledge in more comprehensive ways those thriving environments facilitated by faculty who prioritize connections and relationships with students, and intentionally use these connections to boost student engagement and success. The underlying, and perhaps less political, assumption is that student-faculty relationships are actually developing during experiences such as internships and service learning.

The current demographic trends in higher education suggest that we need to explicitly and intentionally consider more social and cultural approaches to transforming how institutions engage Latina/o students. While the current article will not explain the role that student-faculty connections play in engaging Latina/o students specifically, its importance has implications for Latina/o excellence. Latina/o excellence is suggested as an organizing tool and topic around which to pedagogically engage campus stakeholders in conversation, in an effort to engage and facilitate the persistence and success of Latina/o college and university students. Before outlining this excellence framework, it will be useful to provide a brief overview of the author's own educational journey through college/university, as it highlights how a focus on Latina/o excellence can transform opportunities and outcomes for students (Rodríguez, forthcoming).

MY EDUCATIONAL JOURNEY: AN UNLIKELY SCHOLAR
Community College

Late in high school, I discovered I was not eligible to enter a four-year university. Upon review of my high school record with my guidance counselor, I was simply told, "you need to go to community college." Shortly after graduation, I enrolled in community college and so began my career as a first-generation college student, third-generation Chicano, and, according to my community demographics, a working-class student. As a community college student, I worked in an office filing papers for $4.25 per hour, drove a 1977 Chrysler Cordoba, and paid for tuition, books, and other necessities with cash, which was feasible at the time, at a tuition rate of $13 per unit.

There were no immediate sources of support available to me or my peers. After my first semester, I sensed that something was not quite right about "college" and promptly headed to the academic counseling office to speak to a counselor; that turned out to be the best decision I could have made. The counselor set me on a two-year path to complete coursework and then transfer to a local four-year university. This plan virtually jumpstarted my community college experience, whereas before it, I had struggled in some of my classes, and received no social support from my peers, and very little support from the critical institutional agents that should have been looking out for me (Acevedo-Gil, Santos, Alonso, & Solórzano 2015).

It was not until my second year that I encountered a professor who engaged my interests and intentionally communicated to students that she cared about us and our learning. She structured a dialogue-driven classroom, small group discussions, and essay-based assignments and exams. She showed interest in and concern for our thoughts on specific historical events, and often helped us to see their connection to present-day realities. While a one-on-one relationship was not established during my time in her class, I was acknowledged, and that was sufficient; it triggered my engagement and the desire to learn and thrive in her class and in the remainder of my classes at the community college. Moreover, the dialogue-driven nature of her class inspired me to revisit my study habits, redefined my role as a learner, and helped me develop my identity as a student and learner. I always tell people that community college taught me how to be a college student.

What was largely missing from my community college experience was a focus on the end goal. While implicitly and systematically the goal of community college is to transfer to a four-year institution, there were no connections to the larger significance of being an educated Chicano/Latino within our institution, community, and country. There was no conversation about our responsibility to serve or give back to the community; there was no conversation about leadership. There was no conversation about excellence or Latina/o excellence, nor anybody from our community who demonstrated excellence and was now serving our community. Not until recently did I realize, in fact, how vital these critical conversations are to the purpose, motivation, and relevance of pursuing higher education, and vital not only to our own personal excellence, but to community excellence as well (Rodríguez 2015).

Nevertheless, I transferred to CSU, San Bernardino; urged by my mother to fully participate in the college's commencement activities, I thus began the journey to a bachelor's degree. Of the handful of friends that had started community college alongside me, however, I was the only one who persisted beyond the first year, and the only one to graduate with an Associate's Degree and transfer to a four-year university, at least within a reasonable two- to three-year time frame.

Not Quite Yet an HSI

When I transferred, I found myself suddenly on a much larger and much more academically rigorous campus. Fortunately, my emerging academic identity and mental preparation as a self-driven student helped me hit the ground running. While the institution was largely non-Latina/o and much larger in terms of enrollment (roughly 16,000 at the time), I was determined to "succeed" and yet found myself again without any social, cultural, or institutional capital. I lacked guidance and mentorship but I drew support from my grandparents and their legacy, my parents and their hard work and encouragement, and my little brothers, who largely looked up to their older brother for guidance.

After a couple of quarters, I sought further connection. I began attending campus-supported workshops to develop various skills, such as resume crafting and interviewing skills and the like. I attended lectures when I could and continued to work heavily during the evenings, from 6 p.m. to midnight almost every weeknight, and weekends from 10 AM to 7 PM. This busy schedule and the myriad responsibilities that came with it forced me to stay focused and use my time wisely. Time-management decisions, while difficult to make, often led to sacrificing family obligations or attendance of family events (i.e., baptisms) and cutting social time with friends.

One afternoon on campus, I felt my dedication begin to pay off. I was recognized by a peer in the hallway; he was also a Chicano student, but a year or two ahead of me in studies. He invited me to attend an information session about the McNair Scholar's Program. Prior to that meeting, I did not know or understand the full meaning of a Ph.D., but after it, I qualified and was admitted to the program, forever changing the trajectory of my life. I was provided a mentor, encouraged to conduct research, present my research, travel, and continue to strengthen my identity as a student, researcher, and scholar.

The major difference between community college and CSU, San Bernardino was my exposure to others who looked like me and who were thriving scholars. My McNair mentor was a Chicano scholar who earned degrees from Harvard and UC Berkeley. My McNair director was African American, and completing her Ph.D. at a local private university. Many of the campus Vice Presidents were Latino Ph.Ds. who intentionally reached out to McNair Scholars as a gesture of support. For the first time, I had access to people in these positions, to the point where some wrote letters of recommendations for me when I applied to graduate school. My social and cultural capital increased exponentially because of my involvement with the McNair Scholar's Program. In addition, the faculty members mentoring other McNair Scholars from psychology, sociology, history, chemistry, and other programs also profoundly influenced me. There were two women of color who worked closely with the program and indirectly became my mentors as well. They showed me what was possible; they showed me that our role as social scientists was to tell the truth, to speak truth to our experiences, to make sure our stories get told, and that it was OK to be intentional. They were all my McNair mentors, these two scholars and women of color, the university's vice presidents, the McNair director, and my peers—the models of excellence that I sought to find, recognize, and learn from throughout my entire educational journey.

The absence of relevant models of excellence before this point in time in my educational journey is not difficult to explain, nor was it accidental. I grew up in a racially and economically segregated community. I saw no professionals that looked like me; not even teachers. While many years later I learned that there were some thriving Chicana/o/Latina/o professionals in my community, growing up I was unaware of them and never had the fortunate experience of meeting them or benefiting from their mentorship or mere acquaintance. And unfortunately, mentorship by and visibility of minority professionals remains an ongoing challenge.

In proposing the excellence framework, it is important to recognize the influence of earlier research on our model. The first is related to the so-called "Obama Effect." Researchers in the fields of business and social psychology were interested in the extent to which Barack Obama's rise to the presidency impacted the test-taking performance of African American and White test takers (Marx, Ko, and Friedman 2009). Over the course of a carefully designed investigation, the researchers found no achievement gap between African American and White test takers, particularly during the soon-to-be President Obama's most prominent moments (e.g., being nominated for the Democratic ticket and elected as President). The researchers suggested that the presence of a national role model may have diminished any real or perceived barriers that may have existed during a testing situation. Role models matter, and identifying with those role models matters, in this case specifically for African Americans. This research suggests that the presence and visibility of role models may play a significant role in imagining what is possible but also actually shaping one's performance in academic situations.

This study refers to the stereotypes threat research, which suggests that social stereotypes do impact people's performance, particularly people of color, in testing and performance situations (Steele, 1997). For example, if there is a stereotype that Latinas underperform on certain math tests, and, if a Latina test taker believes in the salience of the test itself and is also aware of the stereotype, her performance is likely to be hampered. These experiments have been confirmed in various situations by race, gender, and even athletic ability (see Wasserberg 2009 for an overview of these studies). The research provides a basis for why many people may continue to struggle with certain testing and performance tasks, with direct implications to their success within the formal education system. As this research, along with the Obama Effect research, seems to suggest, positive models of excellence may have a powerful effect on the people who identify with them.

It is essential in this article to acknowledge the power that lies in knowing, acknowledging, learning from, and celebrating Latina/o models of excellence; the right conditions can lead to a transformative paradigm shift when it comes to Latina/o college student persistence and success. My own story is one of many that showcase the tremendous role that mentors and visible models of excellence play in a student's college trajectory and future success. The question becomes which pedagogical and practical strategies will universities follow to use excellence, and Latina/o excellence specifically, as an organizing tool to build an institutional culture that shifts the social and cultural fabric of the institution? In other words, and in the context of some of the developments occurring at many institutions of higher learning that enroll significant numbers of Latina/o students, how can a well-developed and deeply ingrained culture of excellence and Latina/o excellence specifically be used to sustain any policies, programs, or practices that promote Latina/o student success? If Latina/o excellence is intentionally sought, created, and sustained, we are likely to turn the page in our institutional history and begin to shape reality anew for the purposes of our students and the role of our institutions in our community and society.

TOWARD A LATINA/O EXCELLENCE FRAMEWORK

What does a Pedagogy of Latina/o Excellence look like at the university level? What would local policy look like to support these efforts? What is the role of campus and community stakeholders in engaging in this type of pedagogy? For the last ten years, my research has focused primarily on the voices and experiences of Black and Latina/o youth in urban schools and communities. In addition to understanding students' experiences and using their experiences to shape subsequent investigation, I have focused my research on developing practical and policy changes at the school, district, and university levels, particularly in terms of teacher/leadership development. I have also been interested in developing pedagogical strategies that students, educators, leaders, and community stakeholders can use to engage in dialogue about pertinent issues facing the community. For instance, my work has suggested classroom/community dialogues, Participatory Action Research (PAR) approaches such as problem-posing pedagogies, and the use of Educational Journeys as a tool to engage students, parents, and educators (Rodríguez 2014). In all these efforts, the voices and experiences of the community are the driving force. My main role, and that of my collaborators, has been to provide a space and to ask critical questions to push the conversation along. Nevertheless, the ownership, skill development, and the "what next" questions are largely driven by members of the community.

Following those guiding principles, this work has been carried out in the K-12 context over the last several years (Rodríguez 2015). I have worked with elementary, middle, and high schools, their districts and their surrounding community stakeholders in processes related to a Pedagogy of

Excellence. In all cases, excellence was defined by each school community, a series of models of excellence were identified based upon that definition of excellence, and these models were recognized in very public ways. In all these examples, excellence had to be intentional and required the following: the support of leadership, the community's engagement efforts, a focus on process and outcome, and a heightened understanding of the community context. The remainder of this section will discuss the ways in which this framework applies to the university context for the purposes of developing a Latina/o Excellence Pedagogy at the community college and university level.

A Latina/o Excellence Pedagogy

The process associated with a Latina/o Excellence Pedagogy is essential to it. With that said, however, it is also highly important to note that the step-by-step structure is a mere guide. Stakeholders need to understand and acknowledge that each context will vary its approach and will be shaped by the leadership and existing institutional culture. The common thread throughout the process in any context or institution is the intentionality behind the work. Further, the step-by-step model does not suggest that unwavering adherence or, for that matter, a more flexible approach, will yield certain results. In fact, each process will likely—and aims to—reflect the local realities. Nevertheless, there are a series of non-negotiables that I outline in *Intentional Excellence* to serve as a guide.

Leadership. For one, leadership participation is essential. Whether at an HSI or PWI, the leadership must be committed to developing a culture that values, recognizes, and sustains a culture of Latina/o excellence on campus. As colleges and universities continue to inch toward the 25% enrollment threshold, they can and should be poised to respond through the suggested pedagogy. However, the political will must be present. When it is, it sends a strong a message throughout the community, about the institution's goals, vision, and priorities. When the message is conveyed, stakeholders who value similar priorities will engage. However, this does not automatically result in full institutional participation. Members of the existing institutional culture need to be included in the process; the political leverage brought by university leadership is vital, not only symbolically but also practically.

Community engagement. Another point that is non-negotiable, that is, completely vital to the work, is community engagement. Community is defined as both institutional and community/region-wide. At the campus level, this is an opportunity to engage students, staff, faculty, administrators, and other university personnel. Like any institution, each stakeholder has a vital role to play in shaping and defining what excellence means to the community and Latina/o excellence specifically. Another important stakeholder is alumni. To the extent possible, key alumni should be engaged in important ways that demonstrate their value to the institution and tapped for their insight regarding Latina/o excellence, especially if they are Latina/o alumni. Research on Latina/o alumni engagement is still an underexplored field, but the strong desire by this group to find ways to contribute and give back is a visible tendency. The adage, "build it and they will come" has proven true in our work and findings. Beyond the campus community, there are other community stakeholders, and some who constitute untapped community resources, such as respected community leaders, professionals, and other leaders. These people can serve as models of excellence for existing university students and help build a culture of Latina/o excellence.

Contextual mindfulness. It must be noted that, when considering the process by which to incorporate Latina/o excellence into helping shape the culture of the institution, the broader context is key. That is, history, economic context, political challenges, and larger demographic realities will be key factors. What is the nature of engagement between the larger Latina/o community and the university? To what extent are Latina/o faculty represented at the administration and faculty levels? How do language considerations affect the work? What is the climate surrounding immigration and larger policy issues? All these matters require some sensitivity and an understanding of such contextual factors. If there are larger social, political, cultural, and economic challenges in the community, there is a good chance that these issues will spill over into the university, not merely as news but as genuine concerns among the students, faculty, and administrators. These matters must be considered while the work is conducted.

Process and Outcome. A final non-negotiable is the nature of the work with regard to both process and outcome or what I have referred to elsewhere as the process-outcome dualism (Rodríguez 2015). That is, not only should stakeholders be concerned with the outcome of the work, but they should be concerned with the process itself. As mentioned, engaging the community is important and time intensive work. Attention needs to be placed on the people invited, ongoing reflection and analysis on who is at the table, and monitoring of the group process itself is key. In some cases, excellence work can move rather quickly, while for others the work may be slow, and perhaps rightly so, especially if a cultural paradigm shift is what we are seeking. Sometimes the nature itself of the process, is as critical as the outcome. Along the way, community is built, energy is created, and mutual goals and interests are sought, identified, and defined. These moments of process can be just as telling and informative about the institutional culture; nonetheless, the goals of organizing, defining, acknowledging, sustaining, and learning from excellence are always valuable and should always be kept in mind. Now, having identified these guidelines, we can articulate what happens when these non-negotiable elements are put into action.

GETTING THE PEOPLE TOGTHER: THE "HOW"

Organizing for Excellence

Perhaps the most significant step in developing the Latina/o Excellence Pedagogy is getting people together—organizing around excellence. A call for participation should be made and the message should be about using excellence as a tool to boost student engagement and achievement, especially Latina/o students. A series of pedagogical exercises can be used to engage the group (for the purposes of this article, the group will be referred to as the Excellence Committee). For instance, what does excellence mean in general? What does excellence mean in education? What does Latina/o excellence mean, or look like, within the community? What about within the institution? These can be small or large group discussions but the facilitator must be skilled at paying close attention to the group process, including the active, silent, and missing voices. Attention should be placed on truths and the various truths that exist in the institution and community at large. The goal of this initial stage, and part of the Pedagogy itself, is to build excitement and momentum by getting people to engage, discuss, and contribute to a Latina/o Excellence Pedagogy; it is communal, centered on dialogue, and local.

Defining Excellence

Once the Committee is assembled, a list of characteristics associated with excellence must be defined with the local context in mind. To put it simply, we can ask what kinds of actions or evidence should be visible for the definition of Latina/o excellence to be met, as defined for this specific community? In our work at the K-12 level, Latina/o excellence is far more than just academic achievement. Latina/o excellence has been associated with personal and academic improvement. For instance, if a student was getting Ds and Fs in the 7th grade, but turned things around to As and Bs in the 8th grade, it was considered an example of excellence because the implications reach far beyond that one student. If excellence is defined as improvement, then all the students who are struggling their way to improvement can resonate and hold this student as a model of excellence. Similarly, Latina/o excellence has been defined as creating opportunities for others. The Committee that guided our work at one high school defined excellence as creating academic and leadership opportunities for other students. This set of criteria placed greater value on individuals who went above and beyond what teachers or students were expected to do; it recognized work that contributed to developing talent in the community.

When considering the Committee work at the college/university levels, it is important to think critically about Latina/o excellence specifically, and what it looks like inside and outside the institution. There will likely be considerations of specific community concerns and efforts, and cultural and historical acknowledgement of the Latina/o presence within the institution and in the wider community, but there may simultaneously be a consensus that Latina/o excellence mirrors excellence in general. If this is the case, it is important to have conversations about models of excellence that exemplify such definitions, and examine the extent to which Latina/o models of excellence may differ from general models of excellence. The Committee is likely to find that Latina/o models of excellence are working directly to improve the conditions related to Latinas/os in education and in society in general.

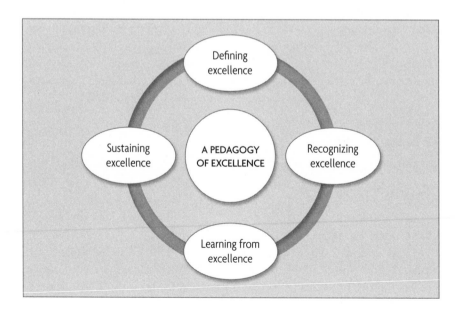

Recognizing Excellence

Once the standard of Latina/o excellence is defined and a list of criteria is set, the Committee should create a nomination process to identify models of excellence in the college/university and larger communities. The Committee should also decide how many models it seeks to identify for the initial Excellence Campaign. Typically, Committees begin with five honorees, predetermining how they allot the honoree spots—two students, two faculty, and one alumnus or similar configuration. At this point of the process, the facilitator and Committee members should remain mindful of the purpose of the work: the goal is to identify Latina/o models of excellence for the purposes of creating a cultural shift within the institution (and community).

How the honorees will be announced and honored is of significance at this point. Once selected, they should be contacted via a personal phone call, a formal letter of recognition, or both. The Committee must also decide how the honorees will be publicly recognized and celebrated. When this work began at the K-12 level, we used district school board meetings, honorees were featured on custom posters, social media and other technology was used to share the news, as well as mailers to announce the honorees. The posters were effective at enabling students to visualize excellence as role models for the public to see. In other words, Excellence posters are tangible and useful artifacts with pedagogical and symbolic utility, both inside and outside the classroom, at the institutional and community levels. In many ways, these posters displaying the role models of excellence aim to be mirrors where students can also see themselves, especially when models are local, and have emerged from the same communities and educational institutions as those around them and current students.

The possibilities of creativity are ample when it comes to poster design and display. One school took the poster concept further and created light-post banners to display across the schoolyard. They also decided to create banners to hang from the gymnasium ceiling. An elementary school created the concept of a walk of excellence (similar to the "Walk of Stars" in Hollywood). Another school thought of a mural, and another of a website.

In any case, the goal is to create processes and practical artifacts that pedagogically engage, motivate, and inspire students, staff, faculty, and community stakeholders. These efforts demonstrate in turn how Latina/o excellence must be intentional.

Learning from Excellence

Perhaps one of the most important and significant insights from our work is the relevance of an institution's ability to learn from its own excellence.

This ability or inability says something critically important about institution's culture—its values, beliefs, leadership, history, capacity, and much more. It is terribly unfortunate that so many of our educational institutions struggle to recognize their own excellence. In *Intentional Excellence,* I refer to this as an Excellence Paradox. That is, while everyone believes in the idea of excellence, how many of our institutions actually pause to define, recognize, and learn from what they already do well (Rodríguez 2015)? I argue that this is not necessarily the fault of teachers, leaders, or the community, but rather a deeply ingrained condition, driven by history and policies, that rewards test score improvement rather than supporting gradual adjustments, or capitalizing on already existing strengths. I argue that every institution and community has strengths and wealth (Yosso 2005), but often lacks the processes to reach their full potential. A Pedagogy of Excellence and a Latina/o Excellence Pedagogy is one such process.

The operative word here is "pedagogy" and that cannot be overemphasized. What I propose and share in this article is an accessible strategy that institutions and communities can use to drive a process. Hence, I am advocating not only for a process by which to recognize and celebrate models of excellence in local communities, but that the entire process itself is an intentional pedagogical act that mobilizes and engages the community in a progressive, communal action related to their own excellence. Through these pedagogical efforts, students, teachers, parents, leaders, and other community stakeholders learn about what is possible and what can be learned, and find an aspirational direction for the community. For a Latina/o Excellence Pedagogy at the college/university level, such spaces are prime for studying what individual students and the community are doing, and for using the Latina/o Excellence Pedagogy work as a case study, to look in the mirror, reflect, and continue growing.

Sustaining Excellence

An equally critical phase in developing a Latina/o Excellence Pedagogy is the promise and possibility of sustaining these efforts. An institution's ability or inability to sustain a gradual and eventually significant shift in culture says something critically important about its potential long term efforts to continue the work. That is, even when there are changes to the leadership, institutional goals, or key players driving these efforts, the extent to which these efforts can be sustained mirrors the extent to which the work has infiltrated the deeply ingrained culture of the institution.

There are several concrete actions that the leadership and Committee can take to ensure that the work continues. There must always be one or more champions committed to carrying the work forward; such individuals provide historical memory of the institution and the efforts and achievements of the excellence work. Another key factor is the use of time, whereas work should be constant and observe frequent milestones. This speaks to the public nature of the work; after a few successful campaigns, the institution and the community begin to expect more. These expectations often reflect hope for something larger and more meaningful even than the honorees and the Committee.

The important symbolism and power that leadership embodies is another feature that cannot be overemphasized. For instance, when launching this work at the K-12 level, one superintendent decided that recognizing and honoring excellence in the district office was going to be a priority for the entire district. With the support of key district leaders and educators, a Committee was assembled, and they decided to "go big" when it came to honoring their models of excellence. They decided the process would cover a period lasting three to six months, and would culminate in a celebration to be held during an official school board meeting in the early spring. The point is that the district's top leader embraced the excellence concept, supported the excellence work symbolically and tangibly, providing resources for needs such as duplicating, food/meals for the launch event, graphic designers, and district resources such as technology specialists to help generate and launch the materials on websites, district television, and media outlets. Clearly, committed and intentional leadership matters.

CONCLUSIONS AND IMPLICATIONS FOR LATINA/O EXCELLENCE AT THE POST-SECONDARY LEVEL

At a time in our nation's history when Latina/o students are an increasing presence on college and university campuses everywhere, it is critical that we look closely both at existing structures, in the forms of programs and policies, and at the culture of the institutions. Institutional culture is reflected in the values, beliefs, practices, responses, actions and inactions, and way of doing things. If we are to consider the persistence, success, and overall wellbeing of Latina/o students on our college and university campuses, we must perform a critical examination of how institutional culture intersects and interacts with Latina/o students (Contreras & Contreras 2015). Similarly, the pace at which an institution inches toward HSI-status should be examined in context with the culture of the institution.

A significant part of the subsequent work is action. In this article, action is framed within the proposed Latina/o Excellence Pedagogy, which serves both as a means by which to engage stakeholders to build something together, and leads finally to the resulting Excellence Campaign. These in turn provide a series of models of excellence whose purpose it is to engage, motivate, and inspire Latina/o students across the PreK-20 educational pipeline.

However, the proposed Latina/o Excellence Pedagogy does require a key principle that is often absent in many institutions across the PreK through 20 pipeline. It was, in fact, absent during my own community college experience and most of my university experience. I am referring to intentionality, and there is no other way around the truth: it was absent until I became a McNair Scholar. Thus, we should remain mindful of the unique nature of programs and practices versus a university-wide pedagogy since it is clear that not everyone will have access to programs and opportunities. Why not then take a critical look the post-secondary culture and place excellence at the center of its educational mission?

Principles for Action to Build
A Latina/o Excellence Pedagogy

A Latina/o Excellence Pedagogy will indeed appear different at each institution, given the unique institutional history and dynamics of each, and the larger community context. Several factors will determine when, how, and at what pace a Latina/o Excellence Pedagogy should be implemented, including the institution's leadership, their will, the tenure of current leadership, the interest and engagement of campus and community stakeholders, and the local and larger context. We must recognize everything from milestone celebrations, to the overall conditions and standing of Latinas/os on campus and in the community, to the broader political context, such as community support or opposition to Latinas/os in general. It all matters.

At the same time, there are some key principles that should inform any Latina/o Excellence Pedagogy. Earlier in this article, a series of non-negotiable considerations were outlined, including the role of leadership, contextual mindfulness, community engagement, and the importance of the process-outcome duality. For A Latina/o Excellence Pedagogy at the post-secondary, I offer a few more suggestions.

Intentionality. Building with intentionality towards A Pedagogy of Excellence is a gesture of equity. At the same time, an absence of this Pedagogy can be considered a gesture of inequity. The same can be said about any research-driven practice that contributes to the persistence and success of Latina/o students at the post-secondary levels.

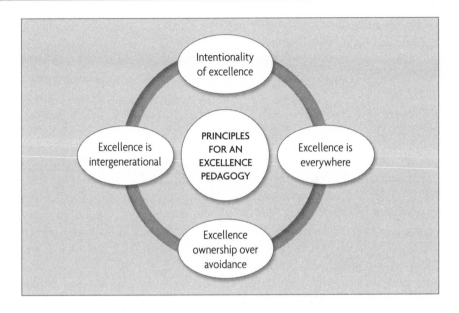

Latina/o excellence everywhere. In most educational spaces across the United States, the historical role and contribution of Latinas/os throughout the Americas and the United States is generally ignored, overlooked, or excluded from mainstream curriculum and pedagogy. The struggle to formally include Latina/o history has been going on for at least 60 years. While our history is still largely excluded at the post-secondary level, except where universities have ethnic studies departments, programs, or courses, Latina/o excellence is largely absent from the spotlight, or just lingering in the shadows. In 2015, there were significant strides to be seen at the K-12 level, while simultaneously several steps backward were taken in places such as Arizona and Texas. I am certain, however, that our excellence is present and ready to be uncovered. A Latina/o Excellence Pedagogy helps us recognize and realize our excellence.

Ownership over avoidance. In *Intentional Excellence* I wrote about the Excellence Paradox and the ways in which our larger educational culture has allowed many educators to disown and dissociate themselves from their own excellence (Rodríguez 2015). It is not the fault of the educators, nor even of the leaders who support them; it is largely due to a deeper current in education that has punished and sometimes denigrated schools, communities, and systems that struggle to serve low-income children of color, and Latinas/os specifically. It has made it difficult for schools to exercise a general Pedagogy of Excellence because they are always functioning in a constant "catch up" mode. Nonetheless, I argue that excellence is present at all levels. We need to move the dial over to a point where our campus and community stakeholders feel comfortable and supported when they own their excellence. This shift is another significant necessity in the context of A Pedagogy of Latina/o Excellence.

Latina/o excellence is intergenerational. In our excellence work across schools, districts, and communities, primarily at the PreK-12 level, it never ceases to amaze us how the spirit, wisdom, and contributions of our ancestors, elders, and families have formed our past, present, and future. One of the guiding principles to follow when defining and identifying models of excellence is the extent to which certain individuals and groups have contributed to our legacy in post-secondary education and beyond. In every institution, there are the trailblazers and list of "firsts," however it is often difficult to know and identify these people, and the same happens at the community level. Yet these very people were instrumental, and contributed to forging the possibilities allowing so many to follow them into these institutions. Because this level of recognition causes us to acknowledge a history of struggle and sacrifice by others before us, we hope to trigger a more profound Latina/o consciousness, and a sense of responsibility to keep the work moving us forward.

CLOSING THOUGHTS

The rising number of Latina/os at the post-secondary level provides stakeholders with significant opportunities to step up and act. The evidence and recent enrollment trends alone suggest we anticipate a significant Latina/o presence on our college and university campuses. The question and challenge, however, remain: are we, as a community of campus and community stakeholders, ready to invoke our moral, historical, and political will, to build a process that engages and intentionally builds intergenerational Latina/o excellence?

REFERENCES

Acevedo-Gil, Nancy, Ryan Santos, Luliana Alonso, and Daniel Solórzano. 2015. "Latinas/os in Community College Developmental Education: Increasing Moments of Academic and Interpersonal Validation." *Journal of Hispanics in Higher Education* 14 (2): 101–127.

Contreras, Frances and Gilbert Contreras. 2015. "Raising the Bar for Hispanic Serving Institutions: An Analysis of College Completion and Success Rates." *Journal of Hispanics in Higher Education* 14 (2): 151–170.

Contreras, Frances, Lindsay Malcolm, and Estela Bensimón. 2008. Hispanic Serving Institutions: Closeted Identity and the Production of Equitable Outcomes for Latina/o Students. In *Understanding Minority Institutions*, ed. Marybeth Gasman, Benjamin Baez, and C.S. Viernes Turner, 72–90. Albany, NY: State University of New York Press.

Marx, David, Sei Jin Ko, and Ray Friedman. 2009. "The 'Obama Effect': How a Salient Role Model Reduces Race-Based Performance Differences." *The Journal of Experimental Social Psychology* 45 (4): 953–956.

Núñez, Anne-Marie. 2015. Hispanic Serving Institutions: Where Are They Now? Paper presented at the Hispanic Serving Institutions in the 21st Century: A Convening conference, University of Texas at El Paso, April 28–29, 2015.

Núñez, Anne-Marie, and Diane Elizondo. 2012. "Hispanic-Serving Institutions in the U.S. Mainland and Puerto Rico: Organizational Characteristics, Institutional Financial Context, and Graduation Outcomes." White paper for the Hispanic Association of Colleges and Universities.

Rodríguez, Louie. 2015. *Intentional Excellence: The Pedagogy, Power, and Politics of Excellence in Latina/o Schools and Communities*. New York: Peter Lang Publishing.

Rodríguez, Louie. 2014. *The Time Is Now: Understanding and Responding to the Black and Latina/o Dropout Crisis in the U.S.* New York: Peter Lang Publishing.

Rodríguez, Louie, Eduardo Mosqueda, Pedro Nava, and Gilberto Conchas. 2013. "Reflecting on the Institutional Process of College Success: The Experiences of Four Chicanos in the Context of Crisis." *Latino Studies Journal* 11: 411–427.

Rodríguez, Louie, and Leticia Oseguera. 2015. "Nothing but the Best: Best Strategies for Latina/o Students Across the Educational Pipeline." *Journal of Hispanics in Higher Education* volume (?) and page numbers missing.

Santiago, Deborah. 2010. "Emerging HSI's (Hispanic Serving Institutions): Serving Latina/o Students." Washington, DC: Excelencia in Education.

Steele, C. M. 1997. A threat in the air: How stereotypes shape intellectual identity and performance. *American Psychologist, 52*(6), 613–629.

Wasserberg, Martin. 2009. Stereotype Threat and the Standardized Testing Experiences of African American Students at an Urban Elementary School. PhD diss., Florida International University.

Yosso, Tara. 2005. "Whose Culture Has Capital? Towards a Critical Race Theory Discussion of Community Cultural Wealth." *Race, Ethnicity, and Education* 8 (1): 69–91.

About the Contributors

Alberto Acereda is Senior Director, Global Education, at Educational Testing Service in Princeton, New Jersey. He provides overall leadership for business development initiatives and academic outreach in global and higher education. More information may be found on pages 5 and 6 of the introduction to this volume.

Nancy Acevedo-Gil is an assistant professor in the College of Education at California State University, San Bernardino. She is an interdisciplinary scholar who uses critical race theory and Chicana feminist theories to examine transitions of Latina/o/x students along the PK–20 educational pipeline. Her research aims to interrupt racist and deficit policies, practices, and ideologies that contribute to the marginalization of Communities of Color.

Rebecca A. Beals is an assistant professor of sociology at the University of Northern Colorado. Her research focuses on how to transform the culture of higher education in order to promote inclusive excellence within institutions.

Estela Mara Bensimón is professor of higher education and director of the Center for Urban Education (CUE) at the University of Southern California Rossier School of Education. More information may be found on page 6 of the introduction to this volume.

Ripsimé K. Bledsoe is a doctoral fellow in the Department of Educational Leadership and Policy Studies at The University of Texas at San Antonio. Bledsoe has extensive experience in faculty and student affairs positions at two- and four-year institutions. Her research centers around maintaining and restoring academic momentum through high-impact educational practices, including classroom teaching and learning, among diverse, low-income, first-generation college students. She is a Barbara Jackson Scholar.

Jorge Chapa, professor of Latino/Latina Studies at the University of Illinois at Urbana-Champaign, died unexpectedly on Monday, October 19, 2015. Jorge, his wife Belinda De La Rosa, and Blanca Rincón were working on a chapter for this volume when he died. For more information, see the *In Memoriam* page in the front matter of this book.

Frances Contreras is an associate vice-chancellor for equity, diversity, and inclusion and an associate professor in the Department of Education Studies at the University of California San Diego. Her research focuses on issues of equity and access for underrepresented students in the education pipeline and the role of public policy in ensuring student equity across a P–20 continuum. Contreras's most recent books include *Achieving Equity for Latino Students, Expanding the Pathway to Higher Education through Public Policy*, and *The Latino Education Crisis* with P. Gandara.

Gilbert J. Contreras Jr. serves Fullerton College as the vice president of student services. As an educational administrator in the community college system, Dr. Contreras has demonstrated leadership in shared governance, community partnerships, and developing data-driven programs that emphasize student success and student equity. He has extensive leadership and research experience in the community college system fostering collaboration between instruction and student services, implementing student life initiatives, and advancing diversity objectives.

Belinda De La Rosa is director of the University of Illinois at Urbana-Champaign Testing Center and director of assessment for the Office of the Dean of Students. She is an evaluator and institutional researcher. Her publications focus on Latino educational attainment, including "The Problematic Pipeline: Demographic Trends and Latino Participation in Graduate Science, Technology, Engineering, and Math Programs," coauthored with the late Jorge Chapa.

Alfredo G. de los Santos Jr., the lead editor of this volume, is a research professor at the Hispanic Research Center of Arizona State University, emeritus vice-chancellor of the Maricopa Community College District, and founding president of El Paso Community College. More information may be found on pages 4 and 5 of the introduction to this volume.

José Del Real Viramontes is a doctoral candidate in the Cultural Studies in Education Program at The University of Texas at Austin. His research explores the transfer receptive culture for Chicana/o/x Latina/o/x community college transfer students at Predominantly White Institutions (PWIs) and how Chicana/o/x Latina/o/x community college transfer students navigate and engage in the cultural production of the transfer receptive culture at PWIs.

Antonio G. Estudillo (PhD Indiana University Bloomington) is an assistant professor in the School of Education at Monmouth University. His research centers on developmental and educational trajectories of children and adolescents as well as equity in the schools and higher education, with particular interest in United States Latina/o education.

Ebelia Hernández (PhD Indiana University Bloomington) is an associate professor in the Graduate School of Education at Rutgers, The State University of New Jersey. Her research on Latina college women has been published in the *Journal of College Student Development, Journal of Hispanics in Higher Education, The Journal of Higher Education, The Journal of Latinos and Education,* and others.

Roberto A. Ibarra is an emeritus professor of sociology at the University of New Mexico, emeritus vice-chancellor of academic affairs at the University of Wisconsin-Madison, and developer of the Context Diversity model. He has over forty years of teaching, research, and administrative experience in diversity issues in higher education.

Vijay Kanagala is an assistant professor of higher education and student affairs administration in the Department of Leadership and Developmental Sciences, The University of Vermont. A former student affairs practitioner with extensive experience in multicultural programming, social justice initiatives, and inclusion efforts, Kanagala explores the intersectionality of education and social identities such as race, class, and gender in higher education contexts. He has successfully secured funding worth $3,858,419 for four major educational research projects that focus on access and success of limited income and first-generation students.

Gary Francisco Keller is Regents' Professor and director of the Hispanic Research Center at Arizona State University as well as publisher of the Bilingual Press. More information may be found on page 5 of the introduction to this volume.

Ou Lydia Liu is senior director of research at the Academic to Career Research Center at Educational Testing Service. Dr. Liu has conducted extensive research in student learning outcomes and is an internationally recognized expert in assessing college-level competencies in higher education. She has published over fifty papers in top-tier, peer-reviewed journals and was the recipient of the 2011 National Council on Measurement in Education *Jason Millman Promising Measurement Scholar Award.*

Walt MacDonald became the sixth President and CEO of Educational Testing Service on January 1, 2014, 30 years after he joined the company as an assessment specialist with an expertise in science. Over the course of his career, he has led nearly every major program, guiding each to grow and achieve the mission of ETS. In the late 1980s, he directed test development for the National Assessment of Educational Progress (NAEP), known as the "Nation's Report Card." Rising through the organization, he directed the Advanced Placement program through incredible growth and later led the College Board®, Higher Education, K–12 and Teacher Licensure divisions of ETS.

Lindsey E. Malcom-Piqueux is the associate director for research and policy at the Center for Urban Education and a research associate professor in the Rossier School of Education at the University of Southern California. Her work focuses on the ways in which higher education policy, institutions, and practitioners contribute to and/or reduce educational inequities experienced by minoritized student populations.

Ross Markle serves as a senior assessment strategist in the Higher Education Division at Educational Testing Service. In this role, he works with colleges and universities to promote the effective use of assessments and data, focusing on the issues of student success and student learning outcomes in higher education. He also works to remain actively engaged with organizations and initiatives throughout the higher education community.

Melissa A. Martínez is associate professor in education and community leadership and school improvement at Texas State University. She researches P-20 equity and access issues for underserved communities, primarily college access and readiness, equity-oriented school leaders/leadership, and the experiences of faculty of color. Some of her work is published in *The High School Journal, Race Ethnicity and Education, Journal of Latinos and Education,* and *International Journal of Qualitative Studies in Education.*

Gilda L. Ochoa is professor of Chicana/o-Latina/o studies at Pomona College. Her books include *Becoming Neighbors in a Mexican American Community,*

Learning from Latino Teachers, and Academic Profiling: Latinos, Asian Americans, and the Achievement Gap, which has received multiple awards for its focus on eradicating racism. Her most recent work analyzes (1) the sexualized policing of Latinas and (2) the sanctuary movement in her hometown of La Puente, CA.

María Elena Oliveri, PhD, is a research scientist at Educational Testing Service and associate editor of *International Journal of Testing.* Her research focuses on fairness, validity, and innovative assessment design in support of learners from diverse cultural and linguistic backgrounds. Her doctoral and master's degrees are in measurement, evaluation, and research methodology from the University of British Columbia (UBC), Canada. Previously, she was a literacy mentor to Vancouver schoolteachers, a teacher of second language learners and students with disabilities, and UBC lecturer.

Laura I. Rendón is professor emerita of educational leadership and policy studies at The University of Texas at San Antonio. She is a nationally recognized education theorist, speaker, and advocate for low-income, first-generation students. More information may be found on page 5 of the introduction to this volume.

Blanca Rincón is an assistant professor in the Educational Psychology and Higher Education Department in the College of Education, University of Nevada, Las Vegas. Dr. Rincón's research agenda is concerned with equity issues in higher education, with a specific focus on access and success for underrepresented and underserved students in STEM fields.

Joseph A. Ríos is an associate research scientist in the Academic to Career Research Center at the Educational Testing Service in Princeton, New Jersey. He holds a PhD in educational measurement and psychometrics from the University of Massachusetts, Amherst. His research interests include test-taking motivation in low-stakes testing contexts, cross-lingual assessment, and increasing diversity in graduate admissions.

Louie F. Rodríguez is an associate professor and associate dean in the Graduate School of Education at the University of California Riverside. His research examines the voices and experiences of students across the educational pipeline to shape educational policy, practice, and pedagogy. He is the author of *Intentional Excellence: The Pedagogy, Power, and Politics of Excellence in Latina/o Schools and Communities* and *The Time is Now: Understanding and Responding to the Black and Latina/o Dropout Crisis in the U.S.*

Luis Urrieta Jr. is the inaugural Suzanne B. and John L. Adams Endowed Professor of Education at The University of Texas at Austin. He specializes in the study of Chicanx, Latinx, and indigenous (P'urhépecha) identities; indigenous education, migrations and diasporas; and learning in family and community contexts. Urrieta is the author of *Working from Within: Chicana and Chicano Activist Educators in Whitestream Schools* (2009) and is coeditor, with George Noblit, of *Cultural Constructions of Identity: Meta-ethnography and Theory* (2018).

Index

Download the index for this book at https://bilingualpress.clas.asu.edu/book/new-directions-assessment-and-preparation-hispanic-college-students

PRAISE FOR *NEW DIRECTIONS*

"Hispanics represent more than 25% of all students and are the fastest growing group in our public schools. Yet national data on high-school graduation rates, college completion rates, and employment outcomes suggest that they are not being afforded the opportunities they deserve to meet their full potential. This should alarm everyone, and this sense of alarm needs to translate into informed action. That is why the data, perspectives, and recommendations presented in *New Directions* make the volume a must read for educational practitioners, advocates, and policymakers."

José Luis Cruz, President
LEHMAN COLLEGE, CITY UNIVERSITY OF NEW YORK

"This is required reading for administrators, faculty, and student services personnel as we seek to raise the level of Hispanic student achievement, access, and completion. I urge you to read this important work."

Larry H. Ebbers, University Professor Emeritus
SCHOOL OF EDUCATION, IOWA STATE UNIVERSITY

"The future viability of our colleges and our workforce depends on our growing Hispanic population. *New Directions* is a great source of policies and practices we can use to improve not just opportunities but also outcomes for the new wave of Hispanic students arriving at our institutions every year."

Joe García, President
WESTERN INTERSTATE COMMISSION FOR HIGHER EDUCATION

"*New Directions* makes a critical contribution to research and practice related to Hispanic students. The issues explored in this volume are essential to our students, institutions, and national educational attainment."

Manuel J. Justiz, Dean
COLLEGE OF EDUCATION, THE UNIVERSITY OF TEXAS AT AUSTIN

"[*New Directions*] represents an essential source addressing the multitude of issues affecting the higher education experiences of Latino students. The authors also review and propose programs that not only support the students socially, culturally, and intellectually but also seek to 'educate the educators' about the needs and strengths of these students. It is an outstanding contribution to its field of study."

Luis C. Moll, Professor Emeritus
DEPARTMENT OF TEACHING, LEARNING & SOCIOCULTURAL STUDIES
UNIVERSITY OF ARIZONA

"The number of Hispanics in community colleges across the country is growing at a phenomenal rate. It has never been more important to have the collaborative entrepreneurial spirit of PK-16 drive the way for economic prosperity. The book is an invaluable resource for students and communities to use the research to help transform the future for Hispanic-Serving Institutions and Hispanic students."

Richard M. Rhodes, President/CEO
AUSTIN COMMUNITY COLLEGE DISTRICT

"The essays in *New Directions* are rich in variety of topics as well as ideas on how to improve educational opportunities for Hispanic students. The appearance of this book could not be better timed as we witness a record enrollment of young Hispanic students across rural and urban communities of America. A very welcome edition to an important topic."

Ricardo Romo, President
THE UNIVERSITY OF TEXAS AT SAN ANTONIO